齊物
逍遙
2022

黃效文————著

ENLIGHTENED
SOJOURN

Authored and Photographed by Wong How Man

Wong How Man

Time Magazine honored Wong How Man among their 25 Asian Heroes in 2002, calling Wong "China's most accomplished living explorer". CNN has featured his work over a dozen times, including a half-hour profile by the network's anchor. Discovery Channel has made several documentaries about his work. The Wall Street Journal has also featured him on its front page. Wong began exploring China in 1974. He is Founder/President of the China Exploration & Research Society, a non-profit organization founded in 1986 specializing in exploration, research, conservation and education in remote China and neighboring countries. Wong has led six major expeditions for the National Geographic. He successfully defined the sources of the Yangtze, Mekong, Yellow River, Salween, Irrawaddy and the Brahmaputra rivers.

He conducts projects in Mainland China, India, Nepal, Bhutan, Laos, Myanmar, the Philippines, and also Taiwan. In these countries or regions, he has set up centers, theme exhibits, or permanent operation bases. Wong has authored over thirty books and has received many accolades, among them an honorary doctorate from his alma mater, the University of Wisconsin at River Falls, and the Lifetime Achievement Award from Monk Hsing Yun of Taiwan. He has been invited as keynote speaker at many international functions.

黃
效
文

《時代雜誌》在二零零二年曾選黃效文為亞洲二十五位英雄之一，稱他為「中國最有成就的在世探險家」。*CNN* 報導過黃效文的各項工作超過十二次之多，其中還包括主播 *Richard Quest* 的三十分鐘專訪。探索頻道也為他做的工作製作了好幾個紀錄片。《華爾街日報》也曾用頭版報導過他。

黃效文自一九七四年開始在中國探險。他是中國探險學會的創辦人和會長，這是個非營利組織，致力於在中國偏遠地區及鄰近國家的探險，研究，保育和教育工作。他曾經在美國《國家地理雜誌》帶領過六個重要的探險。他成功地定位的源頭包括長江，湄公河，黃河，薩爾溫江，伊洛瓦底江及雅魯藏布江。

他的學會主導的文化和自然保育項目橫跨中國和鄰近的國家，包括印度、尼泊爾、不丹、寮國、緬甸、菲律賓還有台灣。黃效文著作的書超過三十本並獲得過許多榮譽，他的母校威斯康辛大學頒發給他名譽博士學位，星雲大師也贈與他「華人世界終身成就獎」。他也是許多國際會議裡的專題演講人。

Preface

The sky is open again, and my journey resumes. I write this on a Drukair flight out of Bhutan. I have just completed a two-week sojourn and exploration of Bhutan as guest of the Royal Grandmother of this Himalayan kingdom. In another week, Bhutan will be reopening its border to tourism, and a huge influx of tourists are in line to enter.

After an overnight in Bangkok, I will then fly to Myanmar to continue our work there, something I had left behind two and a half years ago. The last time I was in Myanmar, I was boarding the very last Dragonair flight to Hong Kong, leaving the country in March 2020. Dragonair would soon after stop operating forever as the Covid pandemic hit globally. It seems ironic that two airlines with similar name, Druk meaning Dragon in Bhutanese, should meet such different destinies. One dragon went down while the other survived and is taking to the air again into a changed world as my journey continues.

During the first year of the pandemic, I promised myself to stay home for one year, and thus I started a number of small projects within Hong Kong. That year also allowed me to revisit the *huge archive in my library of books, notes, photographs and raw film footage that I had collected over almost half a century. Thus, that sojourn yielded retro writings and films that otherwise would have been left to gather dust. Once the self-imposed full year limit was reached, I hit the road again, quarantine notwithstanding.*

This fourth book in a series by the same name, Enlightened Sojourn, covers mainly my two long journeys in China during 2021. Both these trips were taken after twenty-one-day quarantines, required before I was allowed to travel relatively freely. I made good use of my hotel stays to read and write. It goes to show that, within certain confines and restrictions, old-school discipline could keep our minds wandering, though limits may be imposed on our physical parameters.

I am delighted that the restrictions in overseas travels gave me more opportunity to reacquaint myself with central China and the coast. By doing so, I brought myself up to date with the huge changes to the country, while reminiscing about China's past, which I also had the good fortune to observe since the 1970s. Through this book, I hope to share those experiences with others who also yearn to explore, both into our past as well as into the present.

序

晴空萬里，我的旅程重新啟動。我在飛離不丹的「不丹皇家航空」(Drukair) 上完成這篇序言。我以不丹皇太后的賓客身分，在這喜馬拉雅王國逗留兩週，完成又一段不丹探索之旅。再過一週，不丹將重新開放邊境，翹首以待的大批遊客，迫不及待等著排隊入境。

在曼谷過了一夜，我將馬不停蹄飛往緬甸，繼續我兩年半前尚未完成的工作。我還記得上一次準備離開緬甸時，是二○二○年三月，我搭上當地最後一班飛往香港的「港龍航空」(Dragonair)。緊接著，席捲全球的新冠疫情爆發，不久便傳來「港龍航空」終止營運的消息。巧的是，「不丹皇家航空」的 Druk 字原意也是「龍」，兩家航空公司同名不同命，一條龍倒了，另一條則僥倖存活，在我延續旅程之際，再度騰空飛入一個改變後的世界；令人不勝唏噓。

疫情大流行的第一年，我答應自己會好好待在家裡一整年，於是，我在香港展開了一些小項目。我也在那一年，重新檢視一些我收藏了近半個世紀的龐大檔案資

料庫——書籍、筆記、照片與未經後製處理的原始影片。若沒有這段安居於室的時間使我埋首回顧許多文字書寫與電影，這些作品恐怕要被塵封而不見天日。如期完成自我設定的「全年不外出」之大限以後，儘管還須隔離而進出各地，我仍再次上路。

這是《齊物逍遙》(Enlightened Sojourn) 同名系列的第四本書；主要敘述我在二〇二一年踏上中國境內的兩次長途遠行。值得一提的是，兩段「逍遙」之旅其實都是在二十一天隔離的限制要求之後進行的。我充分善用飯店隔離期間閱讀與書寫。這樣的體驗足以說明，在足不出戶與特定限制下，即使身體受限、障礙重重，老派的紀律還是可以讓我們的思緒暢遊無阻。

海外遊歷的限制，反倒讓我有更多機會重新認識中國中部與沿海地區，這令我喜出望外。我藉此而發現這個國家翻天覆地的變化，也同時憶起中國的過去；那是我有幸自一九七〇年代以來曾經見證的歷史。我希望藉由本書，與其他也渴望探索的人分享這些歷程與體驗，深入這塊土地的過去與現在。

目次

隱
藏
秘
境
—
澳
門

MACAU hidden ENCLAVE

Macau – April 29, 2021

MACAU hidden ENCLAVE
Post quarantine exploration

April 2021 - The upgrade was better than a birthday gift. After two weeks of hotel room quarantine, I was allowed to go out of my hotel room to roam around town during the day, yet must return to the same hotel, though now in a different wing, for another week of self-quarantine. That is kind of like a half-way house out on drug remedial probation.

So the final break-out at the end of the third week was a little like liberation, from slavery or jail, or for those with spiritual pursuit, enlightenment after an ashram or retreat. Looking back at what others have had to go through, say during the three years and eight months of Japanese occupation of Hong Kong during WWII, my confinement was a minimal detention per se.

At end of quarantine for the three weeks of stay in Macau, we must move out of our hotel and into another. I thus booked the Grand Lapa which was priced only around HK300 per night. Martin, our CERS director, insisted on upgrading me to the MGM, a posh casino hotel at the waterfront. Checking in, we were given a two-bedroom suite; each came with separate spa tub, and a living room with panoramic view. I obliged with grace, accepting a last bit of decadence before entering into the field on expedition and a more spartan lifestyle.

MGM Macau / 澳門美高梅

The third week of partial release actually allowed me to explore Macau (or Macao as it is spelled by the Portuguese) - a consolation prize. I've visited Macau maybe a score of times, but never at such length. Avoiding all the tourist sites I have already visited, now I could penetrate into some niche areas.

As my room at the Lisboeta Hotel looked out toward the ocean with a green hill to the right, I was eager to check out that hill upon being allowed to exit the hotel to roam around. That turned out to be Gau O Shan (Nine Bay Hill). On the hill is Our Lady of Sorrows Church, first opened in 1934 in this remotest corner of Macau. Adjacent to the church used to be a small leper colony with a hospital next to the church. While the church remains, the lepers have long gone. Today, a café is taking up the former small Portuguese style lodge, and again quite Portuguese, open only according to its operator's will.

Further down through a foot path is Gau O Village. Few realize that in the year 1910, a major battle was fought

at this site between the then ruling Portuguese and the marauding pirates of the Pearl River Delta. Eighteen young students from nearby China were kidnapped and kept near here at Coloane for ransom. The pirates managed to beat off two brigades of soldiers and even occupied a small fortress nearby. After several unsuccessful engagements by the government, more relief forces were sent in.

The pirates managed to escape by sea while the army swooped in and burned the entire village. Over forty pirates were captured, with eight of the most recalcitrant ones being sent off to Africa for 28 years of hard labor. The army, while chasing the pirates, killed many innocent villagers, triggering the local community to plead to the Qing Government to take back Macau from the Portuguese. It fell on deaf ears, as the Imperial Court was preoccupied with its own survival.

My next stop is another church and fortress on another hill with a commanding view of old Macau. The Guia Lighthouse and Fortress is situated on the highest point of Macau. The Chapel of Our Lady of Guia, first built in the early 1600s, sits next to the fort of the same era and the lighthouse, built later. Both structures are European and Mediterranean in their architectural style. Two old cannons still watch over the delta mouth of the Pearl River. The lighthouse is believed to be the first western style

Lighthouse & Cannon / 燈塔＆大砲
Church & Lighthouse / 教堂＆燈塔

lighthouse along the China coast, built in the year 1864. It preceded the first one in Hong Kong, built in 1875; one that I am quite familiar with, as it is near my studio in Cape D'Aguilar in Hong Kong.

My high school mate Joseph Lee has recently taken up the post of President of Macau University of Science and Technology (MUST). It allows me a chance to visit this very new yet dynamic private university. Small as its campus is, it has now exceeded enrollment above the much older Macau University and is still growing. While its faculties of Chinese Medicine, Business and Space Sciences are all extremely well regarded, I was fascinated by its tourism school, an integral faculty to complement Macau's world heritage properties and many casinos.

During my visit, a leading Portuguese executive chef was teaching students about the intricacy of the European ham delicacy, including the best method to hand-slice a piece of ham. Due in part to my own background in Fine Art, the university gallery, presenting works of its Masters and PhD candidates, fascinated me with their very high standards. The art displayed, I was told, was mostly from graduate students who are already art teachers or professors. The design workshop, likewise, caught my attention.

Lung Wah is an old-style tea house in an old-style beige building next to the old-style market, painted in the traditional pink color used for government buildings in the Portuguese colonial period. The restaurant, first opened in 1962, is decked out with antiques, porcelain display and paintings on the wall, complementing a long line of bench seating, most popular during the 1950s and 60s. The dim sum is also old-style, likewise a large image of Chairman Mao on the wall indicating Macau's closeness to China during that same period.

Not far away - everything is "not far away" in Macau - in a garden covered area is another "tea kiosk" where bird-

lovers bring their cages of song birds each morning. A red New Year lucky paper stuck to the post reads, "Bird Luck Enjoy Throughout". The "songs" may be music with loving lyrics to the bird lovers, but not necessarily so for the uninitiated, including yours truly.

My favorite tea house, however, is Tai Lung Fung Restaurant, which I visited twice during my week-long furlough in Macau. This is perhaps the only teahouse with a tiny performing stage for Cantonese opera in the entire Pearl River Delta region, including Hong Kong. The owner Ha Jia is not only a Cantonese opera fan, but loves to sing as an amateur. Thus, she brings in an orchestra every afternoon for "high tea," allowing customers to enjoy the singing, or participate in it on stage. This just may become my hang-out joint if CERS ever starts a future project in Macau. And I am ready to clear my throat for an audition.

Another "not far away" relic is the Wing Lok Theater. Its architectural style is part Art Deco, part Bauhaus with its rounded corners. It is most lovely to look at during the night, when the neon lights are turned on. In the rain when I visited, it was both retro and romantic.

"Nearby", for need of a shorter term, is a rather disappointing Burmese restaurant. Macau boasted over ten thousand Burmese Chinese who immigrated there from the mid 1960s onward. Many of them business families or industrialists, they made Macau their home. Hong Kong, on the other hand, despite being a British colony at the time, did not give refuge to these "refugees" driven from another former British colony. This seems quite in line with its established colonial policy since exit; unless it has good political or economic benefits, nothing about moral or ethics. Quite

Grad students exhibit / 研究生展

Central market / 中央市場
Bird pavilion / 賞鳥亭

understandable, as everyone should learn to expect.

Since CERS just started a project on Lantau Island regarding the only Hua Guang Temple in Hong Kong, I was naturally attracted to the Lien Kei New Temple that was specially built to honor Hua Guang in Macau. "New" because it was rebuilt in 1830 upon the collapse of the old temple. A wooden tablet dates the rebuild to that particular year, whereas the date of first-construction is rather dubious. Unlike the small and remote temple in Hong Kong, the one in Macau is in the heart of the city, "nearby" to Wing Lok Theater and the Bird tea pavilion.

There are many worshippers offering incense and money everyday. Outside is a wall mural depicting the travels and route of the three-eyed Hua Guang deity, and another mural pinpointing where other Hua Guang statues are located within Macau; quite a few. There are also street stands and antique venders on the main street and side alleys within range of the temple.

The main chamber is as usual devoted to the higher deity of Good Fortune. But the immediately adjacent pavilion to its right is where Hua Guang takes up his seat. A tablet tells the tale that the three-eye statue was first brought to Macau in 1943 by someone related to the British expeditionary force to China, and procured along the Yangtze River, perhaps from

Zhenjiang. It was then given to a lady as an antique. Upon leaving Macau, it was put up for sale and bought by a gentleman who in turn raised the money to restore the pavilion to house it.

Performing artists, musicians and all stage hands related to Cantonese opera hold Hua Guang in revere. Since 1876, there would generally be a small Cantonese opera performance on site each year during Hua Guang's birthday on the 28th day of the Ninth Moon, according to the lunar calendar. From one of the more recent restorations, that of 1950, a stone tablet remains listing many of the dignitaries, wealthy individuals and opera artists who had donated. Among them are familiar names of artists like Ma Si Jeng (馬師曾), Hung Sin Nui (紅線女), Leung Sing Bor (梁醒波) and Law Yim Hing (羅艷卿).

My final stop in Macau was at a tiny street corner store, King Yin Jan (景 然 棧), my favourite Cantonese sausage and snack shop. The owner knew my face and soon I left with several bags of fatty pork and liver sausages, enough to last a few weeks as supplement to my otherwise dire diet while on expedition.

Hua Guang Temple / 華光殿

Hua Guang statue / 華光神像

Mural of temple / 殿裡壁畫

隱藏秘境－澳門

後隔離期間的城市探索

升級版，比生日禮物好太多了！歷經長達兩週的飯店隔離，我獲准可以在白天時離開飯店外出，到城裡溜達溜達；然後，必須返回同一家飯店不同一座的房間，再進行自我隔離一週。這有點像給癮君子戒毒的中途之家，隨時得「緩刑與回報」。

及至第三週完全結束隔離時，那種身心大解放，猶如被奴役或監禁後的重獲新生，也類似付上高價追求靈性的修道者從閉關所退隱出關時，深獲啟迪般，「法喜」充滿，喜逐顏開。我想起許多也曾被囚被禁之人的困頓，譬如那些曾在二戰期間躲過日本長達三年八個月侵佔的人，相較之下，我拘役般的隔離，實在微不足道。

澳門的三週隔離期一結束，我們必須搬出飯店，再入住另一家飯店。因此，我預訂了價格僅每晚港幣三百元左右的「澳門雅辰酒店」。「中國探險學會」(CERS)董事馬丁 (Martin) 堅持要替我升級到一家位於濱海區的豪華賭場飯店「澳門美高梅」。我們住的大套房配有獨立水療浴缸，與一覽無遺的全景觀客廳。在展開餐風露宿、近乎斯巴達的冒險旅程之前，能擁有這般近乎「頹廢墮落」的奢華享受，我就恭敬不如從命，欣然領受了。

事實上，第三週獲准部分外出的「類緩刑」期間，我把探索澳門 (Macau)，視為老天賞

予我的安慰獎。我對澳門並不陌生，前後到此遊歷不下數十次，但從不曾花那麼長時間待在這裡。這次我刻意避開曾經去過的旅遊景點，好整以暇地，深入一些少有人注意的冷門區域。

澳門葡京人飯店房間面向大海，右邊一座綠色山丘映入眼簾，令我心動。當我獲准離開飯店外出時，我迫不及待想近距離看看那座山丘。原來那是九澳山。山上有座「九澳七苦聖母小堂」，一九三四年，小教堂在澳門最偏遠的角落，首次對外開放。聖母堂旁邊有家醫院，那附近曾是痲瘋病院區。教堂猶在，痲瘋病人早已離散。今天，前葡式風格的建築已被一家咖啡館取而代之，咖啡館造型保有原來的傳統葡式風，就連經營方式也很葡萄牙——開不開門營業，看老闆心情。

再往下走遠一點，穿過一條人行道，便是九澳村。很少人知道，一九一〇年期間，當時的葡萄牙統治者曾與珠江三角州的海盜在此大動干戈。十八名來自臨近中國的年輕學子被綁架，關在澳門路環附近，等著勒索贖金。海盜成功擊敗兩隊葡萄牙士兵，甚至一度乘勝追擊，佔據不遠處的小堡壘。清朝政府多方交涉不果後，只能派更多救援軍力進駐當地。

海盜最終從海路逃跑，後方軍隊追趕而至，雙方短兵相接，整座村莊被燒毀殆盡。超過四十名海盜被捕，其中最頑強抵抗的八名

Former leper's lodge / 前痲瘋病院

硬頸海盜被送往非洲從事長達二十八年的勞役。軍隊在追捕海盜過程中，許多無辜村民遭殃被殺，無助的村民轉而懇請清政府從葡萄牙殖民者手中奪回澳門政權。但村民所託非人，清政府當時自顧不暇，也只能對此訴求置若罔聞。

我的下一站，是另一座山上的教堂與堡壘，高得足以俯瞰整個舊澳門——位於澳門制高點的「東望洋燈塔」與堡壘。東望洋聖母堂於一六○○年初期創建，與同期蓋建的堡壘與後期的燈塔，比鄰而居，建築設計兼顧歐洲風與地中海型設計，兼容並蓄。兩座古老的大砲至今仍忠心守著珠江三角洲河口。說起這座於一八六四年蓋好的燈塔，它被視為中國沿海第一座西式燈塔，與香港一八七五年建成的第一座燈塔相比，足足早了十一年；而香港這座燈塔我可熟了，因它就在我香港鶴咀海角的工作室附近，與我日夜對望。

我的高中同學李行偉 (Joseph Lee) 最近被聘任澳門科技大學 (Macau University of Science and Technology) 校長。他帶著我參觀這所嶄新而活力十足的私立大學。校園不大，但目前報名就讀的學生人數，不僅已超越資深的老牌澳門大學，且人數還不斷增加中。雖然澳門科大的中醫醫學院、商業與空間科學學院都備受推崇，口碑甚佳，但我卻對它的觀光旅遊學院深深感興趣，這與澳門備受矚目的世界遺產與享譽盛名的許多賭場，正好相輔相成。

在我訪視期間，一位著名的葡萄牙行政主廚正教導學生有關歐洲火腿美食的精緻與複雜性，包括火腿的最佳手工切片法。另外，我在大學畫廊欣賞博碩士生所展示的藝術作品，從我的純美術背景來看，他們高超的藝術表現，令我刮目相看。我後來被告知，

Chef with students / 廚師與學生
Design workshop / 設計工作室

Tai Lung Fung Tea House / 大龍鳳餐廳
Lung Wah Tea House / 龍華茶樓

這些展出的作品大多出自研究生，而他們早已是藝術老師或教授了。此外，大學內的設計研討會，也同樣引起我的注意。

充滿懷舊風的龍華茶樓，位於舊市場旁一棟老式的米黃建築裡，餐廳牆壁一片傳統粉紅色，那是葡萄牙殖民時期政府單位的建築慣用塗漆。這家老餐廳於一九六二年首次開業，餐廳內有古董與瓷器裝飾，古色古香，牆上掛著大畫，牆邊是一整排的長凳子；五〇與六〇年代，最時興這類長椅，和那幅毛主席斗大的肖像畫，相映成趣，澳門在那時空背景下，與中國之間的親近，不言而喻。當然，就連端上桌的港式點心，也是老式的。

不遠處——是的，彈丸小島如澳門，一切都是「不遠處」——被錦簇花團遮蔽的公園一角，是另一個「茶亭」，吸引愛鳥人士帶著關在籠中鳥到此聚集，聊聊「鳥事」。柱子上貼了張賀新年的紅色春聯：「雀運亨通」。此起彼落的鶯歌燕舞，唰啾唧唧，聽在愛鳥人士耳中，鳥聲嚦嚦，猶如填滿情愛歌詞的旋律，聽出耳油，但對初次體驗者——包括敝人我——或許不以為然。

不過，要說我個人最喜歡的茶館，則首推大龍鳳餐廳。在我長達一週的澳門休假期內，我便已去了兩次。這茶館設了個讓粵劇表演的小舞台，這可能是包括香港在內的整個珠江三角州地區，唯一一家有室內粵劇小舞台的茶館。茶館主人霞姊，不僅是粵劇大

粉絲，還是業餘愛好者，閒來小露身手，上台唱幾曲。她每天下午都會帶領一支管弦隊來個粵曲「下午茶」時光，讓來店賓客邊吃邊欣賞演出，或邀請來賓上台參與，賓主盡歡。未來如果「中國探險學會」計畫在澳門「展店營業」的話，眼前這地方或許可以成為我們聚會的好所在。我已準備好為試鏡清清嗓子，熱熱身了。

另一個「不遠處」，則是澳門遺跡——永樂戲院。戲院的建築風格包含部分裝飾藝術，另一半則以「包浩斯主義」的圓角形等現代藝術風為主。黑夜裡的戲院，在霓虹燈閃爍下，顯得格外嫵媚動人。我當時置身雨中，既復古又浪漫。

比不遠更「近」的地方，是一家令人有些失望的緬甸餐廳。回顧一下澳門的移民史，自一九六０年代中期開始，遷居澳門的緬甸華人移民已逾一萬人。他們當中不乏卓然有成的商人或企業家，落腳此地後便以澳門為家。另一方面，當時身為英國殖民地的香港，雖然身不由己，卻也沒有為這群被另一個前英殖民趕來的「難民」，提供任何庇護。不過，這看來似乎也無可厚非，既有的殖民政策

Pawn shop strip / 當鋪街　　　　　　　　　　　Theater by night / 夜間的戲院

向來如此，除非背後有政治優勢或經歷利益的考量，則另當別論，否則的話，也無關乎道德與倫理。心有期待，人皆有之，這道理不難理解。

不久前，「中國探險學會」在大嶼山啟動了香港唯一的「華光寺」計畫，這一次來澳門，一間特為紀念華光而蓋建的「蓮溪新廟」，深深吸引我。說它「新」，是因為它是經由舊寺廟倒塌後重新於一八三〇年原址重建。我看到寺廟有塊木板，上面標示重建日期，但首次動工的日期則有些含糊難辨。有別於香港小而偏遠的華光寺，澳門的蓮溪新廟大剌剌地位居市中心，就在永樂戲院和鳥茶館附近，都算相去「不遠」。

蓮溪新廟香火鼎盛，每天到此拜拜與添香油錢的信眾不少。廟宇外圍是一幅描繪三眼華光大帝雲遊四海的壁畫，另外還有一幅壁畫，精準定位澳門其他華光雕像的位置圖，由此看來，當地華光雕像似乎還不少。寺廟周遭的主要街道與小巷，攤販與古董攤，零星散置。

廟內的主殿，一如既往，供奉位階更高的財帛星君，一旁右側則是華光大帝坐臥之處。有塊碑文講述了三眼雕像如何輾轉於一九四三年，由英國遠征中國隊裡某位不具名人士，首次帶到澳門，他是循著長江流域或鎮江一帶，沿途蒐集採購，最後再當成古董，轉送給一位女士。女士離開澳門前，將這些古董大禮出售，最終由一名紳士出手買下，再籌募經費修復亭子，安置這些神像古物。

無論表演藝術家、音樂家，以及所有與粵劇相關的舞台工作人員，大家對華光神明都心存敬畏。自一八七六年以來，每逢農曆九月二十八的華光誕辰日，寺廟現場都會舉

辦小型粵劇表演。一九五〇年——最近一次修復中，一塊石碑列出了許多捐贈者大名，其中不乏非富則貴的政要名人與歌劇藝術家，包括大家耳熟能詳的馬師曾、紅線女、梁醒波與羅艷卿。

我在澳門的最後一站，是巷尾一家小店，景然棧，那裡有我最愛的粵式香腸和小吃。小店主人認得我的臉，因此當我離開時，手上已拎著好幾袋肥豬肉與肝腸，主人的盛情，塞滿行囊，使我滿載而歸，也恰好為我出發探險前，糧草先行，應該足以當我好幾個星期的食物呐！

King Yin Jan / 景然棧

西藏北方朝聖—啟程

NORTHERN TIBET PILGRIMAGE

Kunming – June 25, 2021

NORTHERN TIBET PILGRIMAGE; *The Journey Begins*
An expedition during pandemic

Expedition Background:

Many expeditions depart with launching parties, pomp and display of zealous ambition, yet return, if at all, with little or nothing claimed of what they tried to achieve. No expedition of exploration is guaranteed success. If it were so, it would not be called exploration. Thus, celebration before a trip is usually premature, unless it is as a farewell, assuming they may never meet again!

As for me, it is customary that I stay incognito before or during expeditions, never bothering with any high-profile fanfare, not even after I return. Before there were mobile phones, and even later when we traveled with a satellite phone, using it only in case of emergency, I kept my plans and progress under wraps. Even now in the mobile and internet age when a remote antennae provides me with connection to the world, I've always chosen to remain isolated and insulated from the world, such that I can fully indulge in and embrace nature, and more fully be among people living as a part of nature.

But on my current expedition, the situation has changed. After three weeks of hotel quarantine in Macau, I roam quite freely in Mainland China. Along the way, I share photos and short notes with my small circle of WeChat friends, especially among our CERS directors. Under normal circumstances, such intermittent news from the field might not entice them from their rather busy daily routines, since many of these friends might be traveling the world on their own, living the so-called life in the fast lane. Whereas my field trips are always the opposite, life in the slow lane.

Now however, few people are willing to sustain mandatory time in quarantine in order to meet their usually brief traveling needs, be it for pleasure or for work. Thus, most people have been stuck in their home town for a year or more, hoping the pandemic would come under control or go away and traveling freely would resume once again. As such, my sharing of expedition highlights in real time suddenly seems more meaningful, to bring my friends along on my journey vicariously.

Furthermore, there is added value to launch an expedition during a global pandemic while others are under lock-down or in a semi-locked-down predicament. Not so much that I feel better roaming free compared to others still locked down, but to spend a three-week quarantine in order to have the pay-back of months of roaming in China seems rather equitable, a more than fair return on investment.

Ready to start / 準備出發
Loading cars with equipments / 裝備上車

Wiping phone / 擦乾手機

It is somewhat anticlimactic to begin my expedition story by stating that I missed several of my primary goals. But accounts of disaster-filled mountaineering or oceanic expeditions tend to captivate an audience who enjoys the anxiety and excitement of the disjointed episodes as a most seasoned explorer falls apart into pieces. So, I should not shy away from recounting some of the set-backs, and a few salvaged triumphs, of my recent encounters on yet another exploration trip.

So, here are the twists and turns, where "turn" means "turning back": Goal Number One, reconnaissance of the source of the Indus River, and possibly reaching it to get this seventh major river source under our belt. Armed with multiple satellite images, pre-processed to pinpoint the source at the western glacier tip of Mount Kailash, we reached Lhasa and asked for the usual border permit to western Tibet and Kailash.

No permit can be issued to anyone from outside China, Hong Kong included. Military operations for over a year since the border tension between India and China have effectively closed the western Tibet borders to all outside visitors. I sent Qijala, an old friend and former chief of Zhongdian (Shangri-la), a text message. He has since been promoted to become governor of Tibet. But I waited and received no reply. Military priorities obviously trump administrative power.

I adjusted our plan and we went north, towards our second goal on this trip, which again would in time be dashed. Then the third objective, to move into northern Xinjiang, which in turn, was curtailed. Though at the time a disappointment, the details have become only punctuations now, as my sentence of exploration continues before reaching a period.

And so, the Journey begins:

This is the most expensive spa I have ever had. At HK8600, or US1100, even the Aman Resort would not charge such exorbitant prices. Not that I'm much of a spa person, but the truth is that I was struck by the very organic look of this natural hot spring high on the Tibetan plateau, at an elevation of 4100 meters.

It much resembles a huge mushroom growing out of the earth, as condensation of white gypsum spilled over its top and, dripping downward, hardened into crystal-like formations. As it also somewhat resembles an elephant, it is known as the Elephant Nose Hot Spring. At its base are natural-looking pot holes, in which the bather can sit to enjoy the warmth of this unique hot spring. I was further enticed by the weather. It had just started to snow with feather-like flakes drifting down through the sky. How wonderful it would be to make a photo to raise the envy of all my friends back home stuck in the heat of an approaching summer.

Perhaps due in part to my selfish thought, just as I was pondering taking off my shoes and pants, my latest Huawei phone jumped out of my pocket and took a dive into a pothole of the hot spring. The flakes of snow drifting down from the sky must have prompted it to hurry into the steaming water before I could do so. There goes the US$1,100 entrance fee for me!

A Tibetan looking on quickly rolled up his sleeves and put his full arm into the steaming water, fishing for my phone. Five minutes passed and no luck, then another five minutes and yet he could not feel the phone. I thought it would be futile now to try to retrieve it. Off with my clothes and pants, I went right in to enjoy the hot bath to make-up for my loss. While I sank and sat up to my shoulders in the bath, I slowly felt the bottom and realized it was sand and mud. As my hand searched the soft silt below for a few minutes, suddenly I came upon the phone and fished it out. It was dripping wet, and I decided it was gone beyond repair. Perhaps staying longer in the pool would heal a little of my own pain. After all, this is locally famous as a medicinal hot spring, good in repairing all sorts of pain.

My crew looked on and was amazed at how well I took in stride the huge entrance fee I had just paid to enter into the natural spa. Two of them quipped that the latest Huawei phone is supposed to be hardy and waterproof. Li Na, our logistics manager on this expedition, quickly wiped it off and suggested we put it inside a sack of rice, which can act as a good drying agent. I concurred and gave up my phone, with the latest sophisticated Leica lens, while lamenting that I had just taken some very nice pictures with it. We pulled out the memory card, and luckily it still worked with my older Huawei phone.

Jumping ahead a week or so later, then in Lhasa, I tried the spa phone again and it came back to life. So I got back my entrance fee, and the spa was free after all. And the medicinal hot spring lived up to its name, healing even my phone!

Now this was not just any hot spring spa, and not even just any natural hot spring spa. It sat at the foothill of a very unique monastery on the border of Qinghai with Tibet, in a most remote part of Nangxian County in Yushu Prefecture of southern Qinghai province. Dana Gomba was originally a Bonpo monastery some 1400 years ago and was changed to a Kargyu sect monastery in the year 1188. As such, it is considered one of the oldest monasteries in Tibet with its oldest building being listed as national protected architecture. It is now the only remaining Kargyu monastery belonging to the Yerpa sect, one of the smallest and least known sects of the Kargyu "white" sect within Tibetan Buddhism. Through revival of this one monastery, the Yerpa now have several small sub-monasteries spread out on the pleateau.

Da meaning horse and Na meaning ear, the twin peaks of the mountain right above the monastery resemble a pair of ears of a horse. Without a local guide, the monastery, standing at 4300 meters and hidden among limestone hills, would be extremely difficult to find. We came once just four years ago, yet without the help of Jangju, a monk from nearby, I doubt if we could have rediscovered Dana Monastery easily. Because of its remoteness and high elevation, many Tibetan Eared-pheasant and Tibetan Partridge, and at times even Blue Sheep, visit the vicinity frequently.

Dana is also known as the monastery of Ling, the homeland of Gesar of Ling, the legendary king of the Kham region on the Tibetan plateau. He was born in Dengke, today's Dege, beside the Yangtze. His root guru was Sangye Yerpa, thus connecting him to Dana Monastery. Gesar many battles as he unified the entire region, thus making him famous as the most brilliant and courageous fighter throughout Tibetan history. Dana is said to be the only monastery remaining among of those that had Gesar's direct patronage. Today many relics, including battle weapons and armor, are preserved within the valued collection of Dana Monastery.

General's stupa / 將領的佛塔
Da Na view / 達那山

King Gesar's most gallant generals, also ministers of state, numbered thirty altogether. Each has a stupa (pagoda) dedicated to his memory. These white stupas, styled in the ancient bell shape, are lined up in two grottoes along a precipitous cliff higher up the mountain, at perhaps 5,000 meters above sea level., Although perilously high, they can be seen from Dana monastery whenever the fog lifts and does not obliterate the view.

The presiding head monk Ngodon Nyima, a young Rinpoche of 46 years of age, was very pleased to see me again. After all, who else would revisit such a distant temple, besides those worshippers from nearby communities. As a young monk of 16, Ngodon studied under Tai Situ Rinpoche at Palpung Monastery, one of the most important monasteries of the Kargyu sect, situated in Dege of Sichuan Province. CERS supported a research and conservation project there thirty years ago, coinciding with Ngodon's time there. So today he felt particularly close to us. Our team of eight took up quarters at his home. His ageing mother and aunt also live in an adjacent room within this traditional Tibetan premises.

After the long three-day drive from our Zhongdian Center, we all settled in for the night early, as we were told to join the early morning chanting at the main Assembly Hall. However, when I rose early and walked out of the house, I found that there were several inches of snow on the ground, and all our cars were covered in white. All the better for my photography, as there had been construction within the monastery and things there were kind of messy. Now the snow caste a wonderful cover on everything, and what remained in sight was just wonderfully beautiful. Even two meditation retreat abodes on the slopes of some pinnacles above looked more pronounced in the snow.

Currently, there were even a few monks inside the caves, finishing one year retreats with two more to go before exiting as full lamas.

At the entrance of the Assembly Hall, above on the ceiling and pillars were hung many animal specimens. They included a snow leopard, a bear, a huge wolf, an eagle and a vulture. Inside the Assembly Hall, there were but a few monks for the morning service, as most had been sent home during the cordyceps season to harvest the much-valued caterpillar fungus, a most important economic life-line on the high plateau. At its peak, Dana monastery boasted over 300 monks, but now there were only 130. A stupa was being constructed in an aft chamber to hold the ashes of the former Rinpoche, Phuntso Tashi, who passed away in 2013. He was father of the current head Ngodon Nyima, as is the custom in the Kagyu branch. At a side chamber of the main hall was the Gesar Lhakang, holding a statue of King Gesar on a shiny brown horse.

Phuntso had mentored eight students in his life time; three of them were Rinpoches and two others acquired the title of Khenpo, the highest

Gesar statue / 格薩爾王
Animal specimens / 動物標本

scholastic achievement, while the last two had reached the level of meditation master. Phuntso's son Ngodon, though only 46, had already mentored five successive groups of students, each reaching at least the meditation level involving three years of isolated retreat. In all, he had had 54 graduating students, with the last group of nine soon to graduate once two more years of meditation was completed. Besides these higher level students, he had taught another hundred or so student monks.

There are fifteen events, ceremonies and festivals during the year at Dana Monastery. At the time of our visit, there were no activities, though we recorded the timeline and hope a future visit may coincide with those functions, be it an examination debate or the much awaited monastic dance performance.

While the main Assembly Hall, gradually rebuilt since the 1980s, may be considered grand and beautifully decorated, it was a small and rather nondescript building that put Dana Monastery on the map of China. Standing on the top and along a steep hillside of Dana's ensemble of buildings is Kar Ga'u Lhakang. This is the oldest of the buildings that survived the Cultural Revolution. It is because of this ancient architecture that Dana Monastery is listed as one of China's national protected sites. Today, surveillance cameras are set at multiple corners outside the building to monitor this nationally designated structure. Even seismic instruments are positioned at crucial spots.

The small gate to the building was locked every time I circumambulated this sacred red structure, *but on the second morning I found one side of the door opened. Tucked in my down jacket from the cold outside, I walked in. I could hear drum and bell and chanting coming from above. In front of me was a set of steep stairs to the second floor. I gingerly climbed the stairs and saw lights coming through another door into the dark stairwell landing area. The chanting had momentarily become clearer and mesmerizing while the deep drum beat was captivating my every step as I got closer to the door.*

I shook off the snow from my boots, and took off my shoes and hat to enter. Once through the threshhold, in front of me was a small and ancient chamber of a chapel with many volumes of Buddhist sutras on the wall and Buddhist statues lining the altar. By a window through which morning light barely shone, sat a middle aged monk chanting while beating a drum with intermittent bell and cymbal punctuation. I sat quietly and listened. After thirty minutes, his chanting ended. I walked over to where he sat cross-legged and introduced myself.

Awang Tushem is the lone caretaker of this national treasure of an ancient religious building. I found out his

A monk / 僧人   Assembly hall / 主殿

spoken Mandarin was excellent and we could communicate without trouble. He remembered seeing me four years ago at Dana Monastery. Not only that, he remembered seeing me nearly thirty years ago attending the enthronement of the Karmapa at Tsurphu Monastery outside of Lhasa on September 27 in 1992. At that time the Karmapa was barely seven years old, and I, as a young journalist from Hong Kong, was an honored guest, seated with the parents and siblings of the young Karmapa.

Yet another surprise – he had seen me running around at Palpung Monastery in Dege Sichuan, when thirty years ago in 1991 we made detailed measurements of the monastery, which led to

Thangtong Gyalpo cliff face / 貌似唐東傑布的懸崖

subsequent preservation of that renowned Kargyu monastery. What karma it must be that we should meet again at this remote chapel. As a parting gift, he gave me a small Thangka painting of the Usnisa Vijaya, one of the noted Tara protectors. The Thangka is said to have come from Palpung Monastery where we worked, and so was indeed a perfect parting gift before I took leave of Dana Monastery.

As my team got ready to leave, I saw a perfect pinnacle peak at the opposite side of the ancient temple. Nordeng was on hand to see us off. He pointed to the peak and said to me, "This is one of the most special peaks in all of the Tibetan Plateau. You can see on the cliff face the face of Thangtong Gyalpo, with his long hair and beard."

Thangtong Gyalpo is the much-revered saint who is the most famous architect in Tibet, known for designing and building many famous temples, including some in Bhutan. He is also the master bridge-builder, having constructed over sixty iron chain suspension bridges throughout the plateau. In order to achieve such difficult feats, he invented Tibetan opera and drama as a means to raise funds for his many projects. CERS has been fortunate in being involved in preserving one of his temples in Bhutan, and lately has been conducting research about his history and heritage.

Thangtong Gyalpo is known also as a medicinal deity. With his multiple skills in both the arts and sciences, he is considered by some the Leonardo de Vinci of Tibet. His bearded statue now sits at temple altars and homes throughout Tibetan areas, especially during this time of global pandemic. With this peak of Thangtong Gyalpo seeing us off as parting scene, I felt more than blessed to continue with our onward journey.

西藏北方朝聖—啟程

疫情時代的探索之旅

背景說明：

許多探險隊熱衷於大排場的行前派對與盛會，滿懷壯志又豪氣地準備出發，但卻常因目標不若預期或事與願違，而黯然返回。當然，沒有一趟探險能保證成功，若然，那就不叫探險了。因此，啟程前的慶祝不免為時過早，除非是一場不再相見的永別！

至於我，我習慣在探險前或旅途中隱姓埋名、低調遊走；不擅於高調宣傳，旅途歸來後亦然。未有手機到來之前，我們全程都備有衛星電話——但除非緊急狀況，不輕易派上用場，大多時候，我傾向對行程計畫與進展，保密到家。即便在行動電話與網路無處不在的時代，再怎麼遙遠偏僻的角落都能與世界保持緊密聯繫，但我始終選擇與世隔絕，好讓我能心無旁騖地沈浸與擁抱大自然，完全融入當地人生活中，更成為大自然的一份子。

只是，當下這趟遠途，因為疫情，而情勢大不同。我在澳門被隔離三週，之後才獲准在中國境內自由行動。我把旅途中的照片與「中國探險學會」(CERS) 的幹部與好友圈分享；對生活繁忙又經常環遊世界的這群朋友而言，這些斷斷續續傳來的照片，以往一般情況下，其實對他們沒啥吸引力。尤其我實地考察的慢步調總是與他們快車道的

速度大相徑庭。

只是，這段期間，無論是出於享樂或工作出差，大部分人不願為了短暫出遊而接受強制隔離的限制。因此，我的許多朋友已被困在家中超過一年或更久了，他們一心期待疫情早日受控或消失，儘速恢復自由進出的旅行好時光。於是，我那些即時的旅途亮點與分享，恭逢其時，忽然變得意義非凡而彌足珍貴，彷彿把朋友們帶在身邊，一路參與我們的探險之旅。

此外，在全球疫情大流行之際──當大部分區域屬於全封鎖或半封城的狀態下──發起探險旅程，其實更顯其附加價值。與足不出戶的他人相比，我能如此自由漫遊，與其說感覺特別好，不如說，耗費三週時間被隔離以換取數個月在中國境內的遊走探索，是極高的投資報酬率，也很公平，對我而言，是比投資更划算的回報。

如果我把旅程中錯過的目標當故事序言，似乎有些掃興。但其實，即便災厄頻傳的登山或遠洋惡水之旅，甚至那些幾乎把身經百戰的探險家難倒的情節，仍然是能吸引特定讀者，因為他們總能從危亂的插曲中，咀嚼出兼具不安與興奮的閱讀樂趣。由此看來，我大可不必掩飾近日和未來旅程中的挫折，包括一些費盡艱辛才勉力達成的目標。

且讓我從迂迴轉折處，細說從頭。所謂轉折，指的是「轉」頭，「折」返。第一個目標，印度河 (Indus River) 探源。如果成了，這將是我們完成的第七條河流探源行動。藉助多元衛星影象功能，預先進行資訊處理以尋找與鎖定目標──我們首先要到岡仁波齊 (Kailash) 峰的西部冰川頂端。抵達拉薩 (Lhasa) 時，我們開始申請通行證，準備進入西藏與岡仁波齊峰。

通行許可證無法在中國境外申辦，包括香港。近一年多以來，由於中印邊界的緊張局勢與軍事管制，西藏西部邊界已不對外開放。我傳了訊息給一位老朋友，中甸（香格里拉）前州長齊扎拉，他後來已晉升為西藏自治區主席；但我等不到任何回音，看來是軍令如山，恐怕比行政權還大。

我們只好改弦易轍，調整計畫，轉頭往北走，朝我們這趟行程的第二個目標前進；但最終事與願違，只能再轉頭，重來。於是，我們改往第三個目標：新疆北部也是無疾而終。如此一波三折，不免心灰意敗，但如今回顧檢視，這些遠途冒險的敘述在抵達完結的句點之前，所有細節都只是連結一段又一段的逗號吧。

旅途由此展開。

先從此生最昂貴的水療泡湯體驗開始。我並非溫泉愛好者，但這座位於海拔四千一百公尺、渾然天成的高原溫泉，實在教人難以抗拒；只是，收費太昂貴——折合美金大約一千一百美元——即使以奢華享譽國際的安縵渡假村，泡個浴也沒有如此驚人天價。

這溫泉仿若冒出土的巨型菇，四周的純白岩水溢流而出，往下汩汩滴落，凝固成水晶體。溫泉外型看起來像隻大象，所以被稱為象鼻溫泉。它的底層是個天然熱泉壺穴，泡湯者可以每人一次浸泡其中，享受這獨特的溫泉熱。還有那天氣，最讓我著迷了。不一會兒，漫天飛雪翩然飄下；心想若把此刻美景拍下，肯定羨慕死我那群關在家裡被暑氣蒸騰得冒汗的朋友們。

或許這念頭太自私了，老天不容。我才低頭想脫鞋解褲，我最新的華為手機，彷彿迫不及待般，從口袋裡滑出，大概是冷天飄雪慫恿它比我早一步投奔溫泉熱流的懷抱！美金一千一百元的「入場費」，就這麼隨「機」而「泡湯」了！

一名西藏朋友立即捲起袖子伸手入湯「打撈」我的手機。五分鐘後，一無所獲，再過五分鐘，依舊無功而返。我放棄了，就算搶救回來恐怕也回天乏術。我脫下衣褲，豁出去了，沈入溫泉裡，享受春寒下的泡湯極樂，泡久一些，把損失補回來吧。沉到肩膀下坐在湯池裡，熱氣騰騰，慢慢摸索溫泉底，那是砂石與泥漿，伸手撥弄幾番泥沙，幾分鐘後，我竟摸到自己的手機，立即順手撈出。看著泡過熱湯的手機，意識到大勢已去，我當下就決定不必送修了。或許溫泉泡久一點可以療癒失去的心痛，畢竟這是當地以療效聞名的溫泉，有助於療傷止痛。

隨行隊友看我為此天然溫泉而被迫繳付巨額「入場費」後，還能平常心看待，都詫異不已。其中兩人打趣道，最新的華為手機應該是耐用又防水。我們這次考察的後勤主管李娜趕緊把手機擦乾，並

Elephant nose hot spring / 象鼻溫泉

Bath holes / 溫泉穴

Tibetan Eared-pheasant / 藏馬雞

建議我們把它放在一袋大米裡,大米是優良的天然乾燥劑。我同意,交出手機前,多看一眼手機上最新的精密萊卡鏡頭,扼腕嘆息之餘,心中百般不捨,剛剛用這鏡頭拍下多少好照片啊!我們取出記憶卡,不幸中之大幸,記憶卡還可以在我的舊華為手機上使用。

大約一週後,前往拉薩途中,我試著打開那支泡過湯的手機,它近乎奇蹟地恢復生機。我贖回我的天價入場費,那場溫泉水療是免費的了。以療效聞名的溫泉,果然名不虛傳,連我的手機都起死回生了,唵嘛呢叭咪吽!

事實上,這並非毫不起眼的普通溫泉。它的位置獨特,坐落於西藏青海邊境上一間獨特的達那寺山腳,寺廟隱身於青海省玉樹州的囊謙縣,偏僻深遠。一千四百年前,這裡原是苯教寺廟,一一八八年左右,改為藏傳佛教的噶舉寺廟,不僅是西藏最古老的寺院之一,同時也被列為國家級受保護建築。這間噶舉寺廟隸屬扎葉巴宗派,那是藏傳佛教噶舉派的「白」教派中最小、且鮮為人知的教派分支之一。藉由這間廟宇的修復,高原上開始蓋起了好幾間屬扎葉巴宗派的小廟宇。

所謂「達那」,按原文定義,分別是「馬」與「耳」;寺院正上方的雙峰山形,因狀似馬耳而得名。這小廟位居海拔四千三百公

尺高的奇山險峻之上，四周被群山圍繞，我們四年前曾來過這裡，若沒有附近一位僧侶指點迷津，恐怕如墜雲霧，無法順利找到達那寺。因其高海拔與偏遠，除了旅人外，藏馬雞、高原山鶉與俗稱「藍羊」的西藏岩羊，都是這裡的常客。

此外，達那寺也被譽為嶺國國王之廟宇。嶺國國王格薩爾，是西藏高原康區傳說中的君王。格薩爾出生於長江旁的德格縣，師承桑傑扎葉巴，就這樣連結到達那寺。格薩爾王執掌嶺國期間，馳騁沙場而一統天下，使他成為西藏歷史中英勇無畏的英雄。相傳，達那寺是接受過格薩爾王資助的眾多廟宇中，碩果僅存的一家。直到今天，走進達那寺，仍可見許多保留完整的聖人遺物，包括在戰場上使用過的武器與盔甲。

格薩爾王身邊總計有三十位最饒勇善戰的將領與官長，每人被賞予一座白色佛塔，佛塔建築是古老鐘型，蓋在五千公尺高峰、沿著山上陡峭的懸崖旁，排列於兩個石窟中。雖然高不可攀，但當雲霧散去時，從達那寺可清楚望見佛塔。

今年四十六歲的俄登尼瑪仁波切，是寺廟住持，當我們再度重逢時，他顯得異常開心，畢竟如此偏遠廟宇，除了周遭信眾外，鮮有人會舊地重遊。俄登十六歲時，便以僧侶身份到四川德格縣最重要的藏傳佛教噶舉派的寺院內，修習佛法。「中國探險學會」曾於三十年前在當地執行過廟宇保護計劃，時間推算起來，剛好與俄登習佛的時間點重疊。如此因緣，使我們的久別重逢，格外親近。我們一行八人，當天就住在他家。他年邁的母親與阿姨，也住在這藏族傳統建築的隔壁房。

從中甸的中心出發，驅車三日，南征北討，抵達當晚，大夥兒都早早就寢，準備參加隔天一早在主殿內的誦經會。隔天清晨，當我起早出門時，竟發現地上已積了好幾寸的厚雪，我們的車都被一層

Car in snow / 雪覆蓋車子
Kar Ga'u Lhakang / 格薩爾拉康

白雪覆蓋了。從我的攝影角度來說，那是可遇不可求的好背景，因為修道院內還有進行中的工程，造成周遭環境混亂。但這下，戶外景物都披上白雪外衣，放眼望去，一片銀光耀眼，美不勝收；山頂上的兩座禪修小廟，在雪地裡顯得格外透亮素淨。目前，山洞裡還有幾位僧人已長期閉關一年，再兩年便可出關，成為大喇嘛。

主殿入口處的天花板與柱子上方，懸掛了包括雪豹、熊、巨狼、鷹和禿鷹等動物的標本。堂內只有少數幾位僧侶參與早會，因為當時正逢冬蟲夏草季，大部分僧侶已被送回家去採收珍貴的蟲草——高原上最重要的經濟命脈。達那寺的鼎盛期，有高達三百多名僧侶在此修習，但目前只有一百三十人。寺廟後方蓋了座佛塔，供奉二〇一三年圓寂的前仁波切平措扎西的骨灰。按照噶舉派的傳統習俗，他是現任掌門俄登尼瑪的父親。主殿的側室是格薩爾拉康，裡面有座雕像，是格薩爾王騎在亮棕色駿馬上的英姿。

平措扎西一生親自傳授過八名弟子，其中三位已是仁波切，另外兩位獲得最高佛學學術成就的「堪布」學位，還有兩位則已修得禪俢大師的境界。平措扎西的兒子，四十六歲的俄登尼瑪，年紀輕輕便已接連指導了五組學生，每組至少都已符合三年閉關的條件，修得禪定等級。俄登尼瑪總計傳授了五十四名弟子，最後一批的九位學生，只要完成兩年禪定，便可畢業。除了這些學術領

Monastery in snow / 雪中的寺廟

域的高材生，他另外還教導一百多位僧侶。

達那寺一年舉辦十五場活動、儀式與節慶。在我們逗留期間，恰好沒有任何活動。我們把各場活動的時間表紀錄好，期待未來再訪時能躬逢其盛，無論是精彩的考試辯論會或期待已久的寺廟跳神表演。

自一九八〇年期間逐步重建的主殿，看起來宏偉而精美，但若攤開中國地圖來看，達那寺可說是小而不甚起眼的建築。位於寺廟建築群陡峭山坡頂端的，是尕烏拉康──文革期間僥倖存留的最古老建築。正因為這座歷史老建築，達那寺才會被列為中國其中一個國家重點文物保護建築。今天，寺廟周遭各個角落都架設了監控攝影機，就連地震儀器也派上用場，安置於關鍵定點，小心翼翼地守護這座古蹟建築。

每一回，當我繞道想要進入這座莊嚴神聖的紅色建築時，入口處的小門總是緊閉，但隔日清晨，我意外發現側門敞開。我把自己緊緊包裹在羽絨外套裡，阻絕外頭的寒意。眼前是通往二樓的陡峭階梯，隱約可聞上方傳來的鼓聲、鐘聲與誦經聲。我小心翼翼，拾階而上；一抬頭，瞥見一束光源，穿門投射於梯井平台處。趨近那扇門時，誦經聲頓時清晰起來，剎那間，我有些不知身在何處，沉重的擊鼓聲，牽引我前進的步伐。

抖落靴子上的雪，脫鞋脫帽，我開門入內。過了門檻，眼前是一座古色古香的小禮堂，牆上掛著多卷佛經，祭台上擺滿了佛像。早晨的日光微弱，透進窗裡，前方一名中年僧人盤腿端坐，一邊吟誦，一邊擊鼓，敲鐘打鈸，斷斷續續地念經。我獨坐一旁，坐著靜聽。三十分鐘後，僧人的誦經早課結束。我走到他盤腿坐的地方，自我介紹。

僧人是阿旺土登，這家古老寺廟唯一的管理員。我發現他中文說得流利，聊起話來暢所欲言，相談甚歡。言談之間，我驚覺阿旺不僅記得我四年前曾造訪過達那寺，更出乎意料的是，他居然還記得我年輕時曾以貴賓身份受邀參加大寶法王噶瑪巴的坐床儀式，那已是一九九二年九月在拉薩外的楚布寺所舉辦的歷史事件了。當時的噶瑪巴，還是個不足七歲的孩子，而我當時以香港新聞工作者身分出席，是座上賓，和年輕噶瑪巴的手足與雙親一起坐席。

最令我驚訝的是，阿旺還對三十年前——大約一九九一年發生的往事，記憶猶新——他記得我曾在四川德格縣的八邦寺奔波來去，忙著量測廟宇，最終讓這座藏傳佛教噶舉派主寺及國家級文物保護單位得到一定保護。緣分真不可思議，時隔三十年後，我們竟在崇山峻嶺上的達那寺重逢。離別前，他贈予度母守護者的尊勝佛母唐卡畫。這張唐卡源自當初協助保護的八邦寺，那是我離開達那寺前收到最意義非凡而美好的禮物。

一行人動身離開前，我在古廟對面瞥見一座巍然屹立的完美石峰，躋峰造極。道別前，俄登尼瑪遙指山巔，對我說：「這是西藏高原上最特別的山峰之一，懸崖那一面還隱約可見狀似唐東杰布的長髮與鬍鬚。」

唐東傑布是西藏高度推崇的神人級建築大師，許多遠近馳名的廟宇，都是他一手設計與打造；除了西藏，還有一些在不丹境內。此外，他還是個修建橋梁的大師，整個西藏高原上，總計超過六十座鐵鍊吊橋都是他的建築成品。為了實現如此艱鉅的壯舉，他自行創作西藏獨有的歌劇與舞台劇，以此作為他籌集資金的管道。「中國探險學會」曾致力於維護唐東傑布在不丹蓋建的其中一間廟宇，最近也計劃對唐東傑布的歷史生平與作品，進行相關研究與整理。

唐東傑布也是備受矚目的藥神。他還精通藝術與科學，出眾的才華與卓然的成就，常被人比喻為西藏的達文西。今天，唐東傑布滿臉鬍鬚的雕像，被供奉在許多西藏家庭的神壇上，尤其現在全球疫情爆發之際，唐東傑布的守護神力，更廣受尊崇。有山巔上的唐東傑布來為我們送別，我感覺備受寵幸，對前行的旅程，滿懷信心。

Awang chanting / 阿旺誦經

Awang & HM / 阿旺和 HM

朝
聖
地
變
觀
光
麥
加

PILGRIMAGE SITE TURNED TOURISM MECCA

Kunming – June 25, 2021

PILGRIMAGE SITE TURNED TOURISM MECCA

After exploring a historic Kagyu monastery in southern Qinghai and a surprise reunion with an old acquaintance, we took our leave of Dana Monastery with the image of the bearded saint Thangton Gyalpo visible in the cliff face above. It seemed a most auspicious start to our journey south into the Tibetan Autonomous Region, as the resourceful Tibetan saint and bridge builder was a great remover of obstacles during his lifetime.

We drove south, passing a snow-bound high pass with prayer flags and crossing into Tibet before descending down to the Ji Qu, a fast-running river draining into the upper Mekong. There we passed again a cantilever bridge I remembered, a rare sight on the plateau today. Since part of it had collapsed, it was no longer safe to cross. Hopefully such architectural relics will also be protected in the future as specimens of ancient Tibetan technology, building skills, and heritage.

We passed by old Riwoqe, on the ancient caravan route from Qinghai into Tibet and onward to Lhasa and beyond. The large Sakya monastery stood out along the road with its painted tri-color stripes. We stopped by to make a respectful three circles clockwise around the base of the monastery before moving on. Riwoqe was also made famous by its supposedly miniature breed of horse or pony. Recent explorers had come to search for them, though the end result was somewhat small,

deflated and marginal.

Our next objective was an area known for its Bonpo Monasteries. Often described as the Black Sect, Bonpo originated long ago in western and later northern Tibet, developing out of nature worship and animism. In time, many of its practices were integrated into Tibetan Buddhism, just as Bon adopted meditation and much of the philosophy of the Buddhists. Now the most obvious practice differentiating it from traditional Tibetan Buddhism is the anti-clockwise circumambulation of sacred sites, be it around sacred mountains like Mount Kailash, pagodas or monasteries.

Riwoqe sakya monastery / 類烏齊薩迦派寺廟
Prayer wheels / 轉經筒

Three kilometers outside of today's new Dingqing County was Dingqing Gomba, one of the largest and most famous monasteries among the Bonpo sect. Instead of spending time inside this huge monastery, I went up the hill to a smaller Bonpo temple, adjacent to the large Dingqing Monastery. Richod Gomba, or monastery, was first founded in the year 1844. A single monk, Tsechen Thupshen, was on hand to greet me, not only by chanting with a drum, but he also showed me some old murals in a small chamber and religious masks made long ago. Though all religious practice suffered during the Cultural Revolution, the revival of monasteries began in 1982. At the time, the presiding Rinpoche, Yangdron Gyamtse, led the effort to bring the monastery back to life. He even assisted in the reconstruction of many other Bonpo monasteries in the vicinity. In 2009, he started a religious institute within Richod Monastery.

Today, Richod Monastery has grown from one hundred monks in 1997 to over 500 now. Its regimen of studies is very intense, and daily routine is adhered to strictly. The monks are able to enjoy only one free day each week, on Sunday, and a yearly one-month vacation when they may go collect alms and some pocket money by being invited to pray at private homes or events. Twice a year, student monks would travel over a hundred kilometers away to engage in a three-day debate with monks of another famous Bonpo monastery, Tsedrug Gompa. Despite its renowned religious and scholastic achievements, with Dingqing Monastery right next door, I cannot but feel that Richod will continue to exist somewhat under the shadow of its much larger neighbor.

As Tsedrug Monastery was brought up, I decided to back track for almost one hundred kilometers and head up a very high mountain to over 4800 meters to reach this famous center of Bonpo meditation. What used to be an extremely difficult climb by foot has recently been replaced by a long drive on a switch-backed paved road. It was apparently so remote and peaceful that, soon after climbing the hill, we encountered a large herd of over thirty Blue Sheep grazing across the valley. Such high mountain wildlife are rarely seen together in numbers larger than a dozen.

The best known photo from Tsedrug Monastery is of a huge naturally eroded hole on a limestone peak where some meditation houses have been built on a most precipitous cliff face. As our cars climbed up over a thousand meters from the base of the mountain, I finally beheld this famous scene in front of my eyes. However, I also saw many other cars parked near the top, and there were plenty of tourists around. No doubt this hidden Bonpo

Tsedrug assembly hall / 孜珠寺主殿

Tsedrug monastery scene / 孜珠寺全景

meditation retreat has, like many remote corners of the world, become a tourist attraction because of the internet age. As I got out of the car, I heard more than one drones flying overhead. It was disgusting to watch as one drone flew right past the open natural hole where monks kept tiny quarters for their meditation hideaways.

Tendrin O'dzer Rinpoche is the presiding head of Tsedrug monastery. He was born in 1971 and enthroned as a reincarnation lama at the age of 13. During an interview almost twenty years ago, he said that he would not like to see his monastery becoming a tourist spot. Though that may help in their finances and the buildings may shine with glistening gold roof, but the essence and meaning of the monastery would be lost and becoming just an empty shell, so he said. Apparently, what the Rinpoche feared most has already happened.

I did a little hike toward that part of the monastery, took a look and a few pictures, and decided this remote sacred site has now been reduced to a tourist mecca. I called upon my team and headed down the hill. It was a disappointment for an explorer who is used to making discoveries in places few people have visited. On the other hand perhaps it is karma that has now turned Tsedrug Monastery into one of the hottest spots to visit in northern Tibet.

We continued on our drive to Lhasa. From here on, almost all monasteries were of the Gelug Sect, commonly known as the Yellow Sect. At Sog Xian before reaching Naqu, we passed by the Sog Tsandan Monastery. I had on several occasions driven past this huge edifice, much resembling the Potala Palace in Lhasa. When I first saw it in 1985 during a National Geographic expedition, it was in a much dilapidated state. I passed it again in 1991 and several more times since. Finally, on this trip, I could see that it was now well repaired and looked rather grand, even from a distance.

As someone not much attracted to grandiose eye-catching things, I have often opted for less obscure yet more interesting buildings or even niche structures. Nonetheless, with my team, who may have differing interests, we stopped and made a quick visit of the premises. I found myself somehow more fascinated by the kitchen near the entrance, where a few monk chefs with helpers were just then preparing breakfast for perhaps a few hundred monks.

Monasteries from here on were usually sub-monasteries dominated by the two head monasteries of Drepung and Sera in Lhasa. Gelug is the youngest of all sects of Tibetan Buddhism, being a reformist sect with around four hundred years of history. The Fifth Dalai Lama took the sect to the height of popularity and power during the early part of the Qing Dynasty in the mid-1600s, transforming or obliterating many of the earlier monasteries. Today, the cycle of incarnations of the Dalai is into its 14th generation.

Our team took up abode at the very traditional Shambala Hotel inside the old city section of Lhasa. Belonging to a good friend Laurence Brahm, it has become our CERS dorm hotel over the years, especially since it is situated adjacent to the polygonal Barkhor Street that rings the sacred Johkang monastery. From the roof of our hotel, I had a full view of the Potala Palace, with its golden roof shining during the day and at night, being lit up with flood lights.

Near our hotel, during the day, in particular in the morning and evening, one can find a constant flow of

Tibetans, locals and those traveling into the city from distant parts of the plateau, all engaged in circumambulation of the Johkang by following the Barkhor in a clockwise circle - an age-old tradition. But today, many traditional shops along that route have been turned into photo pop-up stands, offering Tibetan costumes catering to a large influx of tourists, with make-up artists on hand to add red cheeks. There are no shortage of young girls and women lining up for such photo ops. These young ladies are practically all from interior China traveling to the Tibetan capital in order to share their experience with friends and groups online.

Lhasa, represented by the Potala presiding over it, has traditionally been known as the most important religious mecca for Tibetans and other Buddhists of the Vajrayana tradition. But today, it has turned into a city with every modern amenity that the younger generation can expect to find. The clock continues to tick and move forward. Will it ever go backward in time, like the Bonpo monasteries I visited that move in an anti-clockwise circle? At least for this particular person it is somewhat possible, when I reminisce about my first trip to the Tibetan plateau in 1981, exactly forty years ago.

Potala in evening / 布達拉宮的傍晚

朝聖地變觀光麥加

走訪青海南部一座歷史悠久的噶舉寺，並與一位老朋友意外重逢後，我們離開了達那寺，懸崖上滿臉鬍鬚的唐東杰布的聖徒形象，放在心中，一併帶走。這似乎是我們南下西藏自治區之旅的一個最吉祥的開始，因為這位神通廣大的藏族聖人和橋梁建築大師的一生，可是排除障礙的高手，想必可以祝福我們一路順暢。

驅車往南，一路大雪紛飛，我們穿越積雪盈尺的高地，路旁西藏幡旗飄揚，緩行至湍急的湄公河上游吉曲河。我記得我們在那裡跨越一座懸臂橋，至今仍是高原上難得一見的景象。由於部分橋梁已坍塌，不宜硬闖跨橋，太危險。期待未來有朝一日，這些建築遺跡也能被列為重點文物，保障西藏古技術、建築法與珍貴遺產的完善。

進入拉薩與後續的行程，我們得取道類烏齊──走一段從青海到西藏的茶馬古道。沿途可見宏偉的大薩迦派寺院，還有彩繪三色幡旗隨風飄揚，輝映出醒目的繽紛色彩。延續旅途前，我們稍作停留，到寺廟底層，虔心轉了三圈順時針的經綸。類烏齊也以當地罕見的矮種馬或小馬品種而聞名遐邇。近年來越來越多探險者慕名而來，雖然他們成績比預期中的小馬還要小而不起眼。

我們的下一個目標是以苯教寺廟著稱的區域。苯教為西藏本土宗教，源於西藏西方，

再從西藏北方傳入，以自然界神靈與鬼神崇拜為主。隨著時間流逝，苯教的許多信仰實踐開始融入藏傳佛教的習俗，譬如苯教採用了冥想禪定，與大部分佛教的教義與信念。唯一與傳統藏傳佛教最大的差異，在於轉動經輪時，苯教以逆時針方向繞行，無論是在類似岡仁波齊的聖山，或寶塔與寺院。

在今天的新丁青縣城外三公里處，我們抵達丁青貢巴——苯教中規模最大、最著名的寺院之一。我不打算在這座殿宇宏偉的寺院裡消磨太多時間，於是走上山，找到一座較小的苯教寺廟——創建於一八四四年、離大丁青寺不遠的日追寺。一位名叫次成塔才 (Tsechen Thupshen) 的僧人在場迎接我，不僅以鼓誦經，還向我展示了一個精彩小房，室內掛滿古老壁畫與年代久遠的宗教面具。雖然所有宗教活動都曾在文革期間大受影響，但寺院重修早在一九八二年便陸續啟動，由當時住持揚宗江才仁波切主導，修復建築，復興廟宇。除了自家廟宇，他甚至協助附近其他苯教寺院的重建工作。二〇〇九年，揚宗江孜仁波切在日追寺內創辦了佛學院。

今天，在日追寺修習的僧侶，從一九九七年的一百名成長至逾五百位僧侶。佛學院治學嚴謹，僧侶們都得遵守日常作息。除了每週有一天的自由時間，其餘都得恪守學習要求，週日和每年一個月的假期期間，他們可以受邀到私人住家祈禱或主持宗教活

Traditional cantilever bridge / 傳統懸臂橋
Tashilin Gelug monastery / 塔什林黃教寺廟

動，藉此存下一些零用錢。日追寺也規定學員一年兩次，步行到超過一百公里之外的苯教寺廟孜珠寺，在那著名的寺廟裡，與其他僧侶進行為期三天的辯經。儘管學術成就非凡，但因丁青大廟就在隔壁，我總覺得日追寺終究得在大廟環伺的陰影下，辛苦求存。

提起孜珠寺，我最終決定往回走，去看看這間聞名遐邇的苯教寺廟。過去，徒步爬上超過四千八百公尺高山是多麼艱辛費力的事，但現在卻是鋪好車子可開的瀝青路面，省力好走。但它確實靜謐深遠，以致才爬上山後不久，竟與超過三十隻浩浩蕩蕩的岩羊群不期而遇，果然都是「同好」，因為這類高山野生動物很少如此大陣仗群聚。

孜珠寺最為人熟知的指標照片，是蔚藍天空下的自然洞穴四周，幾間修道房舍屹立懸崖邊。當車子開上超過一千公尺高山後，我終於親眼看見孜珠寺！但我也同時發現好多車子與遊客，人聲鼎沸。顯然這個隱秘的西藏苯教重鎮一如其他遠在天邊的角落，不敵網路時代的大肆喧騰，而成了觀光勝地。我才剛下車，從遠處邊聽見好幾台無人機在上空盤旋。瞥見一台無人機大刺刺地穿越大石洞，肆無忌憚地擾亂僧人冥想的禪

Richod Gomba / 日追寺

Blue sheep herd / 岩羊群

Meditation abodes / 閉關場所

修處，真是太可惡了！

仁波切丁真俄色是孜珠寺的住持喇嘛。他出生於一九七一年，十三歲即為轉世喇嘛。我曾在二十年前的一次採訪中，聽他提起心中隱憂，「不希望看到他的寺院成為旅遊景點。」他指出，發展觀光對他們寺廟的營運與財務或許有所助益，寺院建築也可能維修裝飾得光輝閃耀，但終將失落了寺院的本質和意義，淪為空殼。顯然，仁波切最擔心和不願見的事，已不幸成真。

我往寺廟方向徒步前行，看了幾眼，再拍幾張照片，心中惋惜，確定這偏遠幽靜的聖地，已確實淪為旅遊勝地。我召聚了團隊，準備下山。身為探險家，我向來習慣深入杳無人煙之地探索，此情此景，令人扼腕嘆息。另一方面，或許是難以預料的因果業報吧，孜珠寺竟成了藏北最熱門的觀光景點之一。

我們繼續驅車往拉薩去。由此前行，我們後來所見的寺院，幾乎都屬格魯派，俗稱黃教。在索縣到那曲之前，我們經過索贊丹寺。我曾多次驅車路過這座壯觀大寺院，與拉薩的布達拉宮有幾分相似。一九八五年與「國家地理」探險隊初次訪視索贊丹寺，當時它仍處於破敗不堪的狀態。一九九一年我再度途經此處，此後又來過好幾次。最後這一次的舊地重遊，雖然只能遠觀，但仍可清晰看見它修繕完工，殿宇宏偉的外觀。

相對於浮誇瑰麗又眾所矚目的建築，我對獨樹一幟而少見的建築反倒比較感興趣。但那是我個人的喜好，我的團隊成員或許各有不同志趣，所以，我們還是停下腳步，快速參觀瀏覽一下。不自覺走到附近入口處，角落邊的廚房深深吸引我，幾個僧侶與助手正在廚房裡為其他數百名僧侶學員準備早餐。

Sog Zandan monastery circa 1991 / 索縣贊丹寺於 1991 年

朝聖地變觀光麥加

Sog Zandan monastery in 2021 / 索縣贊丹寺於 2021 年

由這裡一路往後的旅途，我們所見的寺院大多是由拉薩的哲蚌寺和色拉寺兩建總寺院所主導的子寺院。格魯派是藏傳佛教所有教派中，最年輕派別，僅有四百年左右的歷史。大約一六〇〇年代中期的清初時期，五世達賴喇嘛大刀闊斧，改造或收編了許多早期零星的寺院，成功將該教派的聲望和權力，推向巔峰，確立格魯派在藏傳佛教的優勢領導地位，直到如今，達賴的轉世輪迴已傳承進入第十四代。

我們一行人在拉薩老城區內一間非常傳統的香巴拉飯店住宿，那是好朋友龍安志 (Laurence Brahm) 的飯店，多年來已成為我們「中國探險學會」的「專用宿舍」。飯店周遭是大昭寺環繞的多邊八廓街，絕佳的優勢位置，是我們的不二之選。從飯店樓頂往外望，布達拉宮盡收眼底，金色的皇宮頂，不分晝夜，閃閃發亮，光彩奪目。

飯店附近，尤其清早與傍晚時分，無論藏人、當地居民或從其他遙遠高原地入城的人，接連不斷地湧入，比肩接踵，人人按照順時針方向的一種古老傳統，繞著八廓佛繞行。但今天，同一條路旁的許多傳統商店，大多已改頭換面，還有不少拍照快閃店，為絡繹不絕的遊客提供藏族服飾，一旁還有造型師隨時為上門拍照的遊客化妝，補上紅腮粉。想要「粉墨登場」的遊客中，不乏少女和婦女，無論老少都耐心排隊，等著拍照留影。大多年輕女士來自中國內地，呼朋引伴到西藏首都一遊，迫不及待要與朋友和線上好友圈分享她們的旅遊體驗。

我走了一段路，發現原來世外桃源的聖地，已淪為觀光麥加，我失望地召聚隊伍，準備下山。我們將繼續往拉薩前進，心中不禁思忖，曾幾何時，這個被藏民與佛教徒視為最重要的朝聖地拉薩，也早已成為年輕族群可親可近的現代都會。身為探險家，我

向來以發現秘境為己任，此番現況不免令我悵然若失，但或許也可解讀為因緣吧，這些寺廟與「聖地」，如今已轉身成為更多人必訪之「勝地」。

以布達拉宮為代表的拉薩，一直以來被認定為藏族和其他金剛乘佛教徒最重要的宗教聖地。但今天，它已逐漸改變，開始以流行時尚與現代設施來迎合年輕族群的期待。時鐘滴答滴答，一刻不停留地，往前轉動。它會不會像我之前參觀的苯教寺院那樣，以逆時針旋轉？這是可行的嗎？我的思緒回到一九八一那年我初次踏上青藏高原的旅程，對我這個特別在乎的人，或許是可行的吧……？時光流逝，悠悠忽忽，回首恰好已滿四十年。

Tourist posing at Barkhor / 八廓街遊客

通
往
羌
塘
以
東

ARTERY OF THE EAST CHANG TANG and
beyond

Zagya Zangbo, Tibet – May 23, 2021

ARTERY OF THE EAST CHANGTANG and beyond

Not much is known, let alone written, about the Zagya Zangbo, a major river of northern Tibet. In Tibetan, it means grayish-white grass river.

Study satellite images covering an area west of the Tanggula Mountain Pass and it will reveal a solid group of mountains with snowfields and multiple glaciers. That is the headwaters of one of the most important tributaries of the Yangtze – the Tuotuohe. It was for a long time considered the source of the Yangtze, with its start at the foot of Geladandong Snow Mountain, the highest peak of the Tanggula range. To be exact, that source starts from Jianggendiru Glacier, which I first set foot on in the summer of 1985, before discovering a longer Yangtze source later that summer at a basin to the east of the range, the Dam Qu.

To the southwest of Jianggendiru glacier is the head of another glacier, also originating from Geladandong Mountain. The meltwater of Gangela Glacier flows in a southwesterly direction, and this is the source of the Zahgya Zangbo, the longest inland river of Tibet. The water will flow for 480 kilometers, with a drop of 470 meters in elevation, before draining into the salty Silin Co, the largest lake of Tibet.

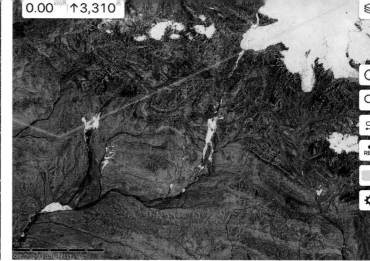

Geladangdong mountains / 格拉丹東雪山   Glacier feeding Zagya Zangbo / 冰河注入札加藏布河

But over a decade ago, the famous Nam Co (Namtso) north of Lhasa was bigger than Silin Co. Due to the glacier melt water of the large body of icefield feeding Zagya Zangbo, not least affected by global warming, rainfall and reduced evaporation, Silin Co has now grown in size and surpassed Nam Co to becoming the largest lake of Tibet.

South of the Tanggula range the watershed is overlaid by a labyrinth of river drainage systems with multiple sources all ultimately converging to join the Zagya Zangbo. This river then meanders to find a path through the extreme high plateau of the east Changtang, a wilderness known for its wildlife abundance and rarefied air, with an average altitude of 5000 meters and above.

The main river changes its name along the way, according to the traditions of the local nomads living and grazing their livestock along its banks. From its source, called Xiang Kar Qu, it would become Ruina Zangbo, then Na Qu Nun, before finally being known as the Zagya Zangbo.

I am camping on the bank of the Zagya Zangbo at a somewhat milder elevation of 4551 meters. The site is, by rough calculation, close to 450 kilometers from the source high up in the Tanggula Mountains, and only twenty or so kilometers from the mouth where the river drains into Silin Co. The estuary, filled with the meltwater of snowfields and glaciers in the Zagya Zanbo, is the largest source of freshwater into Silin Co.

Being a freshwater river, at this point about two hundred meters wide, there are plenty of waterfowl hanging around. Of largest abundance near the end of May are the Brown-headed Gulls, recently arrived from South or Southeast Asia. They hang around the river edge by our camp site, salvaging whatever remains of our food after we wash our dishes by the river. Their acrobatic performance in the air offers a great opportunity as I click away with my camera and long lens. Later they will also fight for the innards that we clean from the many fish caught in the river. These fish are a kind of "snowtrout" carp in the genus Gymnocypris, a fish found only here, and the only species in the lake. These scale-

Camp site by Zagya Zangbo / 札加藏布河旁紮營

less fish grows extremely slowly, yet are so abundant here growing to large sizes that we throw back anything we catch less than thirty centimeters long.

Smaller flocks of Rudy Shelduck hang around and an occasional Bar-headed Goose flies by. Nearby to Silin Co, we encounter several pairs of these geese marshalling their tiny chicks away from us as soon as we try to get closer to photograph them. True to form, like the Shelducks, when humans approach them while they are with young, the geese stretch their necks and lower their heads as if injured while hobbling off, an attempt to lure away the attention of the presumed predator.

Two days ago at Naqu, our team was reduced from three cars with nine members to two cars with seven, after I dispatched one car and two crew to head home due to this third car developing power loss at extreme elevation. We set camp with five tents, four for sleeping and one large one as cooking and dining mess. High wind is normal whereas occasional quiet calm air is most welcome. Deep blue sky is frequent but distant clouds gathering with localized storms can easily be observed over the distant land or on the lake horizon, a most beautiful scene to indulge in when lounging outside our tents.

A small herd of domestic yak grazes nearby, as there is one herder family living within sight. At times, the yaks graze right up to our tents. A few yaks with a red ribbon tied to one horn are considered beneficent offerings, spared from being slaughtered. Niqa Village where we camped is a cluster of simple houses or nomadic huts; seventy eight households spread far apart, each maintaining their own traditional grazing grounds. Each family would also keep a sedentary home at the "village" center called Xongmei, where old folks retire and young kids attend school.

While at camp, I soak up the sun for a much-needed tan to boost my bragging rights when I get home. Meanwhile, I dispatch a team to collect data from the single family, as well as to see if we can also collect some nomadic artefacts.

Dhondrup, now 69 years of age, joined the Communist Party in 1991. He was the village chief of Xongmei from 2001 to 2017, retiring only four years ago. With his wife Padme Tsedron, he has four kids; three boys and one girl. Their eldest son has inherited the father's position and is now the new chief of the village. A younger son is married and living in Naqu, the prefecture town. He is learning to drive and hopes to become a taxi driver in the future. The youngest son is at the county town of Xinja working with the culture and dance troupe. The daughter is attending to the livestock of the family.

They maintain two major herding grounds and one minor one for summer, autumn and winter grazing each year. Currently they are at their summer grazing ground right next to the Zagya Zangbo. Here they usually stay from the fifth to eighth month within the Tibetan calendar. Between the

Bar-headed Geese / 斑頭雁
Brown-headed gull / 棕頭鷗

ninth and tenth months, they will stay at a transitional autumn grazing ground. From the eleventh to the third month of the following year, they will be at a high mountain enclave wintering ground before moving gradually in the spring to the calving ground and summer pasture again.

Their livestock includes a herd of over 300 sheep, about a hundred goats, some 20 yaks and two horses. This spring, they have over 50 newborn lambs, 20 baby goats, and two yak calves. Each year, their income is around twenty to thirty thousand Renminbi, derived mainly from selling yak or lamb meat, accounting for between five to six thousand Yuan. Goat cashmere would yield about another ten thousand, and offering part-time laboring would provide just below eight thousand. Yak hide and sheep skin can fetch about two to three hundred yuan a piece.

With such profitable livestock and associated income, the family owns one car and four motorcycles, and everyone except children has one or more mobile phones. Whatever daily needs they have beyond their nomadic produce they purchase in the neighboring county town of Ban'ge.

Dhondrup and family / 頓珠和家人

CERS team with family / CERS 團隊和頓珠家人

Collected artefacts / 收集文物

The government has provided more basic services recently. Even distant villages are set up with electricity through installation of solar power in 2011. Running water was also piped in as of 2019, at times through drilling of a water well with pump. The village center where each family maintains a sedentary home has a kindergarten and a primary school. But the nearest monastery temple is over a hundred kilometers away. Locally villagers perform their religious observations by circling their village mani stone pile with prayer flags.

We were somewhat successful in collecting a few of their discarded utilitarian relics. They included a yak and sheep wool bag, some livestock bridles, ropes and a baby lamb skin. Such infants are never killed, but usually died from natural causes, like premature birth, lack of milk, or being crushed by the herd at night. Their skins are made into clothes lining, padding or blankets for babies.

Such items, with proper narratives, would further enhance our nomadic tent exhibit back at our Zhongdian Center in Shangri-la. Our exhibits often offer a perfect opportunity for educating students arriving at our Center to learn first hand knowledge from our team, not just internet second hand, third hand, or "infinite hand" dead knowledge. First hand knowledge has authentic and emotional value added, which passive knowledge can never provide.

Today, anyone can claim to be an expert on anything through the internet. But if one were to ask, "When were you there last?" then the expert would likely draw a blank! No doubt with a smart phone connected to the internet, we now have "PhD's" roaming the street. Even for me, who has roamed remote China for almost half a century, I qualify my first-hand gained knowledge by stating when I was last at a place, not assuming it is a static world.

Perhaps using the fluctuating stock market price, comparing quarterly vs. daily quotes, can be a good analogy!

However, today's media and columnists are not shy to speak or write with authenticity, not unlike stock manipulators with their own agenda. Yet the world is so used to accepting everything they say at face value, until that "stock market" would crash one day. Don't many of us just love dramatic stories, fiction or real, as well as subscribing to controversy theory.

Enough lamenting and philosophizing about the next generation of experts, and return to reality at hand, a lovely world with nature and natural people. We left our wonderful camp site and headed north towards my next destination – Shuanghu (Twin Lake) and the wilderness region of northern Tibet. I was last in that area some ten years ago and am really looking forward to returning to this wildlife paradise. It was once a no-man's land, before 1976 when the government started moving nomad families into the region from Xinja County, which ran out of grazing grounds. Over time, seven nomadic "villages" were established.

These nomads are spread out over the second largest terrestrial protected area in the world, The Changtang Nature Reserve, which was first set up in 1993, encompassing over 330,000 square kilometers. Recently, with an adjoining reserve added, the total area under protection grew to close to half a million square kilometers, representing an area as large as the Spain. The reserve was set up to protect both a high altitude ecosystem and many of China's most famous flagship species of plateau animals. They include the Wild Yak, Tibetan Antelope, Tibetan Wild Ass, and an array of other rare high elevation mammals. Before we reached Shuanghu, the county town, we had already encountered herds of many of these animals along the way, a most spectacular sight.

My new objective however was to get to Purog Kangri, arguably the third largest glacier in the world, part of the world's third largest ice sheet after the two in the Arctic and Antarctic. It was first defined as such by glaciologists of a joint China-US expedition in 1999. Situated some ninety kilometers northeast of Shuanghu County, it can be reached in a couple hours of driving. But luck would not prevail to allow an explorer taking another trophy so easily, especially not when he has almost reached the senior age of 72. Although, even reaching 5000 meters in elevation, I have yet to use the oxygen or compression chamber that we brought along for the trip. My plan would be fouled by another man-made hurdle.

What had been dirt roads a decade ago had now been turned into well-paved cement or black-top roads. My spirit was running high as the elevation was also getting higher. Along the way, we saw much wildlife including the

Tibetan antelope / 藏羚羊

Wild Ass and Tibetan Gazelle grazing or resting right near the road. Even the usually shy Tibetan Antelope can readily be seen close up. Such sighting is evidence that animals are no longer being hunted and quite well protected. When we were at Dorma Village, still over 150 kilometers from Shuanghu, there was a police road block ahead. This had become customary during the pandemic, and we thought little of it, expecting a routine health inspection.

A young and obviously junior police officer was at hand, mopping the floor inside the premises. He asked to look at our ID cards, and then told us that no outsiders were allowed to proceed beyond the check point. I pleaded my case and said we were conservationists who had once before been here studying wildlife in the area. He would not budge. I asked him to call his superior on the phone, hoping to plead for permission from a higher up. After all, I said I had come all the way from Hong Kong, even during such an extraordinary time of global pandemic.

We waited and within twenty minutes, a slightly older police officer showed up. We negotiated for a good fifteen minutes. The senior officer stayed firm and said an order was an order. He would not give an inch, let alone the two hundred miles ahead to Shuanghu.

Finally, he explained the rationale behind such a closed door to a visitor from so far away. "We are in the process of moving the entire county out of the Changtang region. Of seven villages, three have already been relocated to Shan Nan region south of Lhasa", said the senior officer. "Within the next two months, all remaining villages and their inhabitants will be totally moved out," he added solemnly. I could feel that his voice was firm and there was little ground to give. "These two days, there will be a major migration out," he further revealed.

Basically, the county name "Shuanghu" would be removed from the map from now on, and the former nomadic land for the last half century would be returned to nature and the wildlife, managed only by the Changtang Nature Reserve staff. Perhaps, I pondered in my mind, in time I can return with some form of conservation agreement for a joint project with the nature reserve.

Disappointed, yes. Defeated, no. Turned back from my attempt to reach the third largest glacier in the world and a return trip to the wildlife paradise of Tibet, I would move on to another target. Not unlike the Brown-headed Gulls, so good at salvaging kitchen scraps and the vultures, also expert scavengers, we also can call up our Plan B and make the best of any predicament, retaining some value for the time and effort we have so far invested.

My old motto to students came to mind again. "When you cannot change the situation, change your attitude." And in this case, also our altitude, going slightly lower. We shall continue our journey with a detour, marching west.

After all, old explorers do not die. They only move on, seeking new grounds.

通往羌塘以東

藏語原意為「灰白玻璃之河」的扎加藏布 *(Zagya Zangbo)* 河，是藏北最大內流河，這是一條少人知曉，也鮮少被提及與書寫的河流。

仔細判讀整片覆蓋唐古拉山口以西地區的衛星圖像，你將發現，扎加藏布河被雪原與無數冰川覆蓋於重巒疊嶂之上。那是長江最重要的其中一條支流——沱沱河的源頭。長期以來，源自唐古拉山脈最高峰格拉丹東雪山腳下的沱沱河，一直被認為是長江的源頭。準確地說，河流的源頭應是姜根迪如 *(Jianggendiru)* 冰川，我曾為了探尋長江源頭，於一九八五年夏天首次踏足此地。

姜根迪如冰川之西南，是另一條冰川之源頭，同樣源自格拉丹東山。甘格拉冰川的融水向西南方向流動，那裡便是西藏最長內陸河流——扎加藏布河的發源地。水流四百八十公里，高地落差達四百七十米，最終匯入西藏最大鹹水湖：色林錯湖。

大約十年前，位於拉薩北方的著名大湖納木錯，曾是西藏大湖之最，但由於冰川與冰原融化，壯大了扎加藏布河，間接深化了色林錯湖，湖泊面積逐漸增大，而超前成西藏最大湖泊。

唐吉拉山以南的分水嶺，被宛如迷宮般的引流系統交錯覆蓋，諸多源頭最終匯聚在扎加藏布河。而這條內陸大河，曲曲折折地在羌塘東部的極高之處，尋找出河口。提起這片海拔五千公尺以上的羌塘高原，向來以其野生動物之眾與空氣之稀薄，而聞名於國內外。

根據當地游牧民族在沿岸生活和放牧牲畜的傳統，這條主要河流之名，也易地而變。從源頭的「相喀曲」，一路到「瑞那藏布」，後為「那曲河」，最後才是「扎加藏布」河。

我就在扎加藏布河岸旁，某個海拔約四千五百五十一公尺左右的高原上，紮營而居。粗估推算起來，這個地點距離唐古拉山脈高處源頭將近四百五十公里，距匯入色林錯河口之分流，僅二十多公里。河口都是扎加藏布雪原和冰川的融水，也是匯入色林錯湖的最大水源。

扎加藏布河的水流清澈，兩百公尺左右的河寬，吸引水禽飛撲戲水，熱鬧非凡。五月下旬的初夏，棕頭鷗紛紛從南亞或東南亞飛來，這群嬌客在我們紮營區河邊閒逛，等我們飽餐後在河邊洗碗時，陸續飛來，搶救一些殘羹菜餚當食物。牠們以柔軟身段在空中飛舞，我把握難得的拍攝瞬間，把相機與長鏡頭都派上用場。稍後，棕頭鷗也會為了搶食我們清洗的魚內臟，而在河上大打出

Car in Northern Tibet / 探險隊在藏北草原
Tibetan gazelle / 藏原羚

手。我們在河中抓的魚，屬裂腹魚的鯉科類，那是當地河川獨有的魚，也是湖中唯一的魚種。這些少見的魚，成長期特別慢；我們一旦抓到身長不足三十公分的小魚，一律丟回河中，這一抓一丟之間，便可一窺魚的數量之多、身型之大。

又名赤麻鴨的瀆鳧，體型較小，一群群在附近晃盪；偶爾抬頭，一隻斑頭雁低空飛過。當我們就近色林錯湖周遭，想辦法要拍攝牠們的身影時，幾對斑頭雁也正想辦法驅離牠們的小雛鳥，不讓雁寶寶與我們太接近。一如赤麻鴨，小小斑頭雁一旦發現人類靠近，則伸長脖子，低著頭，彷彿受了傷般，蹣跚前行，試圖擺脫捕食者的注意力。

兩天前在那曲市，我發現隊伍中的一台車子在爬坡時狀況不佳，於是請兩位團員把車子開回去，將九人三車的團隊，縮減為七人兩車。我們搭起了五個營，其中四個當臥房，比較大的則用來煮食用餐。高山的風大，本是常態，但偶爾也迎來雲淡風輕的好日子。大部分時候，是碧空如洗的湛湛藍天，但偶爾也可見天邊堆疊的雲層與當地常

Fish from river / 河魚

Fish from river / 河魚

見的暴風正面交鋒，在遠方或湖泊上轟雷掣電，那畫面看得我勾魂攝魄。

視線範圍內一戶放牧人家的犛牛，如入無人之境，吃草吃到我們的帳篷外，其中幾隻角上繫著紅絲帶，那是被選為放生供佛的標記，享有免受屠殺當供品的特權。我們紮營的尼加村，是簡陋的游牧人家匯聚區，總計有七十八戶人家，零星散置，每戶相隔甚遠，各有自家的傳統放牧草地。每一家都要在當地「村里」中心設置「松梅」村，作為長久安居的休憩中心，讓長輩安心退休，小孩專心上學。

紮營期間，我想辦法確保自己做足日光浴，猛曬太陽，存夠他日回去向人炫耀的本錢。我同時派了幾位團員挨家挨戶搜集資料，順道看看是否有機會蒐集一些游牧民族文物。

六十九歲的頓珠，一九九一年加入共產黨，曾任職申扎縣雄梅村的村長六年，四年前才剛卸下職位。他和妻子白瑪才忠，共育有四個孩子，三男一女。長子承接父親在村裡的職位，是現任村長。次子已婚，定居縣城——那曲市，並努力在新興城市裡學開車，為自己將來當計程車司機做準備。幼子在申扎縣與歌舞團合作。他們的女兒則待家中，協助放牧。

頓珠一家有兩塊主要的放牧草原，另一個較小片的草地，則作為每年夏、秋、冬放牧用。他們目前的夏季放牧草地，就在扎加藏布河邊，每年西藏年曆的五月到八月，他們在這一帶生活放牧；九月至十月則遷移到季節交替的秋牧場放牧。十一月開始一直到隔年三月，他們往高處爬至高山飛地過冬，直等熬過漫漫長冬，再追隨春天腳步，移至長滿嫩草的夏季草原。

他們擁有的牲畜，包括三百多隻綿羊、大約一百隻山羊與二十頭犛牛，另外還養了兩匹馬。今年春

天，額外增添了超過五十隻新生羔羊，二十隻山羊寶寶和兩隻犛牛犢。像這樣一戶放牧人家，每年收入平均大約兩三萬人民幣左右，其中六、七千人民幣收入以販賣犛牛肉或羊肉為主；而山羊絨的經濟收入則佔大約一萬人民幣，另外，提供兼職勞動也能賺取低於八千人民幣的收入。此外，一塊犛牛皮和羊皮則平均可賣到兩三百元人民幣左右。

牲畜與相關產業所得，獲利不錯，使這家庭有能力購入一輛車，外加四台機車。除了小孩沒有手機，其餘人人都擁有一支或多支手機。若想購買遊牧農產品之外的日常用品，他們會前往鄰近的縣城，班戈鎮購買。

其實，政府最近已在當地提供不少基礎設施；即便是偏遠小鎮，也在十年前陸續配置太陽能發電，近兩年，村裡開始有自來水了，而休憩中心內也設有幼兒園與小學。但最近的寺廟則在一百公里之外。當地村民平日以旋轉村裡的咒文石槺與五彩經幡來履行宗教儀式。

我們在附近找到一些被棄置的東西，包括犛牛與綿羊包，牲畜轡頭、繩索與乳羔羊皮。這些小牲畜一般不會被宰殺，而是死於自然因素，例如早產、缺乏奶水或夜間被同群壓死。這些新生羔羊皮，可以被製成嬰兒的衣服內襯、填充物或毯子。

我們會為這些物品，一一附上詳盡說明，日後可以在香格里拉市的「中甸」中心所舉辦的「遊牧民族展覽」中，更顯生動與真實。我們的展覽經常為學子們提供絕佳的教育機會，那是原汁原味與有血有肉的第一手資訊，而非網路上二手、三手或「無限手

Brown-headed gull / 棕頭鷗
Bar-headed geese / 斑頭雁

Tibetan wild ass / 藏野驢

指」按兩下便輾轉得來的僵化知識所能提供。

拜無所不知的網路之賜，當前是人人都可自詡專家的世代。但當你問他：「你最後一次在當地是多久以前的事？」這些「專家」可能腦中一片空白，無話可答！確實，只要智能手機在手，滿街都是萬事通的「博士」。即便我已在中國上山下海、遊歷過中原的海角天涯將近半世紀，我仍以最後一次到訪的身歷其境為依據，世界之大，變化之劇，絲毫不敢將任何地方視為不變的「靜態世界」。

使用起伏波動的股票市場價格，與每季和每日報價進行比較，或許是個比較貼切的類比！今天的媒體和專欄作家，無論書寫或言談，總是言之鑿鑿，這和股票操盤手按其規劃操弄股市行情，其實沒啥兩樣。只是，世界已習慣接受他們這套言論而信以為真，直到「股市」崩盤的一天，才赫然醒悟。無論劇情虛構或真人真事，我們許多人不只熱衷戲劇性的故事，也對爭議性的論述，照單全收。

好吧，對新一代專家的慨嘆和辯證，到此為止；讓我們返回眼前的現實世界吧——有天然風光與好人的美麗世界。拔營離開湖光山色之地，我們持續旅程，往北前進，到下一個目的地：藏北的雙湖與荒野之地。我十年前到過這裡，至今仍念念不忘何時能重

返那片野生動物天堂。一九七六年以前，這裡曾是無人之地，爾後，政府開始把一些遊牧家庭從草原不足的申扎縣遷來，至今已有七個遊牧「村」。

世界第二大陸地保護區──一九九三年建設、三十三萬平方公里的「羌塘自然保護區」──近日已再擴大至毗鄰區域，保護區的總面積，將近五十萬平方公里，足有一個西班牙國家的大小。羌塘保護區以保護「高原生態與中國旗艦種高原野生動物」為主要目的，包括野犛牛、藏羚羊、西藏野驢與其他大批稀有的高原哺乳類物種。抵達雙湖縣城之前，我們已在路上和遇許多罕見的動物打照面，乍見一群群野生動物，那氣勢驚人而壯觀。

我的新目標，是前往普若崗日 (Purog Kangri)──一個繼北極和南極之後的世界第三大冰川──由中美聯合考察隊的冰川學家於一九九九年，首次為它定義身分與紀錄。普若崗日冰川位於雙湖縣東北

Bar-headed geese / 斑頭雁

約九十公里處，數小時車程便可抵達。但對一個近七十二歲的「資深」探險家而言，面對許多不若往昔的客觀條件，我恐怕難以隨心所欲往極地探索；看看現在，五千公里的高原，就得把高壓氧氣艙派上用場讓我用。不過，想不到阻撓我下一個計畫的障礙，不是大自然，而是人為因素──完全出乎意料之外。

十年前的碎石路已修整成黑亮亮的瀝青柏油路。我的精神隨著車子越走越高、越亢奮。沿途與野生動物近距離會面，包括在路邊休息或在一旁吃草的藏野驢與藏原羚。連向來害羞的藏羚羊也大大方方地現身，無畏無懼的模樣，顯見盜獵已不復見，野生動物的保護也已到位。抵達離雙湖縣外一百五十公里的多瑪鄉時，我們發現前方有警衛哨站。疫情期間，常見類似巡檢站，心想應該只是例常健康檢驗。

一名看起來年輕的初級警官正在室內拖地。他要求檢查我們的身份證，接著，我們竟被眼前這位年輕警官告誡，非當地居民，一律嚴禁進入，不得逾越巡檢站一步。我懇切解釋我們的狀況特殊，是曾到當地進行野生動物研究的環保組織。他堅持不讓步。我讓他打電話給他的上級，希望網開一面，獲得上級許可。畢竟我們是在全球疫情最嚴峻的狀況下，幾經輾轉，迢迢千里從香港來此。

我們耐心等待了二十分鐘，一名較為資深的警官出現。我們談了十五分鐘，一遍遍地努力協商溝通。資深警官態度堅定，禁令如山，只能遵守。他一吋也不許我們跨入，更別說兩百里外的雙湖縣了。

面對我們這群萬水千山趕來的旅人，他解釋了謝絕訪客的背後緣由：「我們準備將整

個縣城搬離羌塘區，計劃正在執行中。原有的七個村落，三個已安置於拉薩以南的山南地區。剩餘的村落與牧民，再兩個月內將全數遷離。」他最後再補充說明：「這兩天還會有大搬遷。」言辭之嚴肅與確鑿，看來，我們的「前途」，恐已無望。

基本上，「雙湖」這兩字從此將從地圖上被移除，之前讓牧民馳騁來去長達半世紀的土地，也將徹底歸還給大自然與野生動物。我心中暗自思忖，或許來日以保育合作協定等形式，再重訪吧。

失望嗎？當然。被擊退了嗎？不。世界第三大冰川與荒野之門既已被關上，我仍會轉向其他目標。一如棕頭鷗擅於處理殘羹剩飯，也像隨時伺機而動的　，我們總有突圍而出的 B 計劃，不讓已投注的時間與努力徒然耗費，更不會無功而返。

我常對學生耳提面命的信念，倏忽浮現腦中：「當你無法改變環境時，那就改變態度。」而此刻，我們要改變的，顯然是把「高度」調降。我們將繼續繞道，往西邁進。

畢竟，老練拓荒者不死。他們只會不斷前行，探索新境地。

西
藏
以
西
，
僧
侶
與
遊
牧
秘
境

MONASTIC AND NOMADIC ENCLAVE OF WESTERN TIBET

Wenbu, Tibet – May 25, 2021

MONASTIC AND NOMADIC ENCLAVE OF WESTERN TIBET

The northern road across western Tibet used to be extremely dismal. It starts from Naqu and ends at Ngari near Mount Kailash and the lake Bagong Co, now a hot spot on the contested border of the Himalayas between India and China. I had been on that "road" in 1993, and again on sections of it in 2002, 2010, and the last time in 2014.

In the early days the road was only multiple tracks on grass or dirt following a generally westerly direction. Today it is all paved and well marked with road signs. Huge 18-wheel trucks travel on it in caravan bringing supplies or construction material westward, returning with little cargo, or empty with no load at all. I would have loved to drive all the way west to Ngari, the prefecture capital of western Tibet, and perhaps to enter Xinjiang again through the Karakoram range. But it was not to be, as no border permit could be issued given the tense political and military stand-off along the border with India.

My team and I would instead head south to explore Wenbu, a dead-end region, south of the new county town of Nyima, that few would bother to visit. This is due in part to its extreme elevation of 4500 meters and higher. Besides, double-back driving is never the preferred route for any tourist. For me however, it is ideal to explore. The region is the heartland of the Bonpo religion, a practice

Multiple tracks in 1993 / 多條軌跡於 1993 年

indigenous to Tibet and started over two millennia ago. Although today it has much in common with sects of Tibetan Buddhism, the Bon religion is distinct and more ancient. Indeed, this area is considered by many as the earliest cultural center of Tibet.

The drive south of Nyima took us past some pristine blue and turquoise salt lakes with white deposits along the lake fronts. On the domestic side, sheep, goats, and sporadic yak herds grazed peacefully along these lakes. Soon we encountered more of the wildlife of Tibet, herds of Wild Ass, Tibetan Gazelle and an occasional Tibetan Antelope. Such animals must have been so rarely disturbed that they crossed the road often, and many small herds stayed within fifty meters of the road. On several occasions, we had to slow down to allow them to pass in front of our cars.

The scenery was spectacular and after climbing over 5000 meters to a high pass marked with prayer flags, we meandered down some switch-backs and reached first a small lake, Dang Qiong Co, beside which Wenbu was situated. It was first set up as a local nomadic administrative unit in 1974. The village with white stone houses was built along the foothill all the way to the lake front.   Adjacent to the village was Dang Qiong Gomba, a monastery of the Kagya sect.   As we stopped our cars in the courtyard and went through the main gate, we found there were a couple hundred people quietly sitting on the ground in the courtyard.   There was a three-day religious ceremony going on and locals had gathered to observe the prayers of the monks in the assembly hall.

We made a short stop and moved onward.   My interest was further on, at two Bonpo monasteries some 120 kilometers from Nyima.   Cutting through a valley, we reached the much larger lake of Tangra Yumco (Tangra Tsho).   Standing at just over 4500 meters, it was the third largest lake of Tibet and the deepest, with depth of more than 210 meters.

Tangra Yumco was famous as being a sacred lake together with Chongzong Relics, a sacred mountain nearby. Both were revered by all Bonpo followers. But the lake was also well known for a mysterious water creature; a kind of Loch Ness monster of Tibet.   Reported sightings of this serpentine giant monster by locals and officials had fascinated even scientists who came and

Dang Qiong Gomba /
當穹錯寺

Local pilgrims with lake behind /
當地朝聖者和湖

Assembly hall of Dang Qiong Gomba /
當穹錯寺主殿

searched for this supposed remnant of Jurassic time. It was said to have a small head, big eyes, long neck, a cow's body and grayish black skin. So far, no photograph had been made, let alone specimen captured. Yet the story continued to circulate. I did not have the pleasure of meeting this fantastic beast during our short visit.

At the small village of Wenbu Nan, some twenty kilometers to the south of the main town of Wenbu, the paved road finally ended and a dirt road began. At this junction were old and unique village houses, now considered cultural heritage for preservation. Near the edge of the village was Wenbu Monastery, first of a series of Bonpo monasteries around the lake.

Wenbu Gomba, though over a thousand years old, was small and had only four monks and one lama. At the time of our visit, all the monks had gone to Chugtso Gomba for a religious ceremony and only one twenty-one year old young monk was left to care for the place. Yondeng Tashi showed us around the small but important assembly hall. It had exquisite murals of the Bonpo style and contents. It was spared from the ravages of the Cultural Revolution, as the locals cleverly made use of the building for grain storage. Yondeng also took us to look at some of the earliest parts of the monastery with some relics and niches in an aft building chapel. He then took us to the back of the monastery where an open garden was filled with mani stones carved with the mantra Om Mani Padme Hum, meaning "Hail to the jewel in the lotus."

The road beyond Wenbu Nan became more precarious as it hugged the mountain side, so that we were left looking down to the lake below. There were also a few steep hills to climb and descend. After another thirty kilometers after passing Jixong Village a bit, we finally reached the destination of this trip and arrived at Yul Bun Gomba. By then we had driven over 150 kilometers from Nyima.

The monastery was set on the side of a cliff face, looking down and beyond to the blue of Tangra Yumco and the sacred mountain in the far distance. Of twenty some monks attached to the monastery, not a single monk was at hand, but we managed to find an older man who was the chef for the monastery. Through him, we managed to secure an unused house and hastily cleaned it up to become our hostel for the night. There were only two beds, so five of our team members had to sleep on the floor using our own mats and sleeping bags. As the most senior in our team, I of course ended up with a bed.

We cooked our own dinner also in the room. On such a summer evening, it did not get dark until almost nine o'clock. Just as we were finishing our dinner, two of the monks returned to the monastery, after a day at the ceremony at Chugtso Gomba, one of the most important Bonpo monasteries, some forty kilometers away. We were able to talk long into the night with 31-year old Tsutrim Namtak, a young but very knowledgeable monk.

Yul Bun Gomba was founded in the First Century, by one of the thirteen most famous Bonpo sages. It was thus among the oldest of any Bonpo monasteries, and became a most important meditation center of the sect. The most recent restoration within memory was in the year 1687 during the early Qing Dynasty. Many of the buildings were subsequently destroyed during the Cultural Revolution. In the 1980s, the presiding 9th Yul Bun Rinpoche, Tenzin Tsutrim, led the effort to rebuild it.

The following morning, I walked over to the old assembly hall and listened to Yanzong, the

Assembly hall of Yul Bung Gomba / 玉本寺主殿

other young monk, chanting his morning prayers. By mid morning when his morning service was over, we had packed to leave Yul Bun Gomba and headed back the way we came.

Along the way, we stopped at a cliff face projecting somewhat into the lake. Here was the site of an ancient palace dating back to the earliest days of Tibetan dynasty, the Xiangxong era, when Bonpo religion ruled the land before Buddhism entered Tibet. Now, hardly any sign of the past could be seen. Kesang Shampa, an 87-years-old nun, was the only person on hand and we chatted with her inside her very humble abode next to a small shrine. She had been in charge of lighting the oil lamp and caring for this little shrine site for over ten years.

We headed back to Nyima and continued east, setting camp this time at the southern edge of the lake front of Silin Co. Here a narrow strip of the road cut through the divide between Silin Co

Tibetan antelope / 藏羚羊

Shrine temple by cliff / 峭壁邊的寺廟

and Or Co. At this point the two lakes were only a few hundred meters apart. Perhaps in time, as water levels continued to rise with glacial meltwater from climate change, the two lakes would become one.

The government had turned the lakefront area into a reserve for wildlife and waterfowl, fencing off much of the water edge to prevent people from entering. We managed to find an opening with a dirt driveway up to a nomadic home - a simple house with a yak tent outside.

It turned out that Ugyen Lhagyal was owner of the household traditionally raising his livestock at this site. His family's area still belonged to one of the villages of the Shuanghu (Twin Lake) administration. His family was also assigned to care for the vicinity of the reserve and protected area, and he was paid 40,000 Yuan a year by the government as subsidy for that role, not a small sum in this area. As testimony to his position, we had to pay an entry fee to him at the rate of ninety yuan, ten for each person and twenty for the cars.

Ugyen's stone house and tent / 烏金的石屋和帳篷

Inside of yak tent / 犛牛帳篷內

Tibetan gazelle / 藏原羚
Blue sheep herd / 岩羊群

Ugyen was 31 years of age and his household had nine members, including his father (63), mother (59), wife Puntso Lhamo, two brothers and three kids. They all lived by the edge of Silin Co tending to the herd, moving camp twice per year based on the seasons. Their livestock included twenty yaks, 360 sheep, 120 goats and three horses. They also were proud owners of two cars and two motorcycles. Each year their income was around 50 to 60 thousand Yuan including the government subsidy of 40,000. Their own income was derived from selling yak and sheep meat, goat cashmere and animal hides. Electricity was provided, since 2009, based on solar panels, and water was piped from a well sunk in 2015.

Our camp was set up a short distance away from Ugyen's house. It was shielded by a small cliff behind while our front view faced the lake. Here we observed the constantly changing sky and water of the vast Tibetan plateau, a most spectacular display of nature to behold from morning to dark. Sunrise could reveal the horizon torched to flame. During the day, the clouds could at times perform dances from heaven to earth. After dark, the star-filled night presented the Milky Way, obvious even to the naked eye.

Nearby roamed freely a pair of Black-necked Cranes, several families of Bar-headed Geese with their newborn chicks, pairing Ruddy Shelducks,

Brown-headed Gulls, small herds of Tibetan Antelope, and a few Tibetan Gazelle. A group of Blue Sheep grazed casually along the cliff a short distance behind our tents.

It was here that I indulged in my last days on the plateau in northern Tibet - by far the best natural setting any explorer can wish for.

Sunrise over Silin Co / 色林錯湖日出

西藏以西，僧侶與遊牧秘境

穿越西藏以西往北之路，曾是一段荒蕪之途。這段路始於那曲，止於靠近岡仁波齊 (Kailash) 峰與班公錯湖的阿里區 (Ngari)，位於喜馬拉雅山的邊界，班公錯湖近年來成了印度和中國之間的爭議熱點。我曾在一九九三年踏上這條「道路」，並在二〇〇二與二〇一〇年，以及最近的二〇一四年，分別幾次重新踏上這條「道路」。

早期，這段大致上往西前進的路，只有草地或泥地的多條軌道。今天，所有道路都已鋪上柏油路面，加上路標。十八輪大卡車的車隊呼嘯來去，將物資或建築材料往西部運送，回程的卡車上貨物極少，有些甚至已完全卸貨而空無一物。我很想一路向西，開到藏西的首府阿里區，或許再翻山越嶺過喀喇崑崙山脈，進入新疆。但事與願違，與印度邊境的緊張局勢和軍事對峙，當局不可能簽發任何邊境許可證。

我們團隊捨西而向南，踏上少人訪視之地：新尼瑪縣城 (Nyima) 南方的盡頭，文部村。人煙稀少的其一緣由，是因其逾四千五百米的極端高海拔。此外，回頭的雙向駕駛從來就不是遊客的首選路線。但對我而言，這卻是深入探索的理想條件。這地方是超過兩千年的原始宗教——西藏苯教的大本營。雖然今天藏傳佛教的派別之間看似大同小異，但苯教卻迥然不同，且更為古老，因此，這地區無疑是西藏最古老的文化中心。

Bar-headed geese with chicks / 斑頭雁幼鳥　　Wild ass crossing road / 藏野驢過公路

往尼瑪縣以南途中，我們經過藍綠交疊的鹽湖，湖邊堆疊了白色沉積物。放牧的綿羊、山羊群與犛牛，成群結隊沿著湖畔走。沒多久，更多西藏野生動物沿途出現，我們陸續與一群群的野驢、藏原羚和偶爾出現的藏羚羊不期而遇。看牠們悠哉悠哉、結伴過路的模樣，想來這些野生動物鮮少被不速之客侵擾，許多小牲畜站在離公路僅五十米以內，我們常得放慢車速，禮讓牠們。

根據路旁的經幡旗所標註的指示，我們已爬上五千公尺高原，稍往下蜿蜒，最先進入眼簾的，是小湖泊——當穹錯湖，一旁便是文部村之所在，一九七四年首次被設立為地方游牧的行政單位。沿著山麓湖泊前的一排白色石屋，便是村落的標誌。村落隔鄰是當穹寺，屬噶舉派的廟宇。我們在院子裡停好車子後，穿過大門，入內時才發現，院子裡聚集了上百人，安安靜靜地，席地而坐。原來當地正舉辦為期三天的宗教活動，在地居民齊聚一堂，專注聆聽僧侶誦經。

短暫停留後，我們持續前行。我的目標是距離尼瑪縣一百二十公里的兩大苯教寺廟。穿越山谷，我

Wenbu village / 文部村

們抵達更大的湖泊，當惹雍錯湖——位處逾四千五百公尺高原，水深兩百一十公尺的西藏第三大與最深的湖泊。

當惹雍錯湖與附近的穹宗遺址，被視為苯教徒的聖湖與聖山。其中與聖湖相關的一則類似西藏的尼斯湖水怪，流傳已久。當地居民與官方都聲稱曾見過此大眼、長頸、牛身與灰黑蛇紋巨獸，甚至吸引科學家前來一探究竟，以為侏羅紀世代在此重現了。不過，至今沒有任何照片可以佐證，更別提有何標本；只是，謬種流傳，難以阻止。我們這趟短暫停留中，倒是沒有這份榮幸見到這隻湖中水怪。

我們在距離文部以南約二十公里外的文部小村落，把瀝青路走完，開始我們顛簸的砂石土路。新舊路交接處，有些老舊而獨特的房子，已被列管文化遺產的保護建築。村落邊緣的文部寺，是湖邊一系列苯教寺的第一間。

超過一千年歷史的文部寺，規模極小，僅有四位僧侶、一位喇嘛。訪視期間，其餘僧侶已前往曲措寺參加宗教祭祀，獨留二十一歲的年輕僧人雲丹扎西，留守顧家。雲丹扎西帶我們參觀小而重要的主殿，牆上壁畫描繪苯教種種淵源，內容豐富而細緻。文革期間，聰明的在地居民把廟宇當穀倉，掩人耳目的作法讓文部寺逃過一劫，僥倖存留至今。雍登也帶我們看看寺廟最早期的建物，

以及珍藏的一些遺物和壁龕。最後，我們一行人被帶到寺院後方，那裡是個開放式花園，瑪尼石上刻了六字大明咒「唵、嘛、呢、叭、咪、吽」，意為「向蓮花中的寶石致敬」。

越過文部南方的路，一路緊貼著山腰，越走越險峻荒蕪，我們只能小心翼翼地低頭俯瞰下方湖泊。曲折蜿蜒的山路，繞著陡峭山丘，上上下下地起伏前行。行過三十公里後，我們路過吉松村，終於抵達此行目的地——玉本寺。彼時，我們已從尼瑪開了一百五十多公里的迢迢遠路。

玉本寺建於峭壁邊，居高臨下，從遠處俯瞰當惹雍錯聖湖與聖山。我們抵達期間，二十幾位駐寺僧人都已外出，只找到一位負責膳食的老僧人。託他的協助，我們得以借宿一晚，倉促把空房打掃清理。房裡只有兩張床，七人的團隊得有五人打地鋪，睡自己的草蓆與睡袋。年紀最大的我，想當然爾，享有特權睡大床。

我們在屋子裡煮起晚餐。如此夏夜，不到九點天不黑。晚餐快吃完時，兩位參加宗教祭祀的僧侶，正好從四十公里以外的曲措寺回來，曲措寺被視為苯教的其中重要寺廟之一。我們有機會與三十一歲的次仁南塔，一名滿腹經綸的年輕僧侶，對話至深夜。

Stone houses of Wenbu village / 文部村石屋

Wenbu Gomba / 文部村寺廟

Old murals of Wenbu Gomba /
文部村寺廟古老壁畫

玉本寺是由苯教十三位傳教大師之一於第一世紀所創建，是苯教最古老、也是最重要的修行道場。有記錄以來最「近期」的修復，是一六八七年的明末清初，爾後大部分建築在文革期間被拆毀，一直到八〇年代，才又在玉本寺的第九任住持丁真次稱（*Tenzin Tsutrim*）的領導下重建。

隔天清晨，我散步經過舊主殿，聆聽另一位年輕僧侶楊忠進行早課與誦經。十點多左右，當他結束早會了，我們也已準備動身離開玉本寺，朝向來時路，回頭前進。

歸途中，我們在一個面湖的懸崖邊，駐足停留。那是古王朝的遺址，可以回溯到最早期的西藏吐蕃王朝前的歷史古國，象雄王朝，而象雄也是苯教發源地，早在佛教傳入西藏之前便已存在。可惜的是，當年的輝煌盛況，如今連一點跡象都已不復見。一位八十七歲女尼格桑強巴，是我們唯一可以找到的人。我們在她簡樸的小住處聊聊，與小神祠僅一牆之隔。她負責打理這偏遠小寺，天黑之後即按時點燈，日日年年，至今已逾十載。

返回尼瑪縣繼續往東，我們在色林錯湖的望南面湖處，紮營歇息。眼前窄小的路徑，把色林錯湖與吳如錯湖一分為二，由此望去，兩湖僅相隔數百公尺之遙。如果湖泊因氣候變遷、冰川融雪而水位不斷上升，或許不稍多久，兩湖終將合而為一。

政府已將湖泊前方大片區域，劃為野生動物與水禽保護地，不准訪客踏入。我們設法找到一個碎石車道的入口處，通往一戶游牧人家──用犛牛帳篷搭起的簡易房舍。

Murals of Yul Bung Gomba / 玉本寺壁畫
Yangzong praying / 楊忠祈禱

原來，烏金拉加是這間傳統放牧家庭的主人。他的起居地，仍屬於雙湖行政區之一的村落。他的家人也被指派負責看管保護區，政府每年付他四萬人民幣當這份職責的津貼，這在當地已算是一筆相當可觀的收入。為了證明他盡忠職守，我們不得不支付入場費九十元──每人十元，每台汽車二十元。

烏金今年三十一歲，一家九口人，包括六十三歲的父親與五十九歲的母親，妻子彭措拉姆，兩個弟弟與三個孩子。他們都住在色林錯湖邊緣，典型的放牧人家，隨季節更迭，而每年遷移兩次。他們所牧養的牲畜包括二十頭犛牛，三百六十頭綿羊，一百二十隻山羊與三匹馬。另外，能買得起兩部車子與兩台機車，對他們而言，是很值得驕傲的事。像烏金這樣的家庭，若加上政府付給的四萬人民幣，一年總收入大約五萬至六萬人民幣。他們自家放牧產業的收入，大多以販售犛牛與綿羊肉、山羊克什米爾與動物皮為主。這裡自二〇〇九年以來便配置了太陽能電板來提供電力，並以二〇一五年沉入井中的管線，來輸送自來水。

Kesang Shampa in her room / 格桑強巴在她的房間
Daughter of Ugygen / 烏金的女兒
Our camp site by Silin Co / 色林錯湖旁紮營

我們的帳篷，離烏金家不遠。帳篷被後方的小懸崖遮蔽，而我們前方，則是無限開闊的湖泊。我們就在這片西藏高原上，浸淫於湖光山色之中，旖旎萬變的雲朵在天空搔首弄姿，從日出到日落，輪番舞動出一幕幕最迷人壯闊的景色。天黑以後，夜空銀河燦亮，星月交輝，舉頭凝望，清晰得肉眼可辨。

黑頸鶴、成雙的赤麻鴨、棕頭鷗、一小群藏羚羊與藏原羚，還有幾隻斑頭雁領著一群小雁子在我們附近漫步遊走，如入無人之境，優遊自在。離我們帳篷後方不遠處，一群岩羊沿著峭壁放牧吃草。

旅途結束前最後幾天，我在藏北高原遼闊無邊的天地間悠然徜徉——迄今為止，我已領受大自然賜下的美好厚禮，身為探險家，我已別無所求。

Black-necked crane / 黑頸鶴

Bar-headed geese with chicks / 斑頭雁幼鳥

從黃河到佛教石窟

FROM YELLOW RIVER TO BUDDHIST GROTTOES

June 7, 2021 – Mai Ji Shan, Gansu

FROM YELLOW RIVER TO BUDDHIST GROTTOES

It was in 1982 that I first got a glimpse of the goatskin raft used on the Yellow River. Subsequently, a photograph of it with a Muslim boatman graced a page in my article in the National Geographic Magazine.

I went back in 1984, again under the auspices of the same magazine and managed to float down the river with the same boatman. After I observed him setting up the raft from scratch at his home, I floated on an innertube down the Yellow River in order to film him in action. Later I visited families along the river in Ningxia, a predominantly Hui Muslim province, where use of such skin rafts was even more prevalent.

At the time, skin rafts in Ningxia mainly held together 14 inflated goat skins, whereas those at Langzhou further upriver maintained a standard of 13 skins. Prior to my visit, the National Geographic had already published an article about an expedition led by Federick Wulsin, a Harvard scholar, and his wife Janet Elliott, between 1921 and '24. Wulsin's multi-year journey used in part a raft of 72 goat skins, with a tent set on top flying an American flag. They floated down a good section of the Yellow River from Lanzhou, arriving in Baotou after three weeks.

Yellow river 1984 / 黃河 1984 年

Such early explorers' efforts provide a humbling record for us late-comers. Today, many visitors, tourists or adventure seekers, will snap a selfie and consider they have "arrived" and "have seen" a place. It is not impossible to visit a couple dozen or more countries within a year during our jet age. For that matter, I often ask the younger jet set who brag of places they have visited; "So you have seen all these places; have any of these places seen you?" After all, leaving a positive impact, or even just making a local friend, is not all that difficult.

Massive goat skin rafts used to ply the Yellow River as one of the most efficient and cost-effective means of transportation in the old days, travelling from Lanzhou as far as Baotou in Inner Mongolia. Rafts of sizes upward of 150 skins were not unheard of, with the skins being sold at the far end as goat hide, after which the boatmen would travel home by road.

After almost forty years, I arrive back in Ningxia expecting that, like other primitive methods of transportation, such means of crossing the Yellow River will have disappeared and become obsolete. Instead, surprise awaits me. At Zhongwei, a riverside town I visited before, there are dozens of skin rafts behind a closed gate. The town

1920s Wulsin expeditions / 吳爾森 1920 年代探險
Wuslin on the Yellow river / 吳爾森於黃河

now has been turned into a tourist destination, and families nearby are integrated into this newly developed and fully packaged attraction. Of course, safety measures are also implemented with small groups of up to six passengers to a raft, and everyone must put on life vests. A single oarsman will pilot the raft from the front, using the oar as both sweep and rudder. The 1F journey may last twenty to thirty minutes, of course with additional ticket price beyond the base entry fee onto the premises.

We are lucky to meet Yu Xiao, a young boatman, who takes an interest in my return visit. He later invites us to his village home, to meet his uncle Zhou Chong who is an expert on the making of skin rafts. From him, we not only manage to learn more about such crafts, but also purchase a raft to take back to our Zhongdian Center as a display specimen to complement our yak-skin coracle boat.

While the skin raft has found a modern value and made itself equitable to be sustained through tourism, the traditional waterwheel has met its destiny and receded from history altogether, leaving behind only a single specimen for display. When I visited the area in 1984, there were many big functional waterwheels redirecting water from the banks of the Yellow River to nearby fields through irrigation canals and aqueducts. Such an ancient and ingenious method, though very environmentally friendly, has become obsolete. I was fortunate to see them in action before, and managed to see one now left to waste along the river.

Any explorer like myself who started venturing into China and traveling far and wide as far back as the 1970s would have regrets. Among them for me is Mai Ji Shan, one of the most famous Buddhist grottoes in China. I did have the great opportunity of visiting Dunhuang, Yungang and even Binglingsi grottoes, and have even written about them. But Mai Ji Shan has been on my wish list for a very long time, over forty years, without a visit. Unlike living culture that may disappear in time due to changing times, artistic culture, like religious temples and relics, may be destroyed by natural disasters or even man-made ones like war and revolution. Mai Ji Shan is among those that luckily survived the ravages and rampages of history.

My biggest desire is to see art, both sculpture and affiliated relics, from the Northern Wei Dynasty of the 4th to 5th Century. Since my days of studying Art History as one of two majors at university, I have always been interested in sculpture of the Northern Wei. Why Northern Wei? Perhaps it relates somehow to my special love

Boatman with rafts / 船夫與皮筏

Tourists on rafts/ 遊客搭皮筏

CERS raft purchase /
CERS 收購的皮筏

Binglingsi Grotto 169 / 炳靈寺 169 石窟
Yungang grotto / 雲岡石窟

of El Greco's work; the elongated features and figures of the people, and in the case of the grottoes, also of the bodhisattvas. It is for that reason that I visited Binglingsi grottoes and focused on Cave number 169, which has a concentration of Northern Wei sculptures. Pictures I took in 1979 illustrated my article in Architectural Digest. Back then, picture taking was not a major issue, and I was able to photograph even inside the world famous grottoes at Dunhuang and published a cover story for Asia Magazine, and later for Reader's Digest.

Today, I finally have the good fortune to be in eastern Gansu, making my first visit to Mai Ji Shan, the name of which pertains to its resemblance from afar to a large pile of wheat. We have the double fortune that the home-stay house we picked online is owned by a young couple of whom the wife Xin Mengmeng is one of the most knowledgeable experts in charge of introducing the caves to special guests visiting Mai Ji Shan.

Xin Mengmeng points us to a back door path with an undulating hike to reach the entrance, allowing us a spectacular view of the cliff-side grotto from a unique vantage point. From that angle, Mai Ji Shan actually looks more like a big honey comb beehive dotted with holes and lines.

An entrance fee into the area is a matter of course in today's China, with a

Maji Shan from distance / 從遠處看麥積山

charge of RMB 80. Old as I am, my fee is waived, but not when I want to enter older grottoes of the Northern Wei some twenty times my age. Views of such caves with the best samples of statuary from that era do not come cheap, at RMB 100 and 180 to enter grottoes 44 and 133 respectively. I join a group of three young art students who have come especially to study such older caves. To say "study these caves" is a huge overstatement, as each visit inside must be finished in a matter of ten minutes or less.

The long stairs built to access these cave niches, with twisting route and switch-back climbs, tend to make the grottoes more difficult to reach. The three huge Buddhas carved out on the rock face seems to look down upon us tiny humans as if with a solemn, yet slightly condescending, smile. While most cliff face niches and grottoes are open to public view, the most valuable ones are closed behind locked gates. Even with a paid visit, such caves and the statues inside are not allowed to be photographed. So I mainly satisfy myself by snapping at the free ones, and buy a few books with pictures of the Northern Wei grottoes 133 and 44, the two that I managed to go inside and appreciate close-up.

Inside the duo-chamber grotto 133, I spend my special moment with a little monk, about two-third of my size. He remains one of the most wonderful sculptures of all Northern Wei statues, bringing joy to many who have had the chance to meet him. His charming smile has often been compared to that of Da Vinci's Mona Lisa, though in my view his smile is more innocent and sacred. Though Grotto 44 hosts statues from the later Western Wei era, they are nonetheless worthy of visit, especially with Xin Mengmeng's vivid explanation bringing back some old memories of my long-

Three huge Buddha / 三尊巨佛
Early sculptures at top tier / 上層早期雕塑

forgotten study from my college days.

There are also remains of mural art on the walls and ceilings to complement the sculptures and statues, spanning several dynasties and centuries. Today, some of these artistic relics are over 1600 years old yet each day still attract hundreds of admirers from all over China. One of those who came, 1200 years ago in the mid-8th Century, was the most renowned Chinese poet of the Tang Dynasty.

Du Fu spent his toughest time in nearby Tian Shui, exiled and destitute for three months as wars and turmoil engulfed the capital in Chang An (now Xi'an). During that period, he wrote a hundred and seventeen poems, almost one a day. And on one special day, he wrote about his visit to Mai Ji Shan. At the time, there were few monks remaining at the Rui Yin Temple at the foot of the mountain.

"Shan Si" (Mountain Temple)

Wild temple monks are but few, mountain round and tiny path high;
Musk deer sleeps among stone and bamboo, parrot picks at golden plum;
Running streams man passes by, cliff abode firmly hold;
Evening light approaches upper pavilion;
Bird's autumn feathers seen from a hundred li.

山寺

作者：杜甫

野寺殘僧少，山園細路高。麝香眠石竹，鸚鵡啄金桃。

亂石通人過，懸崖置屋牢。上方重閣晚，百里見秋毫。

Such were the thoughts during the mid-8th Century of one of the most famous Chinese poets of all times – of a remote and natural place.

I leave Mai Ji Shan with the same thoughts that I had had over forty years ago when I visited several of the most important grottoes in China. It is not an after-thought but always my final thought, when I look at such wonderful pieces of art. How come none of these expert artists, artisans, and craftsmen left behind their names and signatures? Compared to our contemporary "artists" who care so much about fame, wealth and glory, who indeed is actually an artist in most pure form?

Whom I admire more is anyone's guess.

Smiling monk / 微笑和尚

從黃河到佛教石窟

我記得第一次看到黃河上使用山羊皮筏時，是一九八二年。隨後，一張穆斯林船夫的照片，刊載於我在美國《國家地理雜誌》上的一篇報導。

兩年後我重返現場，再次在《國家地理雜誌》贊助下，和同一位船夫一起順流而下。我在他家中近距離觀察，看他如何從零開始打造，一步步完成整個羊皮筏；為了捕捉畫面，我在黃河下游的內胎上載浮載沉，想辦法拍攝他製作皮筏的一舉一動。我後來繼續走訪寧夏沿河的家庭，這是一個以回族穆斯林為主的省份，類似的皮筏在當地仍是個極為普遍的交通工具。

當時寧夏地區所使用的皮筏，主要是由十四張充氣山羊皮所製成，而上游的蘭州所製造的木筏，則保有十三張山羊皮的標準。在我採訪前，《國家地理雜誌》已發表過一篇使用羊皮筏子探險的報導——一九二一至一九二四年間，由哈佛學者費德烈．吳爾森 (Federick Wulsin) 與其妻珍娜．艾略特 (Janet Elliott) 領隊的文獻。吳爾森的多年旅程中，其中某些階段採用七十二塊羊皮製成的筏子，頂端還掛上美國國旗。他們從蘭州出發，順著黃河之水漂流前行，三週後，順利抵達內蒙的包頭。

這些早期探索者的用心努力，令人肅然起敬，也為我們後來者提供了一份不得不虛心

領教的記錄。今天，許多遊客或喜愛探險者，熱衷於自拍，拍照打卡上傳後，便已認定自己「抵達」並「看到」了。在這個噴射機的時代，一年內到數十個或更多國家也並非不可能的事。既然這批噴射機的年輕一族總愛吹噓自己遊歷各地的經驗，我為此經常詢問他們：「好了，你已經看遍所有這些地方了；那麼，這些地方是否看到你了？」畢竟，到此一遊之餘，若能留下一些積極正面的影響，或甚至結交幾位當地朋友，應該不會太困難吧？

過去，大型山羊皮筏在黃河上飄流瀚海，一路從蘭州順流至內蒙古包頭，向來被視為成效高又最具成本效益的交通工具之一。一張超過一百五十片山羊皮的筏子，也並非沒聽過，船伕把羊皮筏子送到遠方把載貨出售後，交易完成後，羊皮也賣掉，船伕再轉從公路交通返家。

將近四十年後，我重訪寧夏，心想那黃河流域的原始交通工具，恐怕早已不敵現代化潮流衝擊，而消失得無影無蹤了吧？結果不但出乎預料，還喜出望外。我之前去過的江邊小鎮中衛市，一扇緊閉的大門後方，停放了幾十艘皮筏。如今，這個市鎮儼然已成旅遊勝地，附近家庭全員出動，趕上這波新興產業的觀光熱潮，順勢將搭乘皮筏當旅遊配套，吸引遊客。當然，安全措施也必須到位，至多六人一團的水上「乘筏」活動，人人都得穿上救生衣。一名船伕負責站在前方搖槳，划開木筏，掌控方向。第一段水上

Lanzhou with spectators circa 1982 /
蘭州旁觀者 1982 年
Ningxia 1984 / 寧夏 1984 年

之旅可能持續二十至三十分鐘；當然，除了基本入場費之外，還要支付額外的漂流票價。

我們很幸運認識了一位對我舊地重遊而興致勃勃的年輕船夫，余霄。他邀請我們到他村子裡，引薦我們認識他那位製作皮筏的叔叔，周崇。我們從周崇那兒學到許多關於皮筏手工藝的知識，還跟他買了個皮筏，帶回我們的中甸中心，當成展示品，和我們的犛牛皮甲骨船配對，相互映襯。

透過觀光旅遊，重新賦予舊皮筏予新身分、新價值，甚至得以維繫與存留下去；但是，傳統水車就沒那麼幸運了，終究被新世界淘汰，而隱退成歷史名詞，僅只留下一個供展示的文物。當我於一九八四年初訪該地時，還瞥見許多功能齊全的大型水車，將水從黃河兩岸，藉由灌溉渠和渡槽，引水流到附近農田。這種古老而充滿巧思的灌溉方式，其實很環保，但因不符經濟效益與不合時宜，而被取代。我慶幸曾見證它們廣受重用的全盛時期，而今還能在此看到一個被棄置岸邊的水車。

Waterwheel circa 1984 / 水車 1984 年   Multi waterwheel 1984 / 多台水車 1984 年   Twin waterwheel 1984 / 雙水車 1984 年

其實，任何一位像我這樣早在一九七０年代便已開始深入中國境
內上山下海的探險者而言，難免常面對一些令人抱憾與慨嘆之
處。其中，麥積山——中國最著名的佛教石窟之一——成了我的
遺珠之憾。我曾參觀過敦煌、雲岡石窟甚至炳靈寺石窟，也曾為
此撰寫過相關文章與報導。然而，我心中念念不忘的麥積山，
四十年來，一直列在我覬欲參觀的心願名單上，卻始終無法如願。
一般生活文化會隨著時代變遷與時間流逝而消失殆盡，但藝術文
化如宗教寺廟和遺跡，卻可能因天災或甚至戰爭、革命等人為禍
害而被摧毀。麥積山也曾歷經大時代的歷史摧殘與衝擊，卻是少
數倖存留存的藝術文化。

我此生最大的心願，是親眼看到四至五世紀時期，中國北魏的雕
塑與相關的遺址文物。打從我大學時雙主修其中的「藝術史」開
始，我就一直對北魏雕塑深感興趣。為什麼是北魏？也許這與我
特別熱愛艾爾．葛雷柯 (El Greco) 的藝術作品有關；作品中格外細
長消瘦的人物特徵和形象，與石窟上的菩薩形象，有幾分神似。
我也為此而前往參觀炳靈寺石窟，並聚焦於其中的 169 號石窟，
那裡集結了許多北魏時期的雕塑。我在一九七九年拍下的照片，
後來刊在《建築文摘》裡，與我的文字報導，圖文並茂。當時，
拍照並非什麼大問題，我甚至可以在聞名遐邇的敦煌石窟裡完成
攝影工作，並在《亞洲雜誌》和後來的《讀者文摘》中以封面故
事發表。

Dunhuang grotto / 敦煌石窟

Northern Zhou Cave 7 / 北周石窟 7 號

今天，我終於如願以償——來到甘肅東部，首次親臨麥積山。麥積山，顧名思義，因遠觀似成堆小麥而得名。看來，我們是好運連連了——在網上挑選的民宿，主人家是一對年輕夫婦，妻子辛孟孟竟是麥積山特為貴賓安排最優秀的其中一位石窟解說專家，她對石窟的認識，瞭若指掌。

辛孟孟帶我們走一條後門小路，沿著稍微起伏的徒步路線，我們抵達入口處，由此獨特位置與視角望去，懸崖邊石窟的壯麗幽靜，一覽無遺；從這角度瞥見的麥積山，其實更像個點綴著小孔與線條的大蜂巢。

時至今日，無論你到中國任何地方參觀，入場費是理所當然的要求，麥積山也不例外，每人收費八十元人民幣。我年紀大了，免收費，但如果想進去看看比我的年紀大二十倍的北魏古老石窟，不好意思，一律收費。想當然，要在洞穴裡保有那年代最好的石雕文物，本是一件「代價高昂」的事，我們分別花了一百元與一百八十元人民幣才得以進入 44 號與 133 號石窟。我加入一支由三名年輕藝術學生組成的小組，他們專為了研究這古老洞穴，遠道而來，不過，雖說是「研究」這些洞穴，其實有些誇大其詞，因為每一次的參觀有時限，必須在十分鐘或更短的時間內完成。

為了方便進入這些洞穴壁龕而建造的長階梯，扭曲彎折的構造，

上下攀爬與走位上，反倒讓石窟更難以企及。岩壁上雕刻的三尊巨佛，莊嚴而面帶微笑，居高臨下，俯視渺小眾生如我們。雖然大部分懸崖壁龕和石窟都對外開放，但最有價值的石窟，都被鎖在大門後。即使是付費參觀，這樣的洞穴和擺放裡面的雕像，一律嚴禁拍照攝影。所以，我只能猛拍那些讓我免費參觀的雕像來自我滿足一番，然後再購買數本附有北魏時期 133 和 44 號石窟圖片的書籍，慶幸我能在現場仔細把這兩大石窟近距離看個徹底。

在 133 號石窟的雙室內，我和一位僅有我三分之二身型的小和尚，共度一段特殊時刻。他是所有北魏雕像中最精緻可愛的其中一尊雕塑，為所有和他會遇之人，帶來歡樂。小和尚的迷人笑容，經常被拿來與達文西的蒙娜麗莎相提並論；但在我看來，他的笑臉更加天真無邪與神聖。至於第 44 號石窟，雖然大部分文物屬西魏晚期的雕像，但仍值得一看，尤其加上辛萌萌生動的解說，勾起我大學時代早已忘懷的那段學習時光。

牆壁和天花板上，還有壁畫等藝術遺跡，以補充雕塑和雕像之不足，將跨越幾個朝代與悠長世紀之隔的藝術，呈現世人眼前。今天，這些藝術文物中，有些已是超過一千六百年的歷史古物，儘管年代久遠，每天仍吸引數以千百計、從中國各地慕名而來的旅人。一千兩百年前的八世紀中葉，其中一位到此觀賞者，是中國唐代最著名的詩人，杜甫。

當年的杜甫，曾在不遠處的天水，度過他一生中最艱困落魄的時光——歷經三個月顛沛流離的流放歲月，與席捲首都長安（今西安）的風塵戰亂。杜甫在磨難的日子裡，寫了一百一十七首詩，幾乎一天一首。在某個特別的一天，他把尋訪麥積山的經歷，寫進詩裡；當時，山腳下的瑞應寺，僧人寥寥無幾。

《山寺》/作者：杜甫

野寺殘僧少，山園細路高。麝香眠石竹，鸚鵡啄金桃。

亂石通人過，懸崖置屋牢。上方重閣晚，百里見秋毫。

這是八世紀中葉中國其中一位著名詩人杜甫，對一個自然寧謐的偏遠之地所凝聚的思想，與萬千感慨。

離開麥積山時，有些深藏心中的想法，竟與四十多年前參觀中國其他重要石窟時的思緒一致。每一次瞥見如此不可多得的藝術品時，心中泛起的念頭，並非事後反思，而是我的最終感想──為何這些學有專精的藝術家、工匠與大師們，都不曾在其曠世巨作下署名或留下任何姓名？這與我們當代講究名氣、財富與聲望榮譽的「藝術家」相比，究竟誰才是最不追求形式、純粹的藝術家？

誰更令我佩服？你猜猜？

Mural art at Maiji Shan / 麥積山壁畫

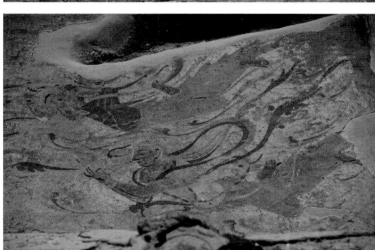

中國沿海—風光明媚之村落與漁港

COASTAL CHINA: FISHING PORTS AND SCENIC VILLAGES

San Sha, Fujian – July 20, 2021

COASTAL CHINA: FISHING PORTS AND SCENIC VILLAGES

"Where is this?"... "You left China already?" Such are the questions from a few friends who received my pictures online. Indeed the pictures I posted seem not to be taken in China. One friend thought I am in Mexico City. Another ventured that I must be in Italy's Cinque Terre. But no, the colorful houses are truly from within China, though somewhat inspired by, but not pirated copies of, the five fishing villages along Italy's Riviera coast.

I am staying on an island headland connected to the mainland in the mid 1980s through a breakwater, and later made fully connected through landfill. Prior to that, villagers coming and going from this Xiao Ruo Island needed to cross to the mainland by sampan or on foot through mud during low tide.

Old village houses on this former island, with less than 500 residents, are made from huge rocks from the seaside. They were recently plastered over and painted with rainbow colors. It was organized and paid for by the local government just a few short years ago in order to do a makeover and establish this little coastal village as a tourist attraction, naming it Colorful Island.

The tactic seems to have worked, as this old fishing village has suddenly become hot on the internet, with many of the houses turning into successful home-stay hostels. Some houses with the best views of the ocean are charging from Rmb 500 to even over 1000 per night. In a reverse of fortune, houses lower down the hill used to be more desirable as people won't need to carry water up the hill. Today, those higher up with commanding view also command higher prices.

My original intent was to check out fishing ports along the eastern seaboard of China. Our tickets purchased online to sail to Da Chen Island were abruptly cancelled due to an approaching typhoon, so I opted to visit Xiao

Xiao Ruo Island / 小箬島

Ruo, a fishing port along the coast of Zhejiang Province. Due to the typhoon as well as being in the middle of a three-month yearly fishing ban, both the oceanic fishing fleet as well as smaller near coast boats were all back and anchored inside the sheltering bay. Nonetheless, we were able to charter a small wooden boat to sail inside the bay and have a closer look at all the various types of boats at anchor.

The houses in Cinque Terra Italy were originally painted in differing colors so that fisherman returning from long periods at sea and longing to get home could quickly identify their house from afar. Here though, the colors mainly are used as an attraction for tourists. Over at Colorful Island, we choose to stay with Chen Sumei, a sixty-some years old owner of a home-stay house. She has operated her four-room outfit for two years. It is located near the top of the hill with a decent view of the bay below. My room comes with a balcony looking out upon all the other colorful houses around me.

Colorful houses / 七彩房屋

Colorful people & houses / 七彩人們和房屋

Across the bay however are cluster of original rock houses, built with huge boulders, sometimes of large suitcase sizes. A few of these walls can still be seen in alleys on the island side. These were the traditional architecture before the government stepped in to plaster the walls and add color to houses on the island hill, making it somewhat foreign looking and catering to a new wave of tourists from within China. With this new touch, even local people and children began to dress more colorfully.

During these two years of pandemic, it has become a popular destination where visitors pride themselves to make a "punch" on their card of travel pictures to circulate among their countless WeChat groups. It seems the weather was cooperative the very morning before my departure - even a distant storm with its rainbow rushed over to add its own "punch" over my photograph of this colorful village.

Leaving Zhejiang, we soon enter Fujian Province, again along the coast. Our next stop is San Sha, another fishing port said to be one of the four most important ones in China. It is barely sixteen sea miles or 30

Colorful island close-up / 近看七彩房屋
Rainbow over village / 村莊上的彩虹
Village at night / 夜晚的村莊

kilometers from Taiwan-controlled Maju Island, and around 120 sea miles from Keelung port at the northern tip of Taiwan. Due to its location close to Taiwan, it has been set up as one of the ports for direct trading across the channel. Even Taiwanese ships, fishing vessels included, are allowed to use the port as typhoon shelter or for ship repair. Such is its strategic location for Mainland China, to be connected to Taiwan in a constructive way.

My interest prompted me to charter a motorized boat to tour the bay, where plenty of the fishing fleet was now at anchor, not so much to avoid the approaching typhoon but due to the three-month fishing ban. It is said that the port can house as many as 2000 boats. On the other side of the fishing port we chose to stay at a new and rather comfortable home-stay lodge with a full view of the ocean and near a former fishing village.

Today, former fishermen use only smaller boats to plant seaweed along the coast as the main stay of their income. After all, going out to sea is now the realm of the big boys with large metal boats, which are often organized as entire fleets during operations far out into the oceans and even to other continents.

In a small bay are tied all these small boats, protected from the waves and rising tide by a breakwater and sand bank. It is amazing to see that high above them is a full line of modern villas. These are homes of former fishermen, now with children who are much better educated and attending universities. Many of these homes, like the one we stay at, are now set up as home-stays, where city folks find tranquility and solace spending a weekend along the coast.

Looking into the sunset, I can envisage that, in the next generation, these fishermen would give up not only their ancient fishing tradition, but also the seaweed growing, and be integrated into the new-found leisure industry of a developing China.

As I have spent almost half a century focused on remote China, my own view of coastal China is rather outdated, with many preconceived notions and even prejudices to feed my superiority complex. It may not be unlike those people who have historic grudges or political and archaic baggage who pray that China would never come to the fore. But with this trip, I realize that China has turned the corner and reached a tipping point. The future and the road ahead are more than obvious, at least for me.

Ocean-going fishing boat / 遠洋漁船

Fisherman modern villas / 現代漁村

中國沿海—風光明媚之村落與漁港

「這是哪裡啊？」⋯⋯「你已經離開中國了嗎？」這是幾位朋友收到我網上傳送的照片後，不約而同的提問。這些照片看起來，的確不太像中國。其中有個朋友誤以為我在墨西哥的城市。另一名友人則猜測我應該是遊歷到義大利的五漁村 *(Cinque Terre)* 了。猜錯猜錯，這些色彩繽紛的房屋，確確實實都是中國的景物，雖然有些建設靈感或許來自義大利里維耶拉 *(Riviera)* 海岸的五漁村，但可不是盜版的山寨村。

我所住的島嶼，一九八〇年代中期，透過防波堤與後來的填海造島工程，而把島嶼岬角完全連接上大陸。在此之前，這個七彩小箬島上的村民，與外界往來互動時，漲潮靠舢舨，退潮則捲起褲管，徒步踏上海灘泥路往返兩地。

這個前身是海島的村落，在地人口不足五百名，大部分房子由海邊巨石蓋建。小箬島居民近幾年紛紛在自家外牆塗上繽紛彩漆，美得像幅畫。幾年前，在當地政府組織的支助下，為小島改頭換面，讓這沿海漁村塗脂抹粉，重設為旅遊勝地，並將其命名為七彩島。

換裝改造的策略似乎奏效了，原來默默無名的樸質老漁村，一夕之間，在網上火紅沸騰起來。許多房子歷經拉皮整形後，轉型成功，變身成風格獨特的民宿。一些可以看

到絕佳海景視角的房子，每晚收費從五百到一千多元人民幣不等。但時來運轉，曾幾何時，過去山腳下的房屋因不需將水辛苦帶上山而廣受歡迎，但「滄海桑田」，過去高低位置的優劣，已不可同日而語；今天，原來乏人問津的高地房舍，因居高臨下與壯闊海景，房屋價格與價值也跟著水漲船高。

我的初衷，其實只想到中國東部沿海的漁港看看。我們原來在網上購買到大陳島的船票，因颱風逼近而毫無預警地取消了，於是，我修改行程，轉往浙江省沿海的小箬漁港。因颱風與每年三個月的禁捕期限，所有遠洋捕魚船隊與較小的近海岸船隻，都紛紛返回，將大小漁船停靠小島的避風港灣裡。雖然如此，我們還是租了艘小木船在海灣內遊航，留意觀察停泊碼頭的各類船隻。

眼前景緻令人聯想起義大利的五漁村海島。靠捕魚維生的五漁村島民，為了讓出門已久、歸心似箭的丈夫回家時，能從遠處一眼立即認出自己的房子，妻子們刻意把房子塗上五彩顏色。繽紛絢爛的彩色房舍，獨樹一幟，把小島裝飾得嫵媚動人，最終竟成了遊客趨之若鶩的觀光景點。抵達七彩島時，我們選擇住在陳素梅的民宿——一名六十餘歲的屋主。她經營這家四房式民宿已兩年。房子位於山頂區，往下俯瞰，遼闊的海灣景觀，美不勝收。我的房間有個陽台，站在陽台上環顧四週，島嶼的朱樓碧瓦，迷人至極。

Xiao Ruo street side / 小箬島街道
Ship at port / 港口船隻

過到海灣對面，則是櫛比鱗差的原始石屋，由巨石建造，有些石頭宛若大型行李箱面積。在島嶼邊境的窄小巷弄間，仍可見其中一些牆壁。在政府接手改裝粉飾前，這些都屬傳統建築，而今，島上房屋都已被淡抹濃妝地登場，也更增添幾分異國情調與風采，並迎來國內的新一波遊客。就連當地居民和孩子們似乎也被這層新氣象感染，而開始穿起了亮麗的衣服，人景皆美。

這兩年的疫情大流行，出不了國的遊客，都湧到這裡，小島瞬間躍居大受歡迎的觀光地，旅人如織，紛紛在照片上「打卡」，也在無數微信社群上，昭告天下。我出發的前一天早上，天氣沒有為難我——即使風雨欲來，還夾雜著趕赴現場的彩虹來湊熱鬧，在我拍攝這五彩繽紛的村莊時，硬是添上它自己的幾抹色彩。

Old village houses / 老村莊的房屋

Old rock walls / 舊石牆

離開浙江，我們很快進入福建省，依舊沿著海岸線遊走。我們的下一站是三沙漁港——另一個中國四大漁港之一。三沙漁港距離台灣的馬祖島僅十六海浬或三十公里，與台灣北部的基隆港約一百二十海浬之遙。由於地理位置與台灣相近，三沙漁港被設置為兩岸貿易直通的港口之一，關係緊密。即使是台灣船隻，包括漁船，有必要時，也被允許進入三沙港口暫避颱風或維修船隻。這其實也是三沙漁港的戰略位置，對中國大陸而言，它以建設性的方式，與台灣連結。

我對海島深感興趣，迫不及待租了艘馬達小船，開始遊覽海灣。海灣港內停放了許多捕魚船，與其說是為了躲避逼近的颱風，不如說是政府頒布的三個月捕魚禁令而讓這些漁船「有志難伸」，擱淺於此。我聽說這港口至多可容納多達兩千艘船隻。我們選擇在漁港的另一頭投宿，挑了間又新又溫馨舒適的民宿，擁有一望無際的大海全景，距離民宿不遠處，是一個過氣的舊漁村。

今天，「卸任」的漁民開著小船在沿海種植海藻，那是他們目前最主要的收入來源。畢竟，出海捕魚這些大工程，不再是小島民

Fishing fleet by bay / 海灣漁船隊
Coastal boats for seaweed / 沿海採海草船隻
Village home we stayed / 我們住的民宿

與小漁船所能做的事，而是屬於那些擁有金屬大漁船的大男孩所主導的事，他們的遠洋行動甚至拓展到全球其他大陸，浩浩蕩蕩，組織周全。

所有小船都綁在一個小海灣裡，由防波堤和沙堤保護好，抵禦海浪和漲潮的衝擊。令人驚訝的是，一旁地勢較高處，蓋了一整排現代化的別墅，美輪美奐。這些地方原是早前漁民的家，他們讓下一代受更完整與高深的大學教育後，生活品質也跟著提升。這一帶有許多類似改造整修後的房屋，就像我們住的民宿；城裡的旅人也可以在週末時，到海邊來度個寧靜與舒壓的好假日。

望著夕陽，我似乎已能想像與預見，年輕一代的漁民不僅會放棄老舊的捕魚傳統，連種植海藻的產業也終將一併捨棄，改弦易轍，轉而投入中國新興的休閒產業。

在中國探索將近半世紀的時日內，我的重心大多集中於內地偏遠的深山幽谷，相對而言，對沿海區域的看法或許已不合時宜，參雜交織了許多先入為主的觀念，其中甚至不乏個人偏見以合理化我的優越感。有些人在心懷歷史恩怨或過時的政治包袱等前提下，或許會暗自期待中國能維持以往現狀貌，保有古國特質，永遠都不要跳躍得太急太快。但這次的沿海遊歷，我開始意識到，中國其實已轉危為安，走到了一個轉折點。至少對我來說，未來和前進的道路，是明確、且顯而易見的。

Coastal Zhejiang / 浙江沿岸

老
汕
頭
的
昔
日
光
輝

OLD SWATOW FADED GLORY

Swatow, Guangdong – July 23, 2021

OLD SWATOW FADED GLORY

It may be more than just a coincidence that I wake up to receive a photograph of my "student" whom I had recommended to attend Oxford's graduate program in archaeology. Jay, pictured hugging an old and worn column of the Canterbury Quadrangle building of St John's College at Oxford, is asking for another reference to attend the university's PhD program.

A quarter of the way around the planet, I am on my way walking to see another old building, perhaps not as old as the one at Oxford, but nonetheless significant and designed with similar baroque style columns and art deco stained-glass windows. The building has had its heydays and gone through ups and downs from the 1930s to today. It even has Cultural Revolution slogans faintly visible on the two front columns; "Long Live The Great Chinese People" on the right, and "Long Live The Proletarian Class" to the left.

The building is situated in a corner at what today looks like an abandoned alley with electric wire and cable overhanging and crisscrossing the approach. Though quite dilapidated today, no one would doubt its grandiosity from an earlier time, as the commanding columns, decorated gateway, and metal balcony railings tell a tale of its glory in the past.

Oxford University / 牛津大學   Tao Fang Restaurant building / 陶芳酒樓

Such prosperity and affluence in old Swatow is to be expected if one were to revisit the history of the city. Soon after the Second Opium War of the early 1860s, Swatow was open as a port city to foreign trade as well as entre port where maritime ships would visit and lay anchor.

At one point in the 1920s and 30s, and well into the pre-war years, Swatow's shipping tonnage rivaled that of other port cities along the China coast, becoming third only after Shanghai and Guangzhou. Even the first civilian-built railroad started in Swatow during the late Qing Dynasty and was completed in the year 1906, though it only travelled 42 kilometers northward reaching Chiu An. It ran for 33 years and ceased operation upon the invasion by Japan in 1939.

I have long been fascinated by an old aerial photograph of Swatow taken in 1934 by German pilot Captain Graf zu Castell for Eurasian Airlines, a joint venture between China's Nationalist government and Lufthansa Airways.

The picture showed a high bridge almost completed, somewhat resembling today's highway overpasses, crossing the delta river of Swatow. Below and adjacent to it was a traditional bridge made from connected boats like a long pontoon. That was during Swatow's prime time in the 1930s.

It was around that time that my mother, born in 1920, left Swatow as a teenager and headed to Hong Kong for her secondary school education. She came from a well-to-do trading family. As a child growing up, she witnessed the prosperity and excesses of the city. Taking up the front middle section seats of the family's own theater, she would attend performances by some of the most famous artists visiting Swatow from Shanghai or Guangzhou. She often mentioned how luxurious homes were then, and the tea ceremony, and how pursuit of the best brew in those decadent days could bankrupt even the richest of tycoons.

The times were also the source of the fortune, and later misfortune, of Tao Fang Restaurant, the majestic building that I am visiting this morning in

First civilian built railroad 1906 / 第一條民建鐵路 1906 年
Swatow from air 1934 / 汕頭空照圖 1934 年

Swatow. Of the four most renowned public places at the time, Yunping Restaurant was famous for its grandness, Central restaurant was best for fun, probably referring to song girls and other peripheral activities, Tao Fang supreme in its shark fin, and Tao Tao theater exceled in its performances. These four premises became the content of a local idiom in those days.

As a corollary to the fun Central Restaurant, there is another old and broken house near to Tao Fang Restaurant. It used to house the Flower Tax Administration Bureau, beautiful name for an agency that levied tax from and issued permits to four kinds of female professionals. Two of these were actually artists performing songs and dances for entertainment, while the other two performed other "more peripheral functions."

Accounts had it that to enjoy a bowl of the most luxurious and delicate shark fin at Tao Fang would cost several taels (each tael was approximately an ounce) of gold. During that time, such an amount was enough for purchasing a small flat. No doubt such luxury could drain the pockets of the type of people who were less well to

Stairs to second floor / 通往二樓的階梯

Steps design decor / 階梯裝飾

Floor pattern and stairs railings / 地板圖案和欄杆

do, yet still eager to impress others. One story, a bit more positive and featuring somewhat more merit than decadence, is worthy of retelling.

It seems that a Shanghai merchant came to Swatow to meet a local businessman regarding a business deal. The local took the Shanghainese for a meal at Tao Fang Restaurant and ordered the best shark fin to impress his counterpart. At the end of the flashy dinner, the deal did not close due to some matter of contention. As the two parties rose to leave, the Swatow man took out a canteen bowl to put away the shark fin that he had not touched. The Shanghainese was a bit taken back and asked why he had not eaten the delicacy and was taking it home. The local man answered, "My father really likes shark fin, so I am saving my bowl for him". The Shanghainese stretched out his arm and offered a hand shake to the Swatownese. "The deal is done. Such a filial person as you - I trust we can do business together."

Though Tao Fang Restaurant closed down in 1951 shortly after liberation, some stories continue to circulate today after seventy years. The building had been turned into a primary school in the 1950s, and later served several functions for the government as offices and even for storage. It finally became quarters for several families and gradually fell into ruin, disused and partly abandoned. Today there are still a couple of persons taking up residence in part of the building - a most destitute abode.

While the glory of Tao Fang Restaurant has faded into history, the colorful tiles of the floor and stairs remain quite vivid, complementing the specially designed railings of the gates, balconies, and *stairways. The dark shadow along the stairwells feed the imagination with images of the past, when high rolling businessmen, perhaps predecessors of the Swatownese tycoon Li Ka-shing of Hong Kong, patronized the restaurant long into the night.*

Shark fin is now not as popular at the dinner table, shunned as environmentally incorrect. I cross the street to have my breakfast at a street side shop. Three Sisters Rice Noodles has been taking up that corner for thirty years. They stay open twenty-four hours in three shifts in rotation. The husband of the eldest sister is currently taking his short shift in the shop, from 3am to 7am. As I sit and taste the thin and delicate rice noodles rolled up with beef and egg, the fragrance and flavor make it most palatable. Unlike Tao Fang's famous shark fin, my dish only costs a meager Renminbi 10 Yuan (US$1.20).

But even the fragrance of my breakfast may not last past this generation, as both daughters of the eldest sister are now studying at university, and unlikely to return to take charge of the noodle shop. It will disappear without even leaving an edifice for future explorers and archaeologists to visit.

Tao Fang& adjacent building /
陶芳酒樓和鄰近的建築物

老汕頭的昔日光輝

醒來時，收到一張「學生」——傑伊 *(Jay)* 寄來的照片，我曾給她寫過報考牛津大學考古學碩士研究推薦函；照片上的她，抱著牛津大學聖約翰學院坎特伯雷四合院大樓一支破舊的廊柱，這一次，她想請我再推薦她升學博士課程。我忍不住想，這巧合也未免太巧了。

距離地球另外四分之一遙遠的路程中，我也正行路前往另一座老建築——或許沒有牛津那棟大樓的悠久歷史，但這座老建築仍有其不可取代的價值，它有類似巴洛克風格的柱子與裝飾藝術的彩色玻璃窗，充滿古意與懷舊設計。這座建築從一九三〇年代一路至今，歷經榮華與敗落，走過高峰與低谷。前兩根柱子上還隱約可見文革時期留下的標語：右邊是「偉大的中國人民萬歲」，左邊則是「無產階級萬歲」。

這座建築位於一條看起來猶如廢棄的小巷一角，整條街道垂掛著電線與電纜，髒亂無序，縱橫交錯。雖然看起來破敗不堪的建築，但那些猶然存在的「雕欄玉砌」——大器的廊柱、裝飾華麗的大門與金屬陽台欄杆，掩不住它盛極一時的往日輝煌與宏偉。

若想重溫這座城市的身世背景，那麼，透過舊汕頭的繁榮與富裕，是理解城市歷史的

切入點。一八六〇年代初期，第二次鴉片戰爭後不久，汕頭市被設置為對外貿易的通商港口，也是海運船隻停靠與進港的碼頭，汕頭因港而興，也因商而盛。

一九二〇至三〇年代，以致戰前時期，汕頭市的航運噸位，僅次於上海與廣州，可與中國沿海其他港都城府相媲美。就連晚清時期於一九〇六年竣工的第一條民建鐵路，也以汕頭作為起始站，向北行駛四十二公里，抵達潮安站。這條潮汕鐵路運行了三十三年，並在一九三九年日本入侵後，才全面停運。

一九三四年，德國飛行員格拉夫·卡斯特 (Graf zu Castell) 為中國國民黨政府與漢莎（德航）航空公司的合資企業──「歐亞航空公司」，拍攝了一張舊汕頭的航拍照，令我深深為之著迷至今。照片中是一座即將完工的大橋，有些類似今天高速公路的跨橋，橫越汕頭三角洲河域。橋下和旁邊是一座傳統的橋樑，由一艘艘船隻連接成類似一個長型浮橋。那是一九三〇年代，老汕頭的黃金時期。

我的母親，也在那前後時期的一九二〇年出生。母親十幾歲時，離開汕頭，前往香港接受中學教育。她出生從商的富裕人家，童年時期的母親，恭逢其盛，見證了這座城市的榮辱興衰。少女時期的母親，經常坐在自家劇院的前中段位子上，觀賞從上海或廣

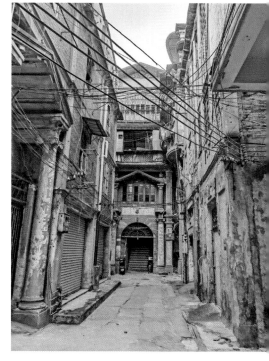

Street alley entrance / 巷口

州到訪汕頭、遠近馳名的藝術家唱作表演。母親經常提及當時的豪宅和茶道，也不忘說起在那些紙醉金迷、飲酒作樂的頹廢日子裡，沈迷酒精如何令最富裕的家族大亨，家道中落，破產告終。

那樣的時代背景，是當時陶芳酒樓的幸與不幸；這家老字號餐館，正是我今早在汕頭所訪視的歷史建築。陶芳酒樓是當時冠蓋雲集的著名四大公共場所之一——永平酒樓以美輪美奐的建築著稱；中央酒家以好玩好架勢而令人流連忘返，其中指的可能是歌女圍繞等活動；而「陶芳好魚翅」的名聲則不絕於耳，最後是陶陶老戲院，以表演著稱。這四大場域之風靡一時，竟傳承為地方諺語，大街小巷，無人不知。

Columns and stained glass / 柱子和彩繪玻璃　　　　　　　　　　　　　Decorative windows / 窗戶裝飾

既有「風趣好玩」的中央酒家，必然有其「相關單位」存在之必要。現在的陶芳酒樓附近，可見一座破舊的老房舍，曾幾何時，那是花稅管理局的所在地。如此溫婉美麗的單位名稱，其實是向四種行業的女性專業人士徵稅和發放許可證的機構——其中兩者是歌舞娛樂的表演工作者與藝術家，另外兩者則是專為執行其他「更外圍功能」的工作者而設。

話說陶芳酒樓，享用一碗最精緻上等的魚翅，據聞要價幾兩黃金（每兩約一盎司）。那個年代，這筆錢已足夠買間小套房的住宅了。可想而知，如此豪奢鋪張之消費，無疑會讓人為了顏面與刻意「裝闊」，而散盡家財。有個流傳已久的故事，或許比頹廢奢靡還要積極正面些，饒富深意，值得再提。

話說有位上海商人，為了與汕頭商人碰面談一筆生意，遠道而來。汕頭商人為盡地主之誼與表達誠意，把上海商人請到陶芳酒樓用餐，還特別點了上等魚翅。一頓奢華晚宴結束後，雙方因為一些歧見僵持不下，生意也談不成了。兩人起身準備離席時，汕頭商人拿出一個碗，將自己沒碰過的魚翅打包。上海人有些遲疑，好奇詢問對方，何以不吃這道美味佳餚而打包帶走？汕頭商人回答：「我父親很喜歡魚翅，所以我把這碗魚翅帶回去給他吃。」上海人一聽，立馬感動得伸出手臂，與這位汕頭商人握手，說道：「這筆交易成交！像你這麼孝順的人，我相信我們可以合作做生意。」

一九五一年，解放後不久，陶芳酒樓隨之關門大吉。雖然老餐館已不復存在，但與它相關的趣聞軼事，七十幾年來，至今仍流傳後世，為人津津樂道。一九五〇年代，這座餐館建築被改造成小學，幾經轉折，也曾為政府單位提供了多種功能，包括辦公室，甚至貨倉。這空間也曾經一度成為好幾個家庭的住所，最終淪為廢墟，某部分已被棄置不用。今天，仍有幾戶人家樓居於這棟樓的部分區域——那是該區最貧困的廢置地。

陶芳酒樓的往日輝煌，已是過眼雲煙，走進歷史；但樓層地板和樓梯的彩色瓷磚，依然亮麗醒目，與大門、陽台和設計獨特的樓梯欄杆，相得益彰。樓梯間的黑影，勾起舊時遐思，那些畫面與想像，彷彿歷歷在目，隨影而動。曾幾何時，富甲一方的商界名流，也許是香港潮汕大亨李嘉誠等富豪的前輩們，就在這家酒樓裡，杯觥交錯，賓主盡歡到深夜。

今天的餐桌上，魚翅的歡迎度與價格，昨是今非，早已不復往日般高不可攀——殺鯊取翅，是生態不正確，人人避而遠之。我過馬路，到路邊小吃店享用早餐。時過境遷，如今，「三姐妹米粉店」，已獨佔這街角地盤超過三十年。這家小吃店輪三班營業、二十四小時無休。大姐的丈夫目前正在店裡當短暫輪班的臨時人手，從凌晨三點到早上七點。米粉將牛肉與雞蛋捲起來，細薄精緻，那四溢的香味，無比美味。不像陶芳酒樓的著名魚翅，這道主食只花了我十元人民幣 (1.20 美元)。

經營米粉店的大姐，兩個女兒都在讀大學，已不太可能再傳承麵館營運；看來就連我這頓早餐的香味與美味，也未必能持續到下一代，不久的將來，不僅消失成記憶中的味道，也無法為未來的探險家與考古學者留下任何可供參訪的實物。

Shadow of the past / 歷史的影子

聖方濟各與中國沿海離島

FRANCIS XAVIER & ISLAND OFF THE CHINA COAST

Shang Chuan Island, Guangdong, July 26, 2021

FRANCIS XAVIER & ISLAND OFF THE CHINA COAST

I owe much of my education to the Jesuits, having spent six years of secondary school at Wah Yan, a school in Hong Kong run by Jesuits. The Order of Jesuits owes its birth to Francis Xavier, one of the six founders of the Society of Jesus, with the priests of this Order commonly known as Jesuits.

These priests are not only devoted, but educated Catholics bestowing their lives to the service of God. In so doing, their missions have spread far and wide throughout the world, even founding centers of higher learning like Georgetown University, Fordham, Boston College, University of San Francisco, University of Santa Clara, etc.

Francis Xavier was born in 1506 in Javier in what is now Spain and co-founded the Society of Jesus in 1534 in Paris, taking vows of poverty and chastity. He left Portugal in 1541 to begin preaching in the Orient, including India, Japan, Malaysia and China. While he evangelized and baptized many at Goa on the west coast of India, and was somewhat successful also in Japan, his main target was China. But while waiting for permission to enter the country through Guangzhou, Francis Xavier died in 1552 from malaria on the coastal island of Shang Chuan, part of an archipelago west of Macao and Hong Kong. He was 46 years old at the time.

The stories of Francis Xavier, later canonized as Saint Francis Xavier, are plenty and need little elaboration by this writer. More personal is perhaps my friend Francis Yam who received his Christian name because he was born on St. Francis Street in Wan Chai of Hong Kong. Then there is our staff filmmaker Xavier Lee, who likewise was named after the Saint. There are more friends on my list.

There is something even more personal to me, which prompted my coming to Shang Chuan with a heart of thanks and pilgrimage to visit the original grave of St. Francis. Before 2006, the premises were in disrepair, and it was restored and funded by the Alumni of Hong Kong's Wah Yan College, my alma mater, to commemorate the Saint's 500th birthday.

Saint Francis' body once rested here and a chapel was built nearby to remember him. However, his remains were removed two years after his death and placed in another grave in Goa, with one arm transferred to Rome and the other to Macao as relics. Some of his other remains are said to be placed in Malacca, Rome and Tokyo as well.

As with much of my work, which looks easy on the outside but actually come with twists and turns, my visit to the grave of St Francis is likewise a mini ordeal. We drove along the waterfront by a road passing Xin Di

HM at Wah Yan circa 1962 /
HM 就讀華仁書院 1962 年
Tang Jigo fisherman / 漁夫唐繼國

St. Francis' graveyard / 聖方濟各的墓

Village that, according to the map, is supposed to dead-end at the grave and chapel. About 500 meters from our destination, the road ended with a gate. As I was reading a sign on the gate notifying closure of the premises for repair, a young man walked up to our car.

"This place has been closed since 2006," said the man. "But I have come a long way to have a look here," I pleaded. "No one can enter, some have even come from as far as overseas, Hong Kong or Macao, none can go inside," he insisted. "But why? What about the church?" I refused to give up. "There are surveillance cameras monitoring inside," he warned as I stood and waited at the locked gate. "The church is no more, taken down." But on my approach, I had seen the steeple of the church with a cross on top.

So be it, within sight, but I must turn back, as obviously his nearby house was considered something of a guard house to keep an eye on anyone attempting to enter further. But as always, I would not take "No" as an answer and sought other means. In this case, by sea.

Five hundred meters back at the village, I stopped to take a picture of a former elementary school. A sampan boat was just returning from sea with its night's catch. I chatted with the wife of the boatman and asked to rent their boat, just for a half hour tour of the bay, but of course with unsaid intention to photograph the graveyard and church from the sea. She asked for Rmb 300, but I quickly talked her down to 100, citing that I am a tour guide and may soon bring groups of tourists back and use their services again.

In no time at all, we boarded the sampan and sailed across the bay. Within fifteen minutes, my goal was accomplished, having a good look at St Francis's grave as well as the nearby chapel, from a most beautiful and unusual vantage point.

The rest of my visit to Shang Chuan Island was less eventful. We spent a night at a bayside hostel near the northwest corner of the island, at Sha Di fishing port. Not many fishing boats were anchored despite this being the three-month "No Fishing" period, soon to end on August 16. About a dozen very large boats, usually fishing at sea near the Spratly Islands, were at anchor. These boats would soon leave port for months before returning home

Sha Di at sunset / 沙地漁港日落

Wooden ferry / 木板渡輪

maybe twice a year.

We chatted with a senior boatman. Sixty-six years old Tang Jigo was repairing a fishing net by our hotel. Tang once lived in Hong Kong's Cheung Chow and worked on a fishing boat for two years, going as far as Indonesia during fishing trips. I had hoped to find a wooden sampan still in use. But everyone had long ago turned to fiberglass boats though there are still a few small wooden ferrying boats left. In the evening, we dined on freshly caught seafood as a small consolation.

The few dilapidated Hakka villages I stopped at had few villagers remaining. Most of the former rice fields were now abandoned as the younger population had left for work in cities, or turned to work for the recently established tourism industry along the sand beaches. The large influx of tourists from nearby Guangdong flooded the island, especially on summer weekends, with entire families, including children, all heading to swimming and dining parties.

The ferry from across the island leaves the pier every hour on the hour, well into the night, plying the strait between mainland Guangdong and the island. We came to the island opted to use the vehicular ferry, which required lining up early, not to speak of all of us having to take the obligatory overnight Covid swab test in order to purchase our tickets.

In short, my visit to Shang Chuan was not as easy and smooth as some might think. Nonetheless, my main goal, to pay respect to Saint Francis, was accomplished. Had the Saint himself known, he no doubt would have pardoned my little lie in order to visit him, Amen.

Sha Di fishing port / 沙地漁港

聖方濟各與中國沿海離島

我這一生所受的一大部分教育，都得歸功於耶穌會，其中六年中學教育，都在天主教耶穌會早年在香港開辦的華仁書院完成。耶穌會是天主教會的修道團體，由六位創始人所成立，其中一位是方濟各 (Francis Xavier) 神父。舉凡天主教組織裡的神職人員，我們一般稱之為耶穌會士。

這些神父不僅信仰上虔敬，而且都是受過高深教育的飽學之士，他們將生命奉獻給天主，也將信仰落實於行動；而他們的宣教使命與足跡，甚至遍布全球各地，其中包括建設許多世界有名的高等學府——美國的喬治城大學、福特漢姆大學、波士頓學院、舊金山大學、聖克拉拉大學等。

方濟各於一五○六年出生於西班牙城市，哈維耶爾 (Javier)，一五三四年時，方濟各在巴黎與其他修士共同成立耶穌會，以服務窮人與追求貞潔生活為創設的核心信念。一五四一年，方濟各離開葡萄牙，開始前往東方傳教，他所踏足之地，既多而遠，包括印度、馬來西亞、日本、中國。方濟各在印度西海岸的果阿 (Goa) 邦致力傳教，影響許多當地人，並為他們施洗；他後來在日本的宣教工作也成效卓著，但其實他一心嚮往的主要目標，是中國。一五五二年，方濟各準備從廣州進入中國內地，在那段等待

入境許可期間，方濟各在中國沿海的上川島——澳門與香港以西的其中一個小島上，死於瘧疾。壯志未酬身先死，得年四十六歲。

方濟各後來被封聖為「聖方濟各」，有關他的奇聞逸事很多，我就無需贅述多言了。若要提起與方濟各比較個人化的牽連，或許是我的朋友任錦鐘 (Francis Yam) 吧，我這位朋友因為出生於香港灣仔的聖方濟各街，而得此教名。另一位與這位耶穌會傳教士同名者，是我們的電影製片人李伯達 (Xavier Lee)，他同樣以方濟各為他的英文名。我所認識的朋友名單上，還有更多與聖方濟各同名的朋友。

其實，有一件更個人的私事，催促我想懷著感恩之情，到廣州上川島走一趟朝聖之旅，參觀聖方濟各的原始墓碑。二〇〇六年，這座墓園因年久失修，狀況不佳，於是，由母校華仁書院的校友們出資，協助修繕整頓，以此紀念聖方濟各誕辰五百週年紀念。

聖方濟各安葬的墓園旁，蓋起了一座小教堂，以此紀念他。然而，聖方濟各去世與安葬兩年後，他的遺體卻被「分置各地」，部分曾被移走而安放於印度果阿邦的方濟各墳墓裡；他的一隻手臂則被取走，送到羅馬去；遺體的另一隻手臂，則被帶往澳門埋葬。據說，他的部分遺體也被安葬於馬來西亞的馬六甲和日本東京。

這趟參觀聖方濟各墳墓的朝聖之旅，與我大部分的工作一樣，表面看來似乎易如反掌，實際上卻是千折百轉，每一個節外生枝，都是考驗。我們按圖索驥，沿著新地村的海濱道路行駛，根據地圖指示，一路走到底，抵達我們的目的地——墳墓與小教堂。就在距離目的地大約五百米之處，我們停在路的盡頭，一堵大門把我們擋下。當我仔細閱讀貼在大門上的標誌時，這才赫然發現，這座墓園因維修而關閉，禁止外人入園。我見一年輕人向我們走來。

「這地方從二〇〇六年起，就關閉了。」男子開門見山說。

「但我千里迢迢走了很遠的路才到這裡，想進去看看啊。」我懇切請他網開一面。但他堅定拒絕：「沒有人可以進去，有人甚至遠從海外各地來，香港或澳門，一律都不准進入。」

我不屈不撓，繼續問道：「禁止的理由是什麼？那可以看看教堂嗎？」我下車，站在緊鎖的門前翹首以待。看管的年輕人警告我：「裡面有監控的攝像機。教堂已不存在，被拆除了。」但當我走近一看時，卻瞥見教堂的尖頂，上面還有個十字架，一清二楚。

明明已在視線範圍內，看得到卻進不去；年輕人一旁的小房子，顯然是個警衛室，負責監控並擋下任何想進入墓園的訪客。我只能被迫轉身離去。但一如既往，我從不輕易接受「不」，此路不通，我就另闢蹊徑，尋找替代管道。在這情況下，那就走水路吧。

開了五百米返回村子，我下車為一所前身是小學的建築，拍了幾張照。一艘舢舨船剛從海上歸來，這趟夜間出海，看來是漁獲豐收。我和船夫的妻子聊天，隨口問起，租他們的船出海半小時，這麼一趟海灣之旅，收費如何？我當然沒有明言要從海上拍攝墓園和教堂的計畫。她開口要價三百元人民幣，我隨即以「導遊身分」為由說服她，因為我告訴她可能很快便會帶一群遊客回來，屆時會再次租借他們的漁船服務。優惠導遊有理，收費調降至一百元。

交易談妥，二話不說，我們很快便登上舢舨出發，駛過海灣。十五分鐘之內，我便已

達成目標——從一個最棒的海上角度、最獨特的極佳位置，仔細端詳了聖方濟各的墳墓，以及附近那座小教堂。

我在上川島的其餘旅程，少了波折，也順遂多了。島嶼西北角的「沙地」漁港附近，有間海灣旅館，我們在那裡住了一晚。儘管當時仍處於為期三個月的「禁捕期」，屈指一算，禁止期限即將於八月十六日結束；只是，漁港內並未見太多漁船停靠；倒是有大約十幾艘大型捕魚船靠岸停泊，這類漁船一般會到南沙群島的周遭海域捕魚。不稍多久，這些船即將離港出海，一去便是好幾個月，每年大約返回兩次。

我們和一位資深船夫談起了話。六十歲的唐繼國，正在我們下榻的旅館旁，修補漁網。唐繼國曾住香港長洲，並在漁船上工作了兩年，也曾遠至東南亞的印尼捕過魚。我之前一直希望能找到一艘仍在使用的木製舢舨，這類舢舨已越來越少見，取而代之的，是今天大家普遍採用的玻璃纖維船；存留下來的小木船，已寥寥無幾。當晚，我們吃了港邊剛捕獲的新鮮海產，就當作折騰了一天後的小小犒賞吧。

Ocean-going boat / 遠洋漁船
Coastal net fishing / 沿岸網魚

我後來陸續停靠幾個破舊不堪的客家村落，走訪之間，發現村裡只剩老弱婦孺，與稀稀落落幾位村民。曾經的稻田，現在都已成了廢棄的荒地，大部分年輕人已離鄉往城市工作，少數留下的，

則轉而舊地重建，在鄰近沙灘上打造觀光遊樂勝地，吸引來自附近廣東的大量遊客湧入，他們在週末假日或夏季暑假期間，攜家帶眷，在這裡游泳度假，吃喝玩樂。

當地的跨島渡輪，每小時整點從碼頭出發，一直到深夜，忠心穿梭於廣東大陸和島嶼之間的海峽。抵達島上時，我們選擇使用車輛渡輪，但仍需提早排隊，而疫情時代下，想當然，我們一行人都必須接受強制性的過夜，以完成新冠病毒的篩檢測試，才能順利買到我們出發的船票。

總之，這一次的上川島之行，不如想像中一帆風順，旅程中一波三折，好事多磨。儘管如此，我已完成心中要向聖方濟各致敬的主要目標，這已足以令我欣慰。如果聖人有知，我想他肯定不會計較我的當導遊小謊言而原諒我，那我下一次才能再來探望他。阿們！

Ferry to and from Shang Chuan / 往返上川島的渡輪
Port of Sha Di / 沙地漁港

澳
門
隔
離
2.0
之
首
日
與
次
日

MACAO QUARANTINE 2.0 Day One/Two

September 28, Macao/Macau

MACAO QUARANTINE 2.0 Day One/Two

Last minute before leaving home, I decided to wear my new pair of Arcteryx shoes, a name brand for outdoor wear and gear. After all, my upcoming expedition would last up to four months, and it would be good exercise to test and break in a new pair.

Almost every time I leave for the field, many friends and supporters ask where will I be going and what I will be doing. I usually refrain from answering, as indeed my plan changes according to situation. Let alone, I focus on delivery of results, not promises of what we set out to accomplish, since there is never a guaranteed result. In fact, often the best work is accomplished through surprises along the way, especially as far as exploration is concerned.

However, I make an exception this time, and give a brief hint of what my own anxiety is about. I have been reading general reports about climate change for well over a decade, maybe even two decades. In brief, such knowledge is gathered and disseminated by scientists and academics, raised to worldwide attention by public media and educated followers at large, embraced by countries and governments to devise future policy to contain or mitigate the problem, and manipulated by politicians to gain fame or win votes.

Much of the scientific work has been conducted from space, monitoring our changing globe. However, I rarely read climate change news or coverage based on storytelling of what is happening on the ground, beyond that temperature and sea level are rising, and ice caps melting faster. I have always believed that climate change would be most apparent at extreme places where human habitations are on the edges of bearable existence.

The Tibetan plateau has many such places, especially at the highest allowable elevations, usually only inhabited during the summer by nomads using such places for marginal summer pasture. CERS expeditions have taken us to some of these places, for example during our work to identify several major river sources. However, during such trips, we have not been focused on the climate situation. Now is time to revisit those places, observe some of the receding glaciers with visible footprints of years of recession. If we can interview nomadic people living close by, we will be able to set up some baseline through first hand narratives and stories told by people on the ground.

This would become the first of three phases of our current expedition to Tibet and its adjacent area. Exciting? Yes, at least for me, in probing a different angle to deliver a story on climate change - something CERS has never attempted. The second and third phase and objectives of the current

Entering Macao / 入境澳門
New shoes and luggage at rest /
新鞋和行李休息中

Temporary snack bar / 臨時點心吧檯
Restaurant menu / 餐廳菜單

expedition will be revealed later on, perhaps in future field reports.

Oh yes, one other hint. Our old friend Mariasol, matriarch of the Ewenki tribe, which is composed of only around 200 individuals, will turn 100 on October 3. I hope to be spending Christmas with her in the northernmost part of China, bordering Russia. Unlike the virtual reindeer imprinted on online Christmas greetings, we would be among the last herd of real domesticated reindeer in China. If that should happen, we hope to send our friends our own Christmas greetings, with bells chiming as I drive the reindeer herd out of the forest of the Hing An Mountains.

Below are some notes and a few thoughts on Day 1 of my Macau quarantine:

-As our bus left Hong Kong for Macau, we passed to the north of Shum Wat in Lantau. There, in a remote village, CERS just started our next phase project on natural inventory. Such projects in Hong Kong necessitate longer stays each time I return to Hong Kong, staying for up to six weeks, rather than the short stops in the past, when I could only afford to stay a few days before turning around.

-My new pair of shoes, used half a day, will now take a rest and go into retreat for two weeks, while the slippers will take over inside our three-room suite. Strange that people may brag about going into high-price ashram or other spiritual retreat but never regarding a quarantine. I suppose one is considered heaven, the other hell. Oh yes, I left my Omega watch next to my bed, and in short of second day, it has decided to stop and take a break too.

-Our three-room suite with the living/dining room in the middle, though on lower floor and not facing the ocean with sunrise like my first quarantine six months ago, is providing quarantine in decadence, courtesy once again of Martin Ma, CERS director. Each day his driver and PA will allow me to pick from several restaurant menus and then deliver to the Hotel Lisboeta the cuisine I select, be it seafood, Japanese, Italian, dim sum, or even street food. To top it all off, vintage wine and old Port, fruits, beverage, and snacks are sent ahead in abundance. With nine outside menu and other online menu to choose from, I can create my own Openrice star-selection, perhaps auctioning off such quarantine for future fundraising. F&B in a hotel was never better. Furthermore, each time I sent Martin a photo of our meal, he would write back, "not enough for three persons".

First evening dinner / 第一晚的晚餐　　　Simple breakfast from hotel / 酒店的簡單早餐

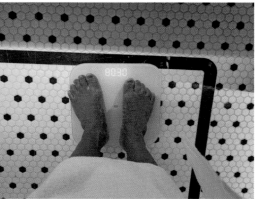

Mural of Leal Senado Square / 議事亭前地壁畫
Weighing in / 秤體重

-The hotel provides three spartan meals per day in addition to Martin's daily feast, with enough left-over for the following day's lunch. His selection of wine are 2003 Lynch Bages red, 2005 Domaine de Chevalier white, and a bottle of my favorite Vallado 20 Years Port.

-There is a huge mural photograph of Leal Senado Square, with the historic Portuguese-style edifice built in 1784 set above my bed. I cannot help but look at the four costumed riders on horseback, as one of the horses' butt and long flying tail is right above my pillow and head. I rushed to wash my hair early the first morning, having slept below that for a night.

-My late night snack of cheese and chips, plus the previous days' swab test in poking my throat and nose at the Sanitorium Hospital, may have contributed to my mild sore throat this morning.

-As expected, same as at my doctor's office, the scale is malfunctioning, as I weighed in at 80.5 kilos last night. This morning after a bath, I weighed only 78.5. Sleeping burns calories I discovered.

-I must begin cleaning up my own messes, including the bath tub, as there will be no in-room cleaning service over my two-week stay.

-While in the tub, I read my Weekend FT with an op ed piece on the newly released ranking of UK universities. John Gapper, a columnist for the FT, rants about ranking of universities and the biases and uselessness of such a list, as St Andrews came in as Number One, topping both Oxford and Cambridge. Checking his background afterwards, I find out Gapper has forgotten to declare his own bias, having graduated from Oxford himself. Sweet grapes have just gone sour.

-Sept. 28, I call Peter Goutiere, our HUMP pilot friend living in New York, to wish him well on his 108th birthday. Pete was born on this day in 1914. I should model after him, toasting myself with whisky each day.

-Last but not least, a small episode yesterday which may just give us some pause and food for thought. A couple lined up right in front of me when checking into the Lisboeta Hotel.   They were a middle-aged pair, both dressed in colorful outfits - the gentleman with flowery trousers looked like he had just come from Hawaii and going into their honeymoon suite. They seemed totally enthused and chatted with me, about their anxiety of going into quarantine, and their anticipation of exploring everywhere in Macau upon exit. They said they had been traveling in China as well, and have even gone to Phuket with the same enthusiasm.

Apparently, this couple, unlike most of the people in the world, has not caught what I call the Covid collateral disease of QPS, Quarantine Phobia Syndrome. I look forward to meeting them again at the check-out line in two weeks' time on October 11, and certainly hope that I will adopt also their attitude, and face up to our own challenges ahead.

Now my second bath is calling. I better go lay back there, read my Macau Daily, and recharge my internal battery.

澳門隔離 2.0 之首日與次日

離家出發前的最後一分鐘，我下定決心，穿上我那雙知名戶外品牌「始祖鳥」(Arcteryx) 的新鞋。畢竟，我這趟外出遊歷漫長，前後長達四個月，這是個測試與考驗這雙新鞋的好時機。

每一次出門遠行，許多友人與「中國探險學會」支持者總愛問我——準備去何處、計畫做何事。我通常笑而不答，因為計畫趕不上變化，我的目標確實隨著當下情勢的變數而不斷調整與改變。尤其我向來喜歡聚焦於陳述結果，更何況，永遠沒有保證必達成之目標，也沒有什麼非抵達不可之方向。事實上，尤其從「探索」的角度與定義而言，我所見過最美好的成就與目標，就是一路上出其不意的驚喜。

不過，這一次我破例，簡要陳述一下我心中的焦慮。這十幾年，或甚至近二十年來，我不斷閱讀一些與氣候變遷相關的報告。簡而言之，這些知識由科學家與專家學者們蒐集、彙整，然後公諸於世，進而由公共媒體和廣大知識份子的認同與談論，而引起全球關注，許多國家和政府紛紛表態支持，並製定未來政策以遏制或緩解這看似棘手的氣候問題，也有政客打著這個討喜的名號來操弄議題，以哄抬個人的政治聲望，或為此贏得選票。

大部分科學驗證的工作，都在太空中進行，以監測全球的異常與變動。然而，我很少讀到有關氣候變遷的一手資料新聞故事，或在現實地點居民經歷氣候變遷的真實遭遇與報導；而地表上的遙遠之處，溫度持續暖化，海平面持續升高、冰蓋積雪融化的速度，也越來越快了。我向來這麼相信——在極端氣候的極端地區，那些勉強處於生存邊緣的人們——他們飽受氣候變遷的衝擊最大、最顯著。

青藏高原有很多這樣的地方，尤其在海拔最高之處，一般只有在夏季時，才有遊牧民族遷徙來此居住，以此作為夏季的邊際牧場。「中國探險學會」的探險隊，曾經抵達這些地方，其中一次，是我們投入大江大河的源頭探尋工作期間。但在那些旅程中，我們並沒有太關注氣候變遷的狀況。

現在，該是時候重新尋訪這些區域，回頭檢視與觀察一些正在消退的冰川，這些年來，融化消退的規模與速度，顯而易見而令人憂心。如果我們有機會採訪居住附近的遊牧居民，或許藉由第一手的敘述和當地人講述的親身經驗，可以幫助我們擬定一些報導的初稿與重點。

我們計畫針對西藏與其週邊地區進行三階段的考察，而目前準備展開的計畫，將被設定為第一階段。振奮人心嗎？是的，至少對我而言，從不同角度切入一個氣候變遷的敘事報導——這是「中國探險學會」從未嘗試的工作。至於後續的第二與第三階段的目標，容我稍後再公布，也或許，我會在未來的田野報告中說明。

啊，對了，關於後續目標，我忽然想起，其實我還可以提供另一個提示。我們有位老朋友瑪麗亞索爾，是東北亞鄂溫克 (Ewenki) 部落的族長，那是個約有兩百人的部落——與俄羅斯接壤的中國最北端。瑪麗亞索爾將於十月三日滿一百歲，我很希望和她在蠻荒北國一起過聖誕。和那些在網路上讓人轉貼聖誕祝賀的虛擬馴鹿大不同，在這個被譽為中國唯一使用馴鹿的古老部落裡，我們極有可能

My triple room suite / 我的三房套房
Spartan hotel box meal / 簡單的飯店餐盒

會在白雪皚皚的聖誕節慶裡，成為中國最後一批被「圈養」的馴鹿。若然，我們還是希望以自己的方式來寄出聖誕祝福給各地朋友，卡片上是我帥氣騎著馴鹿群，從興安嶺的森林中悠然而出的畫面，掛在馴鹿身上的鈴鐺，一路叮叮噹噹響個不停……。

以下是我在澳門隔離第一天所紀錄的筆記，和一些想法：

— 當我們的巴士從香港出發前往澳門時，我們經過大嶼山的深屈以北。「中國探險學會」在那偏遠村莊裡，剛剛啟動了下一階段的項目，以檢視大自然為主。若要在香港深耕這一類的工作，則每一次回港都需要停留更長的時間，初步估計最多停留六週，而非像過去那樣，短暫停留幾天便得匆匆離去，遠赴他鄉異地。

— 我的新鞋，用了半天，這下又要放它休息兩週，未來這段期間，拖鞋將取而代之，成為我們這間三房式套房內「帶步」之鞋。心中忽然備感好奇——同樣是遠離塵囂，但為何人們喜歡炫耀走進高貴又高價的靜修所或參加其他靈性退隱活動，但卻這麼害怕隔離。我想，或許是因為前者被認定為天堂，而後者則是地獄無誤。哦，對了，我把歐米茄手錶放在床邊，才進來隔離第二天，竟連它也決定停止運轉，休息一下。

— 我們的三房式套房，中間是客廳與餐廳，雖然位於較低樓層，不像我六個月前第一次隔離那般奢華，面向大海，凝視日出時分，

但這一次，其實也算是享樂頹廢派之隔離；必須再次感謝「中國探險學會」董事馬丁 *(Martin Ma)* 的招待。他的司機和助理，每一天都讓我從幾家餐廳的菜單中點餐，然後將我點好的美食佳餚，送到澳門葡京人飯店來。餐點品項，包羅萬象——海鮮、日式料理、義式料理、香港點心，甚至是街頭小吃。除了美食，還不忘美酒飲品，馬丁特別我們送上陳年葡萄酒、波特酒、水果、飲料和零食等，多到目不暇給，取之不盡。我在香港餐廳指南「開飯喇」*(Openrice)* 的九個外賣菜單和其他在線菜單上，自由選餐，我甚至可以創建屬於自己的明星線上訂餐服務，心想或許可以考慮來拍賣一下這種享樂版的隔離生活，為將來籌款做準備。其實，飯店提供的餐點與飲料，已好得無話可說。我每一次給馬丁發一張我們用餐的照片時，他都擔心嫌不足，回覆道：「不夠三個人吃吧？」

— 除了馬丁的每日盛宴款待以外，飯店每天仍按時提供三頓簡餐，並提前為隔天午餐提供份量足夠的食物。他選擇的好酒，是二〇〇三年的「林奇巴居堡」*(Lynch Bages)* 紅葡萄酒香港人喜歡名為「靚次伯」、二〇〇五年的「騎士堡」*(Domaine de Chevalier)* 白葡萄酒，和一瓶我最喜歡的「瓦拉多」*(Vallado)* 二十年波特酒。

Happy hour break / 歡樂時光   Dessert pastel de nata / 甜品葡撻

— 我的床頭上方，掛了張巨大的壁畫照，是澳門噴水池的「議事亭前地」，搭配一七八四年的葡萄牙式歷史建築當背景。我忍不住端詳馬背上四名盛裝打扮的騎士，因為其中一匹馬的屁股和飛躍空中的長尾巴，就「打」在我的枕頭和頭上。在馬尾鞭策下睡了一晚，我第一天早上便迫不及待衝進衛浴，把我的頭徹底洗乾淨。

— 我把奶酪和薯條當成深夜時分的夜宵，再加上前幾天在養和醫院戳喉捅鼻的新冠肺炎篩檢，我想，那是造成我今早輕度喉嚨痛的原因吧。

— 正如我所預料，眼前這體重計和醫生的體重計一樣，都故障了——因為我昨晚量體重時，上面顯示的數字和醫生辦公室的體重計一模一樣，都是八十點五公斤。今天早上洗完澡後，我再站上去量一量，竟然只有七十八點五公斤。我赫然發現，睡覺居然可以燃燒卡路里欸！

— 我必須開始面對現實，清理整頓我個人的空間與器具，包括浴缸；因為未來兩週的住宿隔離期間，將沒有任何客房服務。

— 我在浴缸裡，閱讀我的週末版《金融時報》，內文附有一篇專欄文章，是《金融時報》專欄作家約翰 . 加普 (John Gapper) 針對最近剛發布的英國大學排名，大肆批判此類榜單內容偏見又無聊。在大學排名的榜單上，聖安德魯斯大學高居榜首，硬是把牛津和劍橋都擠下。事後查了一下作者背景，我發現原來加普先生從牛津大學畢業，他大概忘了自我表態，畢竟人人難免偏見啊。這下，甜葡萄忽然變酸了。

一 九月二十八日，我打電話給住在紐約的「駝峰」(HUMP) 飛虎隊飛行員朋友，彼得．蓋德爾 (Peter Goutiere)，祝他一百〇八歲生日快樂。彼得出生於一九一四年的這一天。我應該效仿他，每天用威士忌為自己乾杯。

一 最後，還有一件事值得記上一筆。昨天發生了一段小插曲，或許可以讓我們沈思反省。入住澳門葡京人飯店時，一對夫婦排在我前方。他們是一對中年人，倆人都穿上色彩繽紛的花衣服——那位穿著花褲子的紳士，看起來就像剛從夏威夷過來，準備入住他們的蜜月套房。我感覺他們渾身散發熱情，果然不久便轉身和我聊天，談起了他們對隔離的期望，也表明結束隔離後，夫妻倆迫不及待要對澳門各地盡情玩樂與探索的期待。他們也常往中國內地旅行，甚至帶著同樣的熱情去了一趟普吉島。

顯然，這對夫婦與世上多數人不同，他們並未染上我所謂的新冠肺炎的延伸疾病——「隔離恐懼症候群」。我期待兩週後的十月十一日，在櫃檯結賬出關時，再見到他們，當然，有為者亦若是，我多麼希望自己也能像他們那樣，以積極正面的態度來面對我們未來的挑戰。

現在，又到我第二次的洗澡時間了。我最好趕緊躺好泡足，好好閱讀我的《澳門日報》，為我的內在精神，充飽電。

我
對
緬
甸
藝
術
界
的
看
法

MY TAKE ON THE MYANMAR ART SCENE

Macau – October 13, 2021

MY TAKE ON THE MYANMAR ART SCENE
Debut at the Asian Fine Art Asia

It was only two weeks until my departure for Macau quarantine preparatory to entering China and heading to the field. My meeting with Andy and Susanna Hei in Shek O was for another purpose - just to catch up since our first meeting months ago. But in passing, the art-loving couple let me know about the Asian Art Fair they founded, which Susanna has been organizing since 2006. And the event, after being suspended for two years due to various circumstances, was to resume again in two weeks' time. It was scheduled to open on October 7 at the Hong Kong Convention Center, coinciding with the peak auction season of the year.

Andy and Susanna kindly offered a complimentary booth to CERS, in case we would like to present anything CERS is working on. That evening, I gave it some thought, and by the following morning had decided we should take the opportunity to present a few Myanmar artists that our organization has been working to promote and represent.

Two of these artists, Zwe and Phyu (recently married to each other), have benefited from a residency program with CERS. They used our Tibetan Center in Zhongdian as a studio, and even spent time painting on our Myanmar HM Explorer boat and at our Inle Lake Center. Zwe is made famous by his use of stamps and money currency as montage portraits, where is Phyu is most prolific with themes of children and abstract exaggeration. So far, CERS has helped commission work to them internally, directly through our circle of supporters and friends. The Art Fair will finally allow their art to be debuted to a larger public.

Despite having to curate the show from remote while in hotel quarantine, we managed to select, set up, and present a show that ultimately caught the eyes and attention of the art world during this Art Fair. Our booth became one of the hot spots for visitors to the fair, and as evidence of that, the South China Morning Post coverage of the Fair used the Myanmar artists' work not only in pictures, but as lead to their story. It is very gratifying.

Artwork by Myanmar artist / 緬甸藝術家作品

Stamp of authority

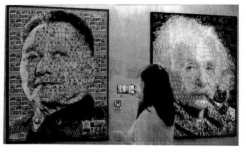

A visitor takes a photo of *Deng with Deng Stamp* by Zwe Yan Naing, which was on display at Fine Art Asia 2021at the Convention and Exhibition Centre in Wan Chai. The artist, who was born in Rakhine state, Myanmar, created the portrait of Deng Xiaoping using stamps issued in honour of China's former paramount leader. This year's exhibition, which ended yesterday, also featured a portrait of Albert Einstein and heralded the beginning of the peak auction season. It featured artworks presented by local artists as well as those from renowned galleries elsewhere. Some international galleries and overseas art lovers took part in the event virtually.   Photo: Nora Tam

Receiving prime media attention / 重要媒體報導

I have always believed that with emerging markets around the world, there are also emerging talents. Perhaps these two emerging artists are fair representation of the Myanmar art scene today. Having worked with them over the last three years, as well as given attention to other Myanmar artists, I have assembled a few observations I can share.

Myanmar, largely cut off from the rest of the world economically and politically from 1962 until 2011, managed to survive, though not without difficulties. The sanctions by western countries, despite being aimed toward the government then in power, certainly did not help civilians at large. Thus, most disciplines of study, art schools included, suffered from a closure to the outside, like all realms of society. So in many ways, Myanmar's art scene, being disconnected from the world media and market, developed only internally, growing from within.

This, however, is both a disadvantage and an advantage. In my view, the art that thus resulted is actually more pure, with little incentives to tie it to the highly commercial predicament in the rest of the world, and thus also free from speculative market agendas. In some ways, it is not different from the China art scene before that market was opened to the West. Furthermore, being a very Buddhist country, Myanmar's art form, theme and style reflect very much the people's religious and cultural heritage. As such, there are also limitations. For example, I personally feel the lack of human body modeling would restrict an artist from portraying the beauty and shape of the human body, whereas portraits would not be constrained by such perimeters.

It is for this reason that Zwe and Phyu, the two artists CERS represents, are very capable of portraits and still life, but may feel uncomfortable in dealing with certain subjects, be they because of the taboos of their religion or established tradition. Yet their works now command a price that is not at all modest, elevating them to a level rarely reached by new artists entering into a matured market. It benefits both the artist as well as their country, as CERS repatriates all our representation proceeds back to Myanmar for conservation and other worthy projects.

This first debut of Myanmar artists has drawn the eyes and attention of many within the art community. They may not have expected, or realized, that this historically isolated country has bred an entirely new generation of contemporary and modern artists, with a genre of style that would rival any to which the rest of the world is accustomed.

Art by a surrealistic artist / 超現實主義作品   Einstein & Van Gough brothers / 愛因斯坦 & 梵谷兄弟

我對緬甸藝術界的看法

首次參展亞洲「典亞藝博」

結束澳門的檢疫隔離，我只有短暫停留兩週的時間，隨後便得準備入境中國，展開探索遊歷之旅。我在香港石澳與黑國強 (Andy) 和盧梓羚 (Susanna) 見面，其實是為了另一個目的——純然因為「好久不見」——距離我們第一次碰面，已是好幾個月前的事了。順帶一提，我從這對熱愛藝術的夫婦身上，理解了他們創辦「典亞藝博」的起心動念；盧梓羚從二〇〇六年便已開始籌組這個別具意義的活動。因為各種狀況與限制，這場備受矚目的藝術博覽會暫停舉辦兩年後，終於訂好兩週內再度登場，眾人引頸期盼。這一次的「典亞藝博」，將於十月七日在香港會議中心開幕，正好趕上一年中的拍賣旺季。

黑國強和盧梓羚為「中國探險學會」提供了一個免費展攤，必要時，可以讓我們的組織隨時把正在進行中的任何成果，在展示平台上分享。那天回去以後，我想了一晚，隔天便決定我們確實該把握時機，引介這段時間以來我們一直努力推廣和推薦的幾位緬甸藝術家。

其中兩位剛新婚的藝術家夫婦 Zwe 和 Phyu，經「中國探險學會」的穿針引線下，在學會「藝術家駐留」的計畫中，受益良多。我們在中甸的「西藏中心」、「茵萊湖中心」

CERS team in action / CERS 團隊工作中　　　　　　　　Exhibition attendees / 參觀民眾

甚至遊走緬甸的「*HM Explorer*」探險號船上，都開放讓他們當工作室，可以隨時在裡面創作。*Zwe* 因使用郵票和紙鈔作為蒙太奇肖像的創作手法，在藝術界大放異彩，好評不斷；而 *Phyu* 的誇張抽象創作與兒童為主題的作品，不但多產，且引人矚目。「中國探險學會」至今仍直接通過我們的支持者和朋友圈，協助他們在內部安排一些相關工作。譬如這一次的藝術博覽會，便是嶄露頭角的好時機，不僅讓他們的藝術作品首次參展，也藉此將他們的創作推向更廣大的群眾眼前。

儘管不得不在飯店隔離期間，遠距離遙控與策劃展覽，但我們還是設法完成篩選畫作、設置攤位和展覽事宜，最終，功成圓滿，我們在本次藝術博覽會中成功引起藝術界的關注。我們的展覽攤位成為參觀者駐足瀏覽的熱點之一，容我以《南華早報》對展會的報導，來佐證我所言不假。該篇報導特別以緬甸藝術家的作品為圖，更以他們的故事為內容的主軸。這確實令人倍感欣慰，也拭目以待。

我一直相信，隨著全球各地此起彼落的新興市場，一定也會「江山代有人才出」。也許，這兩位新興藝術家，便是當今緬甸藝術界的代表。這段與他們合作共事的三年來，加上我對其他緬甸藝術家

Sculpture by Phyu's sister / Phyu 姊姊的雕塑
Another punch card site / 又一個打卡點

的關注，我累積了一些值得分享的觀察與想法。

從一九六二年到二〇一一年間，基本上，緬甸的經濟和政治，與世界其他區域幾乎斷絕往來，儘管面臨鎖國等重重困難，但這個國家仍努力生存下來。西方國家過去對執政的當權派祭出制裁手段，很大程度上也禍及廣大的平民百姓。因此，緬甸當地的教育體制，各方面的學科發展，包括藝術學校等，與當時社會上其他領域無異，都飽受被孤立與封閉的衝擊。也因此，緬甸的藝術界在許多方面與世界媒體和市場，完全脫節，如此斷裂的鴻溝，讓它們只能往內發展，由內而向外生長。

然而，這項特質，猶如雙面刃，既是限制，也是優勢。在我看來，在這樣的土壤所迸發的藝術創作與能量，其實更加純粹，幾乎不受世界其他高度商業化的誘因參雜混淆，也因此得以擺脫投機市場的機制與手段所牽制。就某方面而言，緬甸與當初向西方開放之前的中國藝術界，非常相似。此外，作為一個佛教國家，緬甸的藝術形式、主題和風格，都恰如其分地反映了人民的宗教和文化遺產。當然，這樣的背景也難免限制了藝術的發展向度。譬如，我個人覺得，緬甸普遍上缺乏描繪人體概念的藝術面向，無形中限製了藝術家對人體的藝術美感與想像；幸好，肖像畫不受此限。

也正因如此，「中國探險學會」所代表的兩位藝術家 *Zwe* 和

Phyu，對肖像和靜物畫，駕馭自如，但在處理某些主題時，基於原有的宗教禁忌或根深柢固的傳統觀念，則有些難以突破。儘管如此，他們的藝術創作，在價格上卻一點也不低；而價格與價值的提升，對新創藝術家晉身成熟市場的標準而言，他們其實已達一定的藝術水平。這樣的成就，不論對藝術家個人或他們所屬的國家，都相得益彰，同享好處；最主要的原因是，「中國探險學會」將我們的藝術家代表之所得與獲益，都帶回緬甸，再將這些款項用在藝術家本國值得保存與保護的事物上。

緬甸藝術家初試啼聲即傳來佳績，引起藝術界各方人士的高度矚目；面對這些作品，他們讚賞之餘，也始料未及，或許從未有人意識到，這個長久以來與世隔絕的國家，竟孕育了令人驚豔的新一代藝術家，這些也被譽為當代與現代藝術家的創作風格，和世界其他地方所推崇的藝術成就相比，顯然有過之而無不及。

Hot spot for visitors / 熱門景點

高原上過冬

WINTER ON THE HIGH PLATEAU

Litang, Sichuan – November 5, 2021

WINTER ON THE HIGH PLATEAU
Of Wild Yak and Gourmet Cheese

The edges of the pond around me remains frozen in the morning, though by mid-day it will thaw somewhat. This may not be deep winter yet, but for someone from the south like myself, it is certainly cold enough. Five to ten degrees below freezing may not seem much for someone who has survived four winters in Wisconsin in the northernmost edge for the US, but then that was half a century ago. And once windchill is factored in, it pierces my face like a knife.

That is only the impression of weather on the high plateau for us humans. As for the yak, which are superior to humans as far as nature and the elements here are concerned, the narrative is quite different. With a thick coat of hair, this may just be the right climate for them. And for the Wild Yak, with yet thicker layers of hair, deep winter may well be their preferred temperature. Four thousand meters elevation is ideal pasture for the yak, but for the Wild Yak, they flourish best at 4500 meters and above, be it summer or winter.

And so it is in Litang, a high plateau at over 4100 meters, that the Tibetan former-nomads are experimenting with crossing domestic yak with Wild Yak. Why "former-nomads?" Today every family is living in solid houses and herds their yak or sheep to summer pasture higher up the

Yak herd blacken foothill / 犛牛群染黑山腳

mountain with temporary sheds or tents, and then retreats to their winter homes down lower where usually they are shielded from the brutal winter winds and storms.

My earliest encounter with the wild yak started thirty years ago, when I first went to the Arjin Mountain Nature Reserve in Xinjiang. At that time, it was the largest inland reserve in the world with an area of over 45,000 square kilometers, larger than the size of Taiwan yet with only thirty some Uighur herder families living in it. Subsequently, I became Chief Advisor of the reserve for a number of years, and went there many more times. Later we were to also observe Wild Yak in northern Tibet's Changtang Nature Reserve, as well as those in the Aksay Kazak region of the Qilian Mountains on the border between Qinghai and Gansu. Dr. Paul Buzzard, former CERS field biologist, published several scientific papers on this species of Class One endangered animal.

The largest herd of Wild Yak I have seen numbered over 400, deep inside the Arjin Mountain, blackening the distant foothills. But everywhere we have seen these gigantic animals, almost twice the size of domestic yak and weighing up to a ton, there are single bulls that stray away from the herd.

One might think that these lone bulls are the former kings of the herds that aged and lost mating battles to younger bulls, losing face and dignity, and so strayed away to lead a lonely life from then on. But Paul Buzzard discovered that when females in the herd comes into estrus in August and September, these big bulls can return. In fact, his team only observed copulations during or after frenzies of fighting with intense battles between many large bulls, who often came from outside the herd. So some of these lonely kings, with redeeming value in reproduction, may still exercise their royal authority, when it matters most.

As a herd, the Wild Yaks would move away as humans come closer, protecting the young and infants from potential predators. But the single bulls were generally oblivious to our approach, even to relatively close quarters. Several times when our photographing and filming demanded closer encounters, the yak bull would turn, raise his tail high, lower his head, kick his heels, and charge

Approaching wild yak in car / 駕車靠近野犛牛　　　　　　　　　Yak charging at car / 野犛牛衝向車子

at our vehicles. Engaging our four-wheel drive while accelerating, we always hoped that the ground below would provide enough traction for us to race off before this entire ton of bull hit us. There were times we barely managed to get away from disaster. Such incidents add new meaning to my vocabulary for words such as bulldozing and bullying, and that is no bullshitting.

Excitement of such encounter notwithstanding, these single bulls would occasionally stray far enough to get near to Tibetan herders who drive their domestic yaks high up into the high slopes, at times close to 5000 meters elevation during the summer months. During these times, the Wild Yak would occasionally mate and cross-breed with domestic cows. Their offspring would be enriched with the fresh genes of the Wild Yak, growing bigger and stronger than normal domestic yaks. For this reason, domestic yaks living closer to habitats where Wild Yak roam generally are larger in size than those at lower elevations of the Plateau.

Over the last few decades, nomads have seen their yak herds degenerating to a degree, in that the yaks are becoming smaller and smaller. As such, many would not be able to brave the brutal winter storms on the high plateau. Experimental programs started in Qinghai to capture and crossbreed Wild Yak with domestic ones have shown some early results that are very promising. It was here in Litang on the eastern part of the Tibetan Plateau that I finally witnessed such a program being implemented, over a thousand kilometers from the current stomping ground of the Wild Yak, where they roam free.

We camped at the Huoqu Jixiang pasture co-op. Some 240 families have joined the co-op, which was founded in 2016. Each family contributed purchase of one yak to begin with, and now the herd has grown to over 500 yaks using the pasture nearby.

Wild yak & Lobsang / 野犛牛與洛桑
Wild yak bull of Litang / 理塘的公野犛牛

Drolma and her son Lobsang, our collaborators for almost two decades in pioneering the making of yak cheese, have also moved here to set up shop at the invitation of the government of Litang. It is believed that yaks from high elevation are more pure and do not mate with cows to produce yak/cow hybrids, which the Tibetans call Dzo. Such a mix in a herd would diminish the purity of the yak milk thus produced. The mother and son are just finishing their first season's production of 400 kilos of yak cheese here, and confided to me that the quality is obviously superior.

For yak cheese production, each season is necessarily short, given calves are born usually in March and need to nurse from the mother. Thus surplus milk can only be collected and used beginning in May and lasting until only September when the mother would gradually produce less milk before winter sets in, sufficient only for the calf.

In fact, seasonal changes to the milk on the high plateau are quite unique. For example, during the summer it takes 2.5 kilos of milk to produce 0.5 kilos of cheese, whereas by autumn, the milk becomes much thicker and less than 2 kilos would be adequate to yield the same 0.5 kilo of cheese. Much more data and knowledge are needed to eventually understand the relationship of altitude, pasture, and seasonal changes to define various grades of cheese. Though we arrived out of season, nonetheless Drolma and Lobsang managed to order a small supply just to provide a chance for us to record the procedure on film.

As our team observes the last round of cheese making, I gingerly go out to the back of the farm and approach the few Wild Yak from a safe distance. At last; unlike their relatives in the wilds of Tibet, these beautiful animals of the high plateau can be approached even on foot and observed close up.

In 2018, the co-op started introduction of the Wild Yak. There were six males and a dozen females, all bought and trucked over from Qumalai of Qinghai province near the headwaters of the Yellow River. At that time, a full-grown three-year old bull cost 18,000 RMB for a first generation Wild Yak, whereas a second generation one would cost only 13,000.

Through cross-breeding over the last three years, now each year there are five to six new-born Wild Yak calves. In the beginning, the Wild Yak had more wild character and were very difficult to herd. They resisted being driven back into a ring for the evening, so roamed freely and were difficult to manage. But after these few years, they seem to have adapted to the local climate, pasture, terrain and protocols. Now they mix gladly with the domestic yak herd.

Among new born infants, the survival rate is now quite high, thus achieving the original goal of improving the stock quality of the domestic herd. The co-op does not slaughter any Wild Yak for beef, not even the offspring, hoping the stock will continue to improve. Thus no one can tell how different, superior or inferior, their meat may taste. Caring for these

Freshly made yak cheese / 剛生產的犛牛奶酪

yaks is now of utmost importance, as the co-op hopes that one day these animals would even become an attraction for tourists. Indeed, they have attracted me to make a stop here for two nights.

As of 2020, the co-op had a total of 555 yaks. First and second generations Wild Yak annual production of calves had reached a total of 70, whereas the domestic yak, though many more in numbers, could only reach 25. A heavy snowstorm hit the area between March and April of 2021, and 15 Wild Yak and 20 young domestic yaks died during that period. These figures suggest that Wild Yak probably have dominated domestic bulls in mating battles, thus producing more offspring than their counterparts. Secondly, these offspring are stronger in the fight against nature than the domestic ones.

By late 2021 when I arrive at the scene, there is more good news. The co-op now has a total of 618 yaks in their herd. Among them there are 68 newborn Wild Yak, against only 30 domestic calves. None has died, and, as of now, no yaks have been sold.

In the meantime, we await anxiously to see results of improvement in the yak cheese thus produced. Perhaps in days ahead, the yak cheese production process that has been the hallmark of our collaboration since 2004 would produce yet another cheese type, worthy to be called Wild Yak Cheese.

A customer from Beijing took a wheel of our original artisanal yak cheese, wrapped in bark from the local red birch tree, to the International Contest of Cheeses in Paris in 2015 where it won a Gold

Award. That is not a small accomplishment for a start-up cottage industry, impressing even French connoisseurs, who are renowned for being hard to please.

As I descended from the frozen plateau to where the autumn foliage is still showing a rainbow of colors, I pondered upon the future of the yak cheese project we started two decades ago. This Wild Yak Cheese, so organic and natural, should sweep up more awards and drive the world's cheese lovers "wild" as well; Wild Yak Cheese from over 4000 meters in altitude. That statement is not just catchy, but sets a standard that would be difficult to match anywhere, a unique pedigree from a unique species in a unique habitat.

Autumn view in Litang / 理塘秋景

高原上過冬

野犛牛和奶酪極品

天寒地凍。我住處周遭的池塘邊緣，直到今早，水面仍結凍冰封；午後溫度高一些，湖面才稍稍解凍。這或許還不算「正式進入」嚴冬，但對一個像我這樣的南方人來說，這種冷，實在已夠冷了。零下五度到十度的考驗不算什麼，好歹我這南方人也曾在美國最北端的威斯康辛州完整歷經四個冬天，而存活下來，不過，那畢竟是半個世紀以前的「想當年」了。一想到寒風刺骨的冷咧寒意，感覺就像刀刃般，刺穿我的臉。

這是我們人類對高原天候的印象。至於犛牛，牠們的狀況和我們大相徑庭，無論本質天性與適應客觀條件的元素，都優於人類；彷彿與生俱來就為了在此生存而被覆蓋了一層厚毛髮，低溫寒冷或許是更適合他們的氣候。至於毛髮較厚的野犛牛，雪窖冰天可能是它們的首選與最愛。海拔四千米，是犛牛的理想牧場，而對於野犛牛來說，無論夏季或冬季，只要在海拔四千五百米以上的地方，就是牠們最理想的「宜居之地」，從此幸福度日，而「生生」不息。

就在理塘這個海拔四千一百多米的高原上，西藏的前遊牧民族正嘗試以野犛牛與圈養犛牛交配，孕育混種的下一代。為何說是「前遊牧民族」？那些「逐水草而居」或隨天候變遷而遷徙的遊牧，今天都已住在堅固穩定的房子裡了。時間一到，他們把犛牛

或綿羊放牧到山上的夏季牧場，那裡備有臨時棚子或帳篷；然後，秋末冬至他們便撤退到較低海拔的「冬屋」家裡生活，那一般是他們抵禦嚴冬與狂風暴雨的地方。

推算起來，我最早接觸野犛牛時，已是三十年前的事了。當時我第一次去新疆的「阿爾金山自然保護區」。這個面積超過四點五萬平方公里的自然保護區，比台灣還大，當時還是世界上最大的內陸保護區。廣袤遼闊的保護區內，只住了三十多戶維吾爾族的牧民家庭。之後好幾年間，我成了保護區的首席顧問，前後進出保護區好幾次。後來，我們再到西藏北部的「羌塘自然保護區」，與青海甘肅交界的祁連山阿克賽哈薩克地區，觀察野犛牛。有關野犛牛的知識，前「中國探險學會」的常駐生物學家包樸實 (Paul Buzzard) 博士，曾發表幾篇關於這類一級瀕危動物的科學論文。

我此生見過最大一群野犛牛，是當年在阿爾金山的深山老林處，眼前約四百多頭野犛牛群，黑壓壓一片，遠遠望去，幾乎把整片山麓小丘「染黑」了。無論任何地方見過的野犛牛，都壯碩威武，至少一噸的重量，足有圈養犛牛的兩倍；而且處處可見遠離野犛牛群的公犛牛。

或許有人會以為，這些離群索居的孤僻公犛牛，應是昔日的牛群之王，但因年老體衰，比不上年輕公牛的「雄風」與交配能力，

Escaping from wild yak chase /
逃脫野犛牛追逐
Large domestic yak of western Tibet /
藏西部的大型圈養犛牛

而尊嚴盡失，鬱鬱寡歡，從此落寞地浪跡天涯。不過，對野生動物瞭若指掌的包博士卻指出，每年八月與九月，當雌犛牛發情時，這些公犛牛其實可以雄赳赳地光榮返鄉。包博士的團隊觀察發現，許多大型公犛牛在激烈爭鬥期間或之後，會進行交配，但這些公犛牛大多來自牛群之外。換句話說，一些流落異地的孤獨「國王」，其實在繁殖方面仍有雄風再起的潛力與價值，在至關緊要時期，仍可行使他們的「王權」。

習慣成群結隊的野犛牛，會因人類的接近而漸行漸遠，近乎本能地以離開人類來保護小牛免受潛在獵食者捕殺。但一般落單的公牛，卻對我們的趨近視若無睹，即使在相對近距離內面面相覷，也不驚不擾。不過，有幾次，當我們因攝影與拍攝需求而亦步亦趨時，公犛牛竟轉身，抬高尾巴，低頭踢腳跟，對著我們的車輛往前猛衝。我們急匆匆加速四輪驅動，多麼希望輪子下的地面能為我們提供足夠的引力，讓我們在這隻重達一噸的犛牛撞上我們之前，速速逃離現場。有些時候，我們幾乎來不及擺脫災難。此類事件為我頭腦裡幾個與「公牛」(bull) 相關的英文詞彙——譬如「推土機」(bulldozing) 與「霸凌」(bullying)——增添幾許「血淋淋」的新含義，我真的不是跟你「胡扯」(bullshitting) 喔！真的啦！

儘管如此遭遇令人既怕受傷又興奮，但這些落單公牛有些時候會走得很遠，尤其夏季時分的好幾個月裡，公犛牛會遠走至海拔近五千米高地，遠得足以靠近藏族牧民與他們放牧到高山的犛牛群。野犛牛趁此機會，偶爾也會與放牧的圈養牛隻交配。牠們的混種後代有野犛牛的新基因，身形上，與生俱來比普通的圈養犛牛長得更大、更強壯。因此，生活在野犛牛棲息地附近的圈養犛牛，通常比高原低海拔地區的圈養犛牛更壯碩。

過去幾十年間，遊牧民族已發現他們的犛牛群不斷退化，身形上變得越來越小。而日益瘦小的犛牛，也越來越難以面對高原上嚴酷的冬季風暴。為了取得一些突破性的改善計畫，實驗性的交配計畫，於焉展開。有關單位開始從青海地區捕捉野犛牛，讓牠們與圈養犛牛進行交配，初步取得的成果，令人滿意。我在青藏高原東部的理塘，距離野犛牛悠然漫步約一千多公里之外，親眼見證這些實驗的落實與執行。

我們一行人在理塘的「霍曲吉祥牧場專業合作社」紮營。這個成立於二〇一六年的合作社，基本成員是約有兩百四十個家庭。一開始，每一個家庭都要捐出一隻犛牛，目前，牧場上的犛牛群已繁殖至五百多頭。

卓瑪和她兒子洛桑，是我們開發犛牛奶酪製作的合作夥伴，迄今已近二十年；為回應理塘政府的邀請，他們也遷居當地，開店經營。人們普遍認為，來自高海拔的犛牛，因為不與乳牛交配而品種純正。一般牛牛雜交而產下的混種牛，藏人稱之為 Dzo；當牛群中的品種越混雜，則犛牛奶的純度，也跟著降低。卓瑪這對母子剛剛在這裡完成了他們第一季四百公斤的犛牛奶酪的生產，他們告訴我，這一次的質量，顯著提升。

Tibetan girl milking yak / 藏族女孩擠犛牛奶

Calf of domestic yak / 圈養小犛牛

Wild yak among domestic herd /
野犛牛在圈養犛牛群裡

犛牛奶酪的生產，每個季節都必須在極短的時限內完成；因為小牛一般在三月出生，母牛需優先把小牛餵飽；剩餘的牛奶，只能從五月開始收集和使用，一直到九月，母牛的產奶量會在冬天來臨前，逐漸減少，最終少得僅夠小牛溫飽，再無奶可擠。

事實上，高原上的季節變化，對牛奶有其獨特的影響。比方說，若要在夏季生產零點五公斤的奶酪，則需二點五公斤牛奶，一到秋季時分，牛奶變得較為濃稠，同樣是零點五公斤的奶酪，不到兩公斤的奶量便足矣。因此，若要詳實定義不同等級的奶酪，則要掌握不少數據與知識，才能徹底理解海拔高低、牧場狀況與季節變化之間的相互影響。雖然我們當時的拍攝計畫趕不上奶酪生產的季節，但卓瑪和洛桑還是想方設法訂購了一小部分，好讓我們可以將整個過程記錄成影像。

當我們的團隊聚精會神觀察到最後階段的奶酪製作時，我小心翼翼地走到農場後方，試著接近幾隻野犛牛，但同時與牠們保持一個安全距離。我發現，這些犛牛與西藏荒野中的「親戚」不同，這群美麗的高原動物，不焦不躁，「與人為善」，而且允許人類近距離觀察。

二〇一八年，合作社開始引進野犛牛。六隻公犛牛，十隻母犛牛，都從黃河源頭附近的青海高原的曲麻萊購進。當時，一頭成年三

Wild & domestic yak of Litang / 理塘野犛牛與圈養犛牛

到二〇二一年底，當我抵達現場時，陸續傳來更多好消息。合作社現在共有六百一十八頭犛牛。其中，新生野犛牛共計六十八頭，圈養牛犢則有三十隻。到目前為止，沒有牛隻死亡，亦無犛牛被賣。

於此同時，我們迫不及待想要看看由此生產的犛牛奶酪的優化成果。或許在未來幾年內，將出現另一種全新的奶酪口味，那將是自二〇〇四年以來，我們與合作社共事的里程碑，在一切優勢條件具足下，造就出最純正的「野犛牛奶酪」。

有位來自北京的客戶，帶著我們的原創手工犛牛奶酪，用當地紅樺樹的樹皮包裹，報名參加二〇一五年在巴黎舉行的國際奶酪大賽，一舉成名，榮獲金獎。對於一個新興的家庭手工業來說，這可不是小成就，而是豐功偉績——讓一群向來難以取悅的法國美食鑑賞家評審，驚艷不已，印象深刻。

從冰天雪地的高原下山，返回平地，落葉知秋，天空仍可見彩虹般的斑斕色彩；我不禁回首起二十年前開始的犛牛奶酪計畫，也對此計畫拭目以待，滿懷信心。這種有機和天然的野犛牛奶酪，具備所有先天優勢，如此珍稀美物，理應備受更多獎項肯定，也足以讓全球奶酪粉絲們狂「野」追逐與愛不釋手——產自海拔四千多米的野犛牛奶酪。這不是虛張聲勢的台詞，而是奠定了一個所向披靡的「高」標準——來自獨特棲息地之獨特物種之獨特血統。

青
藏
高
原
最
遙
遠
的
溫
泉

REMOTEST HOT SPRING ON THE TIBETAN PLATEAU

Shiqu, Sichuan – November 8, 2021

REMOTEST HOT SPRING ON THE TIBETAN PLATEAU

Hot springs are treasures anywhere in the world today, let alone a hot spring with medicinal quality, be it real or imagined. Spas have been made popular in resorts and fine hotels all over the world, but are only a derivative of hot springs, most being man-made rather than from natural hot water sources. And their remedial value, marketed as spiritual benefits, health, and tranquility, are the basis for designer branding and price marks.

So it is a treat for us, exploring the deepest corners of the Tibetan Plateau, to places where no brand exists, unknown to the outside world, that we find one of the most hidden hot springs in the world. Not known to the outside world, but among Tibetans it is well known, drawing bathers from far and wide throughout the plateau.

They come for Tsachukha Hot Spring in Gyayi Village of Shiqu County situated at the northwestern tip of Sichuan bordering Qinghai and the Tibetan Autonomous Region. It is purportedly a place where the legendary King Gesar brought his favorite concubine Drukmo and his thirty generals to bathe and enjoy. The legend seems plausible. After all, King Gesar of Ling was born near here and the many stories of his bravery and conquests arose from this region before historic times.

Winter has set in and the chilling temperature provides a perfect atmosphere to locate these steaming holes. Where the climate is cold, a hot spring becomes a refuge for both wildlife and people. Here, at 4,168 meters, as our altimeter shows, the migrating birds should long ago have gone south, but Shelducks are bathing in pairs around the spring as if oblivious to us bathers sharing the warmer climate. Not far away are nomads grazing their yak and sheep herds.

Indeed, it is not just one hot spring, but an ensemble of bathing holes, spread out in the marshes that cover perhaps a quarter of a kilometer along the upper reaches Za Qu, the main tributary of the Yalong River, one of the four major rivers of Sichuan that eventually drain into the Yangtze. One watershed to the west is the upper

Tsachukha hot spring / 察楚卡溫泉

Yangtze where the Tongtian He becomes the Jinsha Jiang. And the watershed to the east is that of the Yellow River, an extension of the Bayangela Mountain Range.

Locals say there are 108 springs, and that they can heal over 400 types of illnesses. Among them, the Gesar Medical Spring can heal all, including pandemic diseases, so perhaps it counts as most useful under our current Covid predicament. The concubine Drukmo's spring is noted for healing the kidneys and women's health problems. Adjacent to the most popular spring is a long wall of mani stones, with each stone carved with a mantra, like Om mani padme hum. Locals and those from afar burn juniper incense by the wall as offering. A naturally formed niche is said to be where King Gesar tied his horse.

Bathing here is said to heal all illness and pain. Each year around September when autumn arrives and heavy agricultural and herding work comes to a close, many from all over the plateau come here,

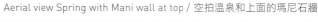

Overview of hot spring / 溫泉全景　　Aerial view Spring with Mani wall at top / 空拍溫泉和上面的瑪尼石牆

from nearby places like Yushul and the Golok areas of Qinghai and from as far away as Chamdo and even Xigaze in inner Tibet. They stay from three to seven days. Some stay as long as two weeks to even a month. When transport was backward in the old days, they would come on yaks and horses, pitching their tents nearby. Today, people arrive in cars and stay at the monastery or hostels nearby.

My team of ten arrives with a camper van and with a local monk. Kunchen, despite only 27, is head of the School of Medicine at Sershul Monastery, having graduated in traditional medicine at the provincial capital of Chengdu. This Yellow Sect monastery is huge, boasting around 2,700 monks, not unlike a major university campus. This is a huge growth from before 1949 when the monastery has 1200 monks at its height, and only 200 some monks when revived in the early 1980s.

Sershul Monastery is the only monastery in Kham, the eastern part of the Tibetan Plateau, that can confer the scholastic title of Geshe, equivalent to a PhD in Tibetan studies. Only four other monasteries, among hundreds on the entire Tibetan Plateau, can provide such highly disciplined academic qualifications. Though we have passed by Shiqu many times since 1991, I have never stopped to visit until now, due to an introduction by a Rinpoche friend to Kunchen, this young monk doctor.

HM with bathers / HM 和泡溫泉的人

Sershul monastery / 色須寺
Monk leaving one of the many halls /
僧人離開其中一個殿

At the monastery we observe the monks' busy morning chanting at various prayer halls of the different schools of study, and their afternoon energetic debate in groups on the main square. Of course, with introduction personally by Kunchen, we visit in greater detail the School of Medicine; the classrooms while students are studying, the workshops for making Tibetan herbal medicine, and the dispensary at the monastic hospital, with its line-up of local Tibetan patients.

Here I would like to reiterate and declare my bias as well as credentials, of having worked in China for almost 50 years, while roaming the Plateau for four decades. This is backed up by numerous awards and accolades I received from mainstream western media, like Time, CNN, the Wall Street Journal, etc. This introduction is preparatory to giving "selective" coverage, brief as it is, about activities at one major monastery on the Plateau.

Unlike many so-called "neutral" foreign journalists who would choose to "select" coverage of clamp-downs at religious sites to report, while not having been there themselves, and using second-hand or creative versions gleaned from others with an agenda or an axe to grind. Such reporting, often citing "anonymous sources" as cover, will lead to wholesale bankruptcy in the long run for the author and even the media they are representing.

Of course, today we can count on readers having short memories and never holding the authors accountable after the next day. As a perpetual student of journalism since college, I need look no further than remembering all the positive reports on China which these same western media outlets ran ten years ago, as compared to their consistently negative coverage now. This is what "selective" reporting is all about; double-standards and hypocrisy. It would be interesting for a leading journalism school to make a case study.

While I may understand the desperado feeling in the West while being challenged by a rising China, such selective reporting today may have a very high hidden cost, in alienating many pro-West Chinese intellectuals, Asians at large, as well as rational-thinking westerners, especially those who have visited China recently. Behind all the negativism is one positive revelation, that such frequency of coverage means China is extremely relevant to the West, and to the world. Otherwise, they would be oblivious to its existence.

Cynicism and political ranting aside, from Sershul Monastery where we stayed we were to drive out early morning after breakfast. It was not easy to pull oneself out of bed with electric blanket and adjacent floor warming devices from the newly finished hotel attached to, and operated by, the monastery.

It took an hour to reach Gyayi, the last village to the northwest of the county. Kunchen had a former schoolmate at Gyayi Gomba, a small sub-monastery of Sershul Monastery, thus he knew the area well. Here in the hills roamed many wildlife species, including Wild Ass, Tibetan Gazelle, Blue Sheep, and even the highly endangered Snow Leopard. And the hot spring was located beyond all settlements, in the wilderness.

Drime Dundrup, 46 years old, together with his wife Tashi Lhamo at 31, manage the tiny hostel by the hot springs. Both are local from Gyayi Village. Drime was identified as a Rinpoche (Reincarnated Lama) when a child and entered Warong Gomba as a monk at the age of eight. His father was likewise head Rinpoche of the monastery. In 2006, he began running both the monastery and a hostel catering to pilgrims and others arriving at Tsachukha Hot Spring. Having met his future wife, Jigme decided to disrobe and leave the monastery in 2015, building another hostel next to the monastery hostel. The two got married in 2020 and now manage the hostel for a living.

According the Drime, the hot spring water here has many minerals and other special contents. According to season, the spring would exhibit different colors. At times, even from morning to noon to evening of the same day, the colors change. There is also a salt-like white deposit in the marshes around the hot spring. Each year in spring around April and in autumn near September, during the time of transition between warm and cold weather, these white salty contents would become more prevalent.

Nomads would collect the salts for use in bathing their feet and legs, believing that it would cure rheumatism and other bone-related ailments. They may also mix it with fodder to feed to their livestock - yak, sheep and horses - to cure their diseases. At times, some would add a little into their very dark tea for drinking, claiming that it can cure stomach illness. Mixing it with snuff tobacco is said to cure sinus problems, a concoction with water can relieve eye disease, and washing hair with it will prevent loss of hair; the remedies are too many to list. In short, a cure-all potion from a magical spring.

Drime in front grandma & father /
智美在祖母、父親前面

While the locals were soaking in the nearby springs fully naked, men, women and children, I opted to keep my heavy down jacket and vest on, bathing only my feet, which have developed numerous cracks in the heels due to the extreme climate.

Perhaps, here I owe an answer to those who may have questions regarding how I found out about this very remote and special hot spring. It was from a set of books in my library published in the mid-1980s about the place names of each county of Sichuan, eighteen volumes in all covering every Tibetan county in western Sichuan. In the book on Shiqu, two words caught my eyes - salt wells in Gyayi Village. Following that small lead, looking for the salt, finally led me to discover these most wonderful hot springs.

As we parted ways to return to Sershul Monastery, Drime revealed a small can of this very precious white salt for me to take home to soak my feet. Hopefully, I will also save some for a time when my silver hair will be thinning out as well.

And for those intent on visiting, including those journalists bent on reporting on China, the coordinates of the hot spring are as follows: xx.xx°N xx.xx°E. After all, they won't need to be there to report on anything.

Furthermore, it may also be useful for the young internet-savvy generation to go and snap a few selfies to share with their followers. My question to this generation of privileged youth has always been, "So you have seen all these places, have any of these places seen you?"

For us, we have made several new friends, and share our friendship with our readers.

HM and team soaking their feet / HM 和團隊泡泡腳

青藏高原最遙遠的溫泉

今天的世界，無論各地，都將溫泉視為珍寶，至於那些具藥用療癒特質的溫泉，不管療效真假或僅止於心理作用，就更顯稀珍寶貴了。由此不難理解，世界各地的渡假村和高級飯店紛紛興建水療中心，一時之間，蔚為風潮；儘管其中大部分水療經營以溫泉衍生的周邊生意為主，且多為人造，而非天然地熱溫泉。這些所謂的療效價值，都在市場行銷與包裝下，按著它們所標榜的各種好處，包括提振精神、強身健體、安神定志……等，成為打造品牌與標價的基本名目。

因此，能夠深入青藏高原最深處的角落探索，在遺世獨立之地發現全世界最隱蔽的其中一個溫泉──無名無姓無品牌──對我們而言，簡直是無上的榮幸與享樂。只不過，這對當地藏人而言，卻是無人不知、家喻戶曉之地，吸引高原上四面八方的沐浴者，前來「泡湯」。

這些人聞「泉」慕名而來，迢迢千里，前來呷依村的查曲卡溫泉──位於四川省西北端與青海和西藏自治區接壤的石渠縣。這是傳說中格薩爾王帶著他最愛的妃子珠姆、和三十名將軍沐浴和休憩之地。從各種跡象顯示，這個傳聞似乎有一定的可信度。畢竟，這附近就是格薩爾王的出生地，而許多有關他英勇戰績的奇聞逸事，從有歷史記

Prayer flag near Shiqu / 風馬旗近石渠縣　　Shelduck pair / 赤麻鴨

錄以來，也都由此傳開。

秋去冬來，風刀霜劍；如此天寒地凍，正是尋找地熱溫泉的絕佳氛圍，此時不找，更待何時？寒氣逼人，直把野生動物與人類都逼到了溫泉區，人畜都在此避寒取暖。根據高度計所顯示的數據，我們當時置身四千一百六十八公尺高處，看來，一般候鳥應該在很久以前便已向南遷徙了，但仍見赤麻鴨，旁若無人般，成雙成對，自在沐浴源泉邊，絲毫沒有留意我們這群和牠們共同取暖的泡湯人士。離溫泉不遠處的牧民，則在放牧犛牛和羊群。人畜無爭，共享天地之暖和與謐靜。

嚴格說來，查曲卡溫泉不只是個溫泉，而是一組浴池，分布於雅礱江的主要支流——扎曲河上游約四分之一公里的沼澤地——那是最終匯入長江的「四川」之一。西部的分水嶺為長江上游，通天河在此匯聚成金沙江；東邊則以黃河為分水嶺，那是巴顏喀拉山脈的延伸。

根據當地人的說法，總計有一百零八個泉池，可治愈多達四百多種疾病，療效驚人。其中，格薩

Bathers & Mani wall in back /
泡溫泉的人和在後面的瑪尼牆
Bathers & CERS team / 泡溫泉的人和學會人員

爾醫療溫泉，可治愈所有疾病，包括流行病，因此，在鋪天蓋地的新冠疫情肆虐下，這醫療等級的泉水，肯定是大顯身手的好時機。其中，格薩爾王王妃珠姆的溫泉，以治愈腎病與婦女疾病而聞名於藏區。其中最受歡迎的溫泉，則由一堵長長的瑪尼石牆相隔，每塊瑪尼石都刻上一個咒語，類似「唵嘛呢叭咪吽」的六字大明咒。當地人和遠道而來的旅人，在牆邊燒杜松香，以此為祭祀。據說，那個渾然天成的壁龕，正是當時格薩爾王繫馬的地方。

在這裡沐浴，可以治愈所有疾病，消除一切疼痛——當地人這麼說、這麼信以為真。每年九月前後，農牧業的繁重工作即將告一段落，來自高原各地的旅人——從青海玉樹、果洛，甚至遠從昌都、以及西藏內地的日喀則——慕名而遠道而來者，絡繹不絕；有人短暫逗留三天至一週，也有待在當地兩週、甚至一個月之久的。過去交通不便，這些人或騎馬、或騎犛牛，不辭千里來，在附近搭帳篷，就近住下來。今時不同往日，人們乘車而來，然後入住附近的寺院或小旅館。

我的十人團隊，包括一輛露營車，在一位當地僧侶的陪同下，抵達目的地。根青，雖然只有二十七歲，年少有為，目前已是色須寺藏醫院的院長，畢業於省會成都的傳統藏醫學院。這座格魯派的黃教寺院規模宏大，總僧侶人數大約兩千七百人，和一個主要的大學校園幾乎沒什麼不同。回顧一九四九年之前的狀況，相比

之下，這已是巨大而顯著的成長，過去寺院最鼎盛時期也不過一千兩百名僧侶，甚至曾在一九八〇年代初期從低谷逐漸恢復時，學員人數縮減至一度只有兩百名僧侶。

色須寺是青藏高原東部康區一帶，唯一可授予「格西」學名的寺院，相當於藏學博士的學位。在整個青藏高原多達數百家寺院中，只有另外四個寺院，能提供如此嚴謹的學術資格。雖然自一九九一年以來，我們曾多次途經石渠縣，我從未駐足停留參訪過，直到這一次，藉由這名年輕僧侶醫生根青的一位仁波切友人引薦，我們終於「有緣相會」。

我們在寺院裡近距離觀察僧侶們的生活作息。所有僧侶一大早便在不同學組的各個祈禱間穿梭，完

Bathers / 泡溫泉的人

成一個接一個功課，祈禱誦經，下午則到主廣場上，分組進行唇槍舌劍的精闢辯論。當然，在根青的親自介紹下，我們能更深入地參觀藏藥醫學院；包括學生學習的教室，藏藥製作的工作室，以及寺醫院的藥房；開放看診時，只見當地藏族病人早已排隊久候。

我想憑藉我在中國工作近五十年、在西藏高原遊歷探索四十年的資歷，在此重申與書寫我的個人「偏見」。這些偏見背後，建基於我從主流西方媒體所累積而得的眾多獎項和肯定，其中包括《時代週刊》(TIME)、《美國有線電視新聞網》(CNN)、《華爾街日報》等。我在此直言，這是一篇「選擇性」的報導，主題明確瞭然——以高原上一個主要寺院的活動為主。

與許多所謂「中立客觀」的外國記者不同，他們篩選並「選擇性」地報導宗教場域的鎮壓事件，但卻沒有親臨其境與現場，而是藉由蒐集轉述的二手資訊，或從其他有意操弄報導方向所彙整的「創意版本」，以片面之詞，權充打手，行抨擊抹黑之實。這種經常以「匿名消息來源」為掩護的報導，長遠來看，將導致作者甚至他們所代表的媒體，失去威信而全面潰散。

當然，我們今天可以因讀者健忘而蒙混過關，反正這群讀者明天以後便「既往不咎」，永不追究作者之責。然而，身為一個從大學起便一直浸淫於新聞學習的學生如我，我不必追究太久遠以前的事，只稍記起十年前這些西方媒體對中國的所有正面表述，再對照他們當前一貫的負面報導，一切所謂「選擇性」報導，攤在雙重標準和虛偽的表象下，不言自明。或許，如此議題與反差，可以讓主要的新聞學院當研究案例來探討，

想必精彩有趣，先選定結果，再找主題編導。

我其實不難理解，面對中國崛起的挑戰，西方世界猶如芒刺在背，深陷絕望情愁，不過，今天這種選擇性的報導，其實有其高昂而隱形的代價──不僅離間許多親西方的華人知識分子，其中尤以亞洲人為大多數，也同時誤導一些理性思維、尤其是那些近期訪問過中國的西方人。隱藏在所有消極主義的背後，有一個積極及正面的啟示──如此高密度的頻繁報導，恰恰突顯中國與西方、乃至全世界之間，牽連至深，密不可分的關係。若非如此，中國的存在早已被遺忘而不復記憶，不值報導。

撇開政治嚷嚷和牢騷，我們在借宿的色須寺用完早餐後，一大早便驅車離開。坦白說，在寺院附屬與經營的嶄新旅館內，要從電熱毯和地暖設備的環境中抽身起床，面對室外的冰天雪地，從來就不是一件容易的事啊！

我們花了一小時車程，終於抵達縣城西北部的最後一個村莊──呷依村。經根青引介一位在色須寺的小分寺──呷依貢巴修習的老同學，我們和他見面。根青的這位老同學，對當地環境與生態瞭若

Monk debating / 和尚辯經

Herbal medicine dispensary / 草藥房

Tibetan patients / 西藏病人

指掌，使我們眼界大開。當地山區原是許多野生動物的棲息地，其中包括野驢、藏羚羊、岩羊，甚至還有高度瀕臨滅絕的雪豹；而溫泉所在，就位於所有人畜定居以外，人煙罕至的荒原沃野。

四十六歲的智美敦珠和他三十一歲的妻子扎西拉姆，經營管理溫泉旁的一家小旅館。倆人都是呯依村當地人。打從孩提時代，智美即已被認定為轉世喇嘛的仁波切，並在八歲時，被送到哇榮寺出家，他的父親是寺院的首席仁波切。二〇〇六年，智美開始經營寺院和旅館，為遠道而來查曲卡溫泉的朝聖者和旅人提供服務。世事難料，當智美遇見未來妻子後，毅然決定還俗，脫下袈裟，並於二〇一五年離開寺院，在寺院宿舍旁蓋建另一間宿舍。這對情侶於二〇二〇年結婚成家，目前以經營旅館為生。

根據智美的說法與介紹，這裡的溫泉水含有多種礦物質與其他特殊成分，這些水質還會隨著季節變換而色澤各異。有時候，不必等到四季遞嬗，就是一天內也會因白天、中午與晚上而呈現不同顏色的水面變化。此外，溫泉周圍的沼澤區，也可見鹽狀的白色沉積物。每年四月前後的春季，與九月的秋季，在乍暖還寒的交替時節，這些白色的鹽粉，更加隨處可見與普遍。

遊牧民族會把這些鹽收集起來泡腳，他們相信這些白色鹽粉具備療效，可以治愈風濕病和其他與骨骼相關的疾病。除此以外，這些鹽還可與飼料混合，餵食他們的牲畜——氂牛、羊和馬——藉此治愈牠們的疾病。有些牧民甚至會在顏色深黑的茶裡，加一點鹽，泡著喝，據稱可以治療胃病。還有當地人深信這些鹽漬若與鼻煙混合，可以治療鼻竇問題，若與水混合，則可緩解眼疾，若以它洗頭，則可防止脫髮……，療效多得

不勝枚舉，幾乎「鹽」來病除，無所不包。簡而言之，十足神奇泉水的靈丹妙藥。

當地人不分男女老少，幾乎全裸浸泡於泉水中；而我則選擇身穿厚重的羽絨外套與背心，單純只泡腳；很可能是極端氣候作祟，我的腳後跟沒兩下便出現龜裂。

或許有人會好奇，我如何發現這遙遠而特殊的溫泉？容許我來釋疑解惑。約莫一九八〇年代中期，四川所出版的系列典藏書籍裡，曾提及四川各縣地名的內文，總計十八卷，內容涵蓋四川西部甘孜州的每一個縣。其中一本關於「石渠」的書中，出現兩個字，格外引發我的矚目與好奇——鹽井，就位於呷依村內。由此小小線索，始於「尋鹽」的起心動念，終於，一步步引領我發現這令人心神俱醉的溫泉。

當我們準備分道揚鑣、各自返回色須寺前，智美拿出一小罐異常珍貴的白鹽，要讓我帶回家泡腳。希望有一天，當我銀髮日益稀疏時，這妙不可「鹽」之禮，真能發揮療效，救我頭頂之髮絲。

對於有意來訪的旅人，包括熱衷報導中國的記者們，溫泉座標如下：*xx.xx*° N *xx.xx*° E。畢竟，他們不需要到現場報導任何事。而對擅於使用互聯網的年輕族群，只要拍幾張自拍照，上傳與追隨的粉絲們分享，應該也稱心如意了。我對這一代「得天獨厚」的年輕人心懷最深的關切，始終是這句提問：「你到過見過這麼多地方，但這些地方是否也見到你了？」

對我們來說，最大的收穫是結交了幾位新朋友，並與我們的讀者分享這幾段友情。

宗薩寺

DZONGSAR MONASTERY

Dege, Sichuan – November 14, 2021

DZONGSAR MONASTERY
Paying homage to the non-sectarian movement of Tibetan Buddhism

This is a story about karma, lost and found. I first heard of Dzongsar Monastery when I came to Dege in 1982 during a National Geographic expedition. I was visiting the Dege Printing House, which at the time had just revived printing the sacred Kangyur sutras after the Cultural Revolution.

In 1991, with a team including a Belgium conservation architect and other scholars of Tibetan culture, we roamed the area and studied in detail 18 surviving Tibetan monasteries. Ultimately, we selected three where CERS got involved, preserving their architecture and murals, and even building earthworks to control landslides that threatened one of the monasteries.

Among these three, Baiya was of Sakya sect, Palpung was Kagyu, and Lumorab (a.k.a. Tumu) was Nyingma sect. Later, we also became involved with Renkang, the house where the 7th Dalai Lama was born, which is important for the Gelug sect. So to some extent we were non-sectarian in our association to Tibetan Buddhism, by karma, not by choice.

Two of these monasteries, Baiya and Palpung, are situated very close to Dzongsar Monastery, in the southwestern part of Dege County. My 1991 foray into Baiya and Palpung, however, was

Dege printing house circa 1982 / 德格印經院於 1982 年　　　　Baiya Gomba in 1991 / 白雅寺於 1991 年

on horseback, carrying our equipment and supplies on pack horses. From Palpung, it would require traversing a couple of hills, a half day's distance to reach Dzongsar, a relatively close distance considering the travel mode of the time. Riding from Dege to Palpung would also take a full day.

Dzongsar is best known for the founding of the Rime Movement, a non-sectarian movement among Tibetan Buddhism, honoring and sharing all four major sects of studies. The Second Generation of incarnated Dzongsar Rinpoche, Jamyang Khyentse Chokyi Lodro, who passed away in Sikkim in 1959, is considered by many Tibetan Buddhist scholars and incarnate lamas to be one of the most revered and knowledgeable Buddhist scholars of modern times. A Rinpoche is a reincarnated lama, or a "Living Buddha" as some may call him.

A story I heard long ago about Chokyi Lodro went like this. When a group of student monks from Kham (eastern Tibet) arrived in Lhasa to try to enter Drepung Monastery for study, the head monk asked them, "Is the Dzongsar

Rinpoche still alive and well?" Upon hearing that he was, the head monk waved them off in dismissal, "Go home! Why would you need to come here to study if Rinpoche is still alive?" Such is the aura the former Dzongsar Rinpoche held among Tibetans.

The venerable Dilgo Khyentse Rinpoche, who wrote Chokyi Lodro's biography, called the Second Dzongsar Rinpoche his supreme and precious master. My old friend the Pewar (Baiya) Rinpoche, who will be turning 90 next month, was an early student of the same Second Dzongsar Rinpoche, contributing one chapter about Chokyi Lodro in Dilgo Khyentse's own autobiography. He was the favorite companion of Dilgo Khyentse, root guru of the current Third Dzongsar Rinpoche. Pewar also gave empowerment and teachings to the Third Dzongsar.

Another old friend, Tupten Nyima, the Zenkar Rinpoche, considered by many as the most knowledgeable Tibetan scholar of this generation, was also a student at Dzongsar. I invited Tupten Nyima to the US and he stayed at my home in Los Angeles in 1988, and later in Hong Kong, as well as at our Center in Zhongdian, a.k.a. Shangri-la. Even the Sogyal Rinpoche, who wrote the famous Tibetan Book of Living and Dying, spent his childhood with the Second Dzongsar Rinpoche at the monastery. It was because of Pewar and Tupten Nyima, our previous connections, that I longed to visit this Sakya monastery.

All the above may sound like name-dropping, but for me it was all karma, connecting all the dots. Notwithstanding that much of my activities over the years were in the vicinity, somehow Dzongsar evaded me. Not so much due to lack of interest, but karma kept taking me around this hill top ensemble of Buddhist "villages" despite passing through the area a dozen times or more. That is, until November 12, 2021.

On that day, we were required to take a swab test before heading out of Dege, so we took one at 10am, being promised to receive the results by 2 pm. I decided to visit the small but important chapel shrine honoring Thangtong Gyalpo, a Tibetan saint considered the Da Vinci of Tibet. It was hidden among some houses in the old section of Dege. Of the few Tibetan Buddhist statues I have received as gifts, the one of Thangtong Gyalpo is especially dear, as it was chosen by Her Majesty the Royal Grandmother of Bhutan for me. So it seemed appropriate to pay my respects at this special and rare chapel.

By 2pm as soon as we received our results, all negative for the ten of us, we drove out of town toward the Yangtze, heading for Dzongsar Monastery. I knew no one at the monastery or at Maixiu Village where the monastery is. But two of our Tibetan staff, Drolma and Tsomo, both knew a local Tibetan woman Dawa who went to the same

Thangtong Gylpo Shrine / 唐東傑布廟   Early mural of Thangtong Gylpo / 早期唐東傑布壁畫   Thangtong Gylpo statue & Baiya Rinpoche / 唐東傑布像及白雅仁波切

English language school in Qinghai before going to the US for college. Drolma went to Duke, Tsomo to Dartmouth and Dawa studied at Bay Path University, a small private college in Massachusetts. They called her and made reservations to stay at a local lodge Dawa had founded a couple of years ago.

From here on, the rest played out according to karma. Dzongsar is now about three hours away from Dege, given that there is a fully paved road leading to the monastery. Traveling on horses is unheard of these days, in contrast to 30 years ago when I visited the area. While in the car, I texted Ashi Kesang Wangchuk, a close friend and princess of Bhutan who has dedicated her career to cultural conservation in the Himalayan Kingdom. I told her that I had just visited the Thangtong Gyalpo shrine. In passing, I mentioned I was on my way to Dzongsar Monastery.

She quickly texted back that Dzongsar was the home monastery of the Third Dzongsar Rinpoche, Jamyang Khyentse Norbu, a Bhutanese Buddhist figure with a huge international following. He is also known for the movies he made and books he authored. It is through Ashi Kesang that I found out the Rinpoche is someone whom Her Majesty the Royal Grandmother had patronized when young, after being authenticated by the Dilgo Khyentse Rinpoche, root guru to the Royal Grandmother. Suddenly everything clicked. We were elevated from a casual tourist to friends of the royal family on a pilgrimage.

Things were set in motion quickly through phone and WeChat, involving the Dzongsar Rinpoche's office in India, his nephew Pawo Choyning Dorji in Taiwan, the Khenpo (head monk) Phuntsho

Namgyel of the monastery, who at the time was in Chengdu, and the caretaker monk Kungyal of the monastery. By 6pm we were already below the expansive ensemble of houses of Dzongsar Monastery after driving through some beautiful valleys and canyons, passing a frozen waterfall, white birch forest and late autumn foliage. But it was getting late and I decided to call it a day, going straight to the lodge.

Fifteen minutes onward and we stopped at Khyenle, Dawa's new lodging house. Dawa came out to greet her school friends from Qinghai times. Dinner was served soon after, with pizza and Tibetan dumplings, just as Dzongsar's caretaker monk Kungyal showed up to join us for a meal. Together we discussed the following day's agenda for our visit. I was delighted that we would have a proper reception and intro to this renowned monastery of the highest scholarship. It was said that Dzongsar had produced over 200 Khenpos (equivalent to Geshe in the Gelup sect or a PhD in the Western tradition) in less than 30 years, a degree that usually requires thirteen years of study to achieve.

Monks at assembly hall / 僧人於主殿裡

Monks studying / 僧人讀書

We started the next morning by visiting the great assembly hall where student monks were having their early morning chant and prayers, followed by the dispensing of butter tea to each monk. At another big hall, only blankets were left on the sitting pads while a few monks gathered to study sutra, or in small group discussions. We were shown the new library and the large and well-organized bookshop, catering to monks as well as the lay public.

Nearby in one of the buildings, a few monks, many lay people, mostly young boys and a few girls,

High view from Retreat Center / 高處看閉關中心

were busy painting religious Thangka scrolls stretched on wooden frames. Their teacher, Tsepal, a well known Thangka artist sat at the head and watched over his students, while also sketching his latest work. The wall was lined with rows of colorful paint in bowls. Most vibrant in color, these were all mineral or plant-based pigments.

Tsepal's 26-years-old son Gonga Lhangyal was showing us around proudly, and explained the process as well as showing us some of the best pieces in their collection that were not for sale. Downstairs, up on a scaffold, six artists were working over an especially large piece of thangka. It is commissioned by a monastery to be put on the wall of the Assembly Hall as a mural.

I was a bit taken aback that each artist, with tiny sharp and pointed hair brush, would dip it in their mouth to get it wet, before picking up some paint and applying the brush to the surface of the cloth or silk painting. I knew some of these minerals were poisonous, for example the cinnabar red that they used was a mercury-based pigment. Such tradition and practice should be modernized and modified to avoid accumulating poisons in their bodies. But then, perhaps with the right prayers, their bodies had developed higher resistance.

The Thangka Center is just one of many cultural activities within Dzongsar. After a most sumptuous lunch prepared by the monastery near the chief abbot's residence, we were led to see other arts and crafts studios, including weaving, pottery, bronze and iron smithing, incense making, and lastly a local Tibetan hospital and its very modern traditional medicine factory. These are all cultural revival projects now fully in motion within the vicinity of Dzongsar, many of which are supported or coordinated through the efforts of Dawa, her Khyenle Guesthouse being a center of dissemination for these activities.

In the afternoon, after seeing an active debate by the monks at the main square in front of the assembly hall, we headed into the mountains and drove for another half hour or so to reach an even higher elevation. Here near the crest of two mountains we looked down to the beautiful valley below with the Dzongsar Retreat Center. These simple abodes were painted with the tri-color of red, white and dark gray stipes, just like all the houses at Dzongsar Monastery. The entire place was very quiet, as literally everyone there was in retreat and deep meditation.

While smaller monasteries may be under stricter supervision by the government, larger institutions with high discipline and well organized internal scholastic structure have been left to operate, even prosper. Dzongsar is one such example. Today, there are around 1200 monks at the monastery, with another 700 additional nuns and 100 monks at a retreat meditation center some thirty minutes away. Its very fine tradition and integrity are being maintained, unlike many large monasteries that aim towards grandeur, luxury and glamor, attracting a very different type of supplicant.

Among the 1200 monks, one stood out different from the rest. Yuanren is from Taiwan and has written a well-received book on his entire journey leading him from his home to becoming a monk at Dzongsar Monastery over a decade ago. We had the good fortune to meet him, as well as 75 year old Lodro Phentso, a lama who became a monk at an early age, but later disrobed and got married during the Cultural Revolution.

In the mid-1980s when religion was revived, Lodro almost single handedly started bit by bit the rebuilding of Dzongsar Monastery after it was razed to the ground during the uprising in the eastern part of the Tibetan plateau in 1958, which was soon followed by more destruction in the Cultural Revolution. Through acute memory of the past, Lodro Phentso began piecing together each structure and their location, rebuilding them to their original shape. As the effort got underway and some early results were shown, others in the area joined in, making the ensemble of buildings what it is today.

Lodro is multi-talented, a Buddhist scholar, architect, carpenter, artist, potter, sculptor, accountant, astronomer, manager, tailor and poet, all in one. Being also a Tibetan traditional doctor, he founded the Tibetan hospital and medicine factory in the village that we visited below Dzongsar. When we met at his modest home to have tea, the most admirable trait was how humble he also was.

As Yuanren describes in his book, illustrated with pictures to match, all the monks, young and old, were pleasant, smiling, and having fun much of the time, besides studying diligently for high scholarship. Such freedom was described in Dilgo Khyentse Rinpoche's autobiography, which also described nearby Katok (Gartok) Monastery in Baiyu as being so strict that any mistake by young monks was punishable with five lashes. In contrast, at Dzongsar, the child monks were all monkeying around and mischievous.

Traditional weaver / 傳統織布人
Dawa & Khyenle Guesthouse / 達瓦和欽樂民宿

The Second Dzongsar Rinpoche actually kept a pet monkey around him.

Not many early photographs of the great Second Dzongsar have been circulated, given the lack of camera and film in such a remote area in the old days. But two pictures little-known to others were taken by Lobsang Dundrup, a Han Chinese named Xing Suzhi, in 1937 while studying at Dzongsar. He is a very fine photographer, traveling with his camera. He later went on to Lhasa and graduated First in debate at Drepung Monastery after seven years of intensive study. He became the first Han Chinese ever to achieve the degree of Geshe.

Xing spent time studying and was initiated with empowerment by Khyentse Chokyi Lodro. He purportedly learned 167 empowerment mantras, including his last lesson from Lodro, what he called the "Disappearing Act". That, perhaps, is the most mysterious and magical practice, which I too would like to learn before I am back in the metropolis of Hong Kong. Being at Dzongsar is close to being in that state of mind and being.

Rime at Dzongsar is like the super conductor that connects all the different sects of Tibetan Buddhism. The karma that it unleashes also brought me to this monastery, after hearing about it for forty years. Om Mani Padme Hum.

Lodro, HM, Yuanren & Drolma / 洛熱、HM、原人和卓瑪

宗薩寺
向藏傳佛教的「無宗派運動」致敬

這是一個與因緣、失而復得相關的故事。第一次聽聞宗薩寺，是在一九八二年帶領美國「國家地理」探險隊初抵德格縣時。當時我正參觀德格印經院，這家印經院剛在文革後首次恢復用木板印製神聖的《甘珠爾經》大藏經。

一九九一年，我們一行人包括比利時籍的文物保育建築師與其他西藏文化的專家學者，組成一個團隊，前往德格縣考察探索，詳細研究了十八座倖存的藏族寺院。我們最終選定由「中國探險學會」參與其中的三家寺院，進行建築保育與壁畫維護，包括地面工程養護，以防任何風雨災害造成土石流而危及寺院安全。

這三家被選定的建築物分別是薩迦派的白雅寺、噶舉派的八蚌寺、寧瑪派的土木寺。爾後，我們又到理塘的仁康古廟，那是七世達賴喇嘛的出生地，也是格魯派的重要聖地。所以，某種程度上，我們與藏傳佛教的連結，其實無關宗派，不管紅白花黃各派，亦非選擇，一切出於因緣。

其中兩個寺院，白雅寺和八蚌寺，位於德格縣西南部，非常靠近宗薩寺。我還記得一九九一年時，當我前往白雅寺和八蚌寺時，是騎在馬背上，用馱馬背著我們的設備

和補給品。往八蚌寺出發，需要穿越幾座山丘，一路顛簸了半天，才好不容易抵達目的地；考慮當時的各種客觀條件，這已是一個相對較快、也較近的交通距離。從德格縣騎到八蚌寺，也需要一整天，而宗薩寺所在地則更遠。

宗薩寺以創立「利美運動」聞名，這項活動是藏傳佛教中的非宗派運動，崇尚和分享所有四大教派。宗薩寺為人所知的另一件事，與一位仁波切有關——一九五九年，在錫金圓寂的第二代宗薩仁波切——蔣揚欽哲確吉羅卓。確吉羅卓被許多藏傳佛教學者和轉世喇嘛認定為現代最受尊敬和知識淵博的佛教學者之一。順道說明，所謂仁波切，是轉世喇嘛，也有人稱之為「活佛」。

我很久以前聽過一個關於確吉羅卓的故事：一群來自康區（東藏）的學生僧人抵達拉薩時，想辦法要進入哲蚌寺修習，大和尚開門見山，問他們：「宗薩仁波切還健在嗎？」學生回答是，仁波切健在；大和尚隨即揮揮手，打發他們離開：「回去吧！如果仁波切還活著，你們何必來此修道呢？」不難看出，前宗薩仁波切在藏人心目中的崇高地位與光環。

Khampa HM to Palpung 1991 /
HM 康巴到八蚌寺於 1991 年
Baiya Rinpoche in HK 2009 /
白雅仁波切於 2009 年

尊貴的頂果欽哲仁波切，是撰寫《碓吉羅卓傳記》的作者，他稱第二世宗薩仁波切為他至高無上的上師。我的老朋友白雅仁波切，下個月滿九十歲了，他是同一位宗薩仁波切的早期弟子，在頂果欽哲的自傳中，曾負責撰寫一章關於碓吉羅卓的內容。他是現任第三世宗薩仁波切的根本上師頂果欽哲最喜歡的夥伴。白雅仁波切還曾給第三世宗薩灌頂和教法。

我的另一位老朋友，土登尼瑪——桑嘎仁波切，是公認最博學的當代藏族學者，同時也是宗薩寺的弟子。我邀請土登尼瑪去美國，他曾於一九八八年住在我洛杉磯的家中，後來也曾到香港，還有我們的中甸中心，也就是香格里拉。著名的《西藏生死書》作者索甲仁波切，也曾在宗薩寺跟隨第二世宗薩仁波切度他的過童年。由於這些過去累積的因緣際會，包括與白雅和土登尼瑪之間的連結，使我一直希望能一訪薩迦寺。

以上洋洋灑灑的名單內容，乍聽下彷彿想借助名人來哄抬我的身分，其實不然；對我而言，這些名字背後都是一段又一段不可思議的因緣，將所有人事時地物，一一牽連起來。儘管這些年來，我大部分的探索行程都在這一區域行動，但不知為何，宗薩寺卻以某種無可名狀的方式，與我擦身而過。與其說是缺乏興趣，倒不如說是業力因緣吧，彷彿一股不可言喻的力量，不斷將我帶往附近的佛教「村莊」群中，兜兜轉轉，儘管旅程中我至少路過該

區十幾次，或甚至更多次，卻從未駐足到過宗薩寺——直到二○二一年十一月十二日。

那一天，我們需要在離開德格縣之前，進行新冠病毒的篩檢測試；於是，我們在上午十點篩檢一次，衛生單位允諾下午兩點前就會告知檢驗結果。在短暫的等待期間，我決定參觀一間供奉唐東傑布的小廟——小而重要的廟宇。神人等級的傳奇聖人唐東傑布，備受藏人尊崇，甚至被媲美為西藏的達文西。這座小廟隱身於德格縣舊區的普通房屋中。在我為數不多的藏傳佛像蒐藏中，唐東傑布的這一尊，尤為珍貴，因為它是不丹皇太后陛下為我挑選的。所以我想，能在這特殊而罕見的小廟裡獻上我的敬意，理所當然。

下午兩點，檢驗結果出來了，我們一行十人都是陰性；健康無虞，於是便驅車出城，前往長江，直奔宗薩寺。我在寺院所在的麥宿村，沒有舊識或朋友。但我們的兩位藏族同事卓瑪和措姆，剛好認識一位當地的藏族女士，達瓦，他們去美國讀大學前，曾是青海同一所英語語言學校的同學。卓瑪後來遠赴美國杜克大學，而措姆則去了達特茅斯學院，這位藏族女士達瓦，則就讀於麻省的朗梅德，一所小型的私立大學。他們打電話給她，並準備下塌達瓦幾年前所開設的旅館。

其餘的連結與關係，由此開始，由因緣牽引與帶領。現在的宗薩寺，距離德格縣大約只需三小時路程，因為通往寺院的道路是鋪設完好的瀝青馬路，不再像過去我做訪時那般顛簸遙遠，三十年前這些騎馬旅行的特殊經歷，早已聞所未聞。在車上，我給不丹的好友公主，艾殊.吉桑.旺楚 (Ashi Kesang Wangchuk) 發了短信，公主傾力為喜馬拉雅王國的文化保護奉獻良多。我告訴她自己剛剛參觀了唐東傑布的小廟，也順便讓她知道，我正前往宗薩寺途中。

公主很快回覆我，告訴我宗薩寺是第三世宗薩仁波切，蔣揚欽哲諾布的家鄉主院，蔣揚欽哲諾布是

一位擁有大量國際追隨者的不丹佛教人物，他也以製作電影與撰寫書籍而聞名遐邇。透過艾殊吉桑公主，我得知這位仁波切在年輕時，曾受過皇太后陛下的恩澤款待，也經后太后的根本上師，頂果欽哲仁波切的認證。一時之間，原來看似毫無關聯的人與事，一一連結起來。在踏上這段朝聖的旅途中，我們就這樣從一個普通的遊客身分，升格為皇室的朋友到訪。

事情通過電話和微信的聯繫，迅速展開，許多單位與負責人紛紛關切，其中包括宗薩寺仁波切駐印度的辦公室、他在台灣的侄子帕沃秋寧多吉、當時在成都的寺院堪布（首席僧人）彭措南傑，和寺院負責看守的僧人坤雅。旅行途中，穿越美不勝收的山谷與峽谷，路經冰凍的瀑布、白樺林與落葉深秋後，下午六點時，我們已抵達宗薩寺寬廣的建築群下方。彼時天色已晚，我決定收工，直接到旅館入住。

Birch forest & foliage / 白樺樹林、葉子

Frozen water fall / 冰凍的瀑布

十五分鐘後，我們停靠達瓦的新旅館，欽樂 (Khyenle)。達瓦出來迎接就讀青海語言學院時期的老同學。晚餐很快就送到了，包括比薩和西藏餃子；宗薩寺的看守僧人坤雅正好出現，便請他和我們一起用餐。期間我們一起討論了隔天的訪問行程。能在如此著名的佛教最高學術寺院，接受那麼高規格的接待與導覽，我備感榮幸，興奮不已。據說，宗薩寺在不到三十年的時間內，培養了兩百多位堪布（相當於格魯派的格西或西方傳統的博士），這個學位通常需要十三年的修習才能完成。

第二天上午，我們參觀了大主殿，學生僧侶們正進行清晨的誦經和早禱；然後，為每位僧侶分發酥油茶。另一間主殿的坐墊上，只剩毯子，眼前有幾位僧人聚在一起研讀佛經，或在進行小組討論。我們還看到嶄新的圖書館和組織完善的大型佛教書店，為僧侶和一般民眾提供服務。

在其中一棟建築附近，幾位僧人和好幾位以年輕男女為主的居士們，忙著在木框壓軸的佛教唐卡捲軸上，埋首繪製。他們的老師澤北 (Tsepal)，是一位著名的唐卡藝術家，他坐在最前面，看著學生作畫，一邊指導一邊自行勾勒出他最新的創作。牆上排列了裝在碗裡的顏料，色澤瑰麗而鮮豔，都是礦物或植物顏料，琳瑯滿目。

Second Dzongsar Rinpoche /
宗薩仁波切二世

策瑟帕的二十六歲兒子吉美南卡 (Gonga Lhangyal)，帶我們四處參觀，一邊導覽與解釋整個繪製過程，自信滿滿地並向我們展示收藏的絕佳非賣品。走到樓下，可見一座臨時搭建的舞台上，六位藝術家正聯手繪製一幅特別大的唐卡。受修道院所託，這幅大唐卡被繪製成壁畫，貼在大主殿牆上。

其中比較令我吃驚的是，每個藝術家會先把尖尖的小毛筆放到嘴裡沾溼，再塗上顏料，繼續在布料或絲綢畫布上作畫。我知道其中一些顏料的礦物質是有毒的，例如他們使用的硃砂紅是一種汞基顏料。我想，為免身體累積毒素，這種傳統畫作法，應該要與時並進和稍作修改。不過，也或許他們可以透過合宜的祈禱，身體會產生更無敵的抵抗力吧。

唐卡繪製，只是宗薩寺內眾多文化活動之一。我們在住持居所旁的寺院，享受一頓豐盛午餐後，隨即便到其他工藝美術工作室參觀，包括紡織、陶器、青銅、鐵匠與藏香，最後是當地的西藏醫院及其非常現代化的傳統藥廠。這些都是當前宗薩寺周遭全面展開的文化復興項目，其中許多項目都與達瓦建立相互支援的合作計畫，她的欽樂旅館更成了這些活動的宣傳站。

下午時分，我們在大主殿前的大廣場，觀賞一場僧侶們精彩的辯論課後，便往深山密林去。開了半小時左右的車程，我們抵達更高海拔的山區。在緊鄰兩座山峰之地，我們俯瞰下方美麗的山谷和宗薩寺閉關中心。這些看起來簡單平凡的建築，與宗薩寺的所有房屋一樣，都塗上了薩迦派花教的紅、白、深灰三色的莖柄。整個地方異常僻靜寧謐，在閉關中心的每個人，幾乎都進入深度冥想的修練中。

Artist painting Thangka / 藝術家畫唐卡
Group paining mural Thangka / 一組人畫唐卡壁畫

Master Tsepal sketching / 澤北大師畫素描

一般規模較小的寺院，必須接受政府更嚴格的監管，相對而言，更大的機構因為具備高度自我管控的紀律，加上內部的學術體制建立在完善的組織架構上，因此，後者反倒享有更大的營運空間，也更蒸蒸日上。宗薩寺便是其中一個例子。如今，該寺院約有一千兩百名僧侶，另外在大約三十分鐘路程之外的禪修閉關中心內，還有七百名尼姑和一百名僧侶。和其他一些追求宏大雄偉與奢華綺麗的大型寺院不同，宗薩寺保留了優良的傳統與簡樸的體質，吸引許多不同類型的求道者慕名而來。

在這一千兩百名僧侶中，其中一位身分獨特的僧侶，格外引發眾人好奇，那是來自台灣的原人——我們很榮幸能見到他。原人在十幾年前，毅然出家，從家鄉台灣遠赴宗薩寺，他後來把這段旅程與出家的心路歷程，寫成一本書，備受關注，也廣受好評。另一位我們深感有幸認識的僧人，是七十五歲的洛熱彭措 (Lodro Phentso)。洛熱彭措是位早年出家的喇嘛，在文革期間脫下袈裟長袍，還俗結婚。

宗薩寺曾於一九五八年在青藏高原東部起義期間受到破壞，及後不到幾年，寺廟又在文革期間被破壞殆盡，遭受攻擊而被夷為平地。一直到一九八〇年代中期，當宗教復興運動紅紅火火展開時，洛熱彭措把握時機，幾乎赤手空拳地展開重建工程，洛熱彭措憑藉頭腦裡對寺廟的記憶，慢慢拼揍，再將寺廟結構，一磚一瓦地

原址重蓋，恢復原有的建築樣貌。隨著這項重建工程的展開，逐漸成型的成果，鼓舞越來越多人投入建設工作，一區一區，一棟一棟，就這麼一步步蓋建起來，錯落有致，成了今天我們所見到的宗薩寺。

洛熱彭措的才華橫溢，集佛教學者、建築師、木匠、藝術家、陶藝家、雕塑家、會計師、天文學家、經理人、裁縫師和詩人於一身。作為一名藏族傳統醫生，他在我們參觀的宗薩寺下方的村子裡，創辦了西藏醫院和藥廠。當我們在他簡陋的家中見面喝茶時，他那謙謙君子的風範，最令人欽佩與充滿敬意。

正如原人在他圖文並茂的書中所描述的，所有僧侶，無論老少，都是法喜充滿，面帶微笑的，即使人人都得勤奮學習以獲得高額獎學金，但大多數時候，他們還是感覺生活精彩有趣。這份自由自在，在頂果欽哲仁波切的自傳中，也可以找到類似的敘事；其中還提及一段插曲：白玉附近的噶陀 (Gartok) 寺以嚴格出了名，年輕僧侶若犯上任何閃失差錯，都得被抽打五鞭當懲罰。相比之下，宗薩寺的小僧侶們則像猴子般調皮搗蛋、撒潑又自由。話說，第二世宗薩仁波切還真的養了隻寵物猴子在身邊。

過去，在偏遠深山裡普遍缺乏相機和膠卷，即使如此偉大重要的第二宗薩寺，早期的歷史照片也極為少見。但有兩張鮮為人知的

Officials of KMT in Lhasa with Li Youyi on left /
國民黨派在拉薩官員，李有義在左
Tupten Nyima with HM in HK /
土登尼瑪和 HM 在香港

照片，是由漢人洛桑珍珠（邢肅芝）於一九三七年在宗薩寺讀書時拍攝，稀有而珍貴。邢肅芝是位非常優秀的攝影師，經常背著相機到處旅行。他後來到拉薩潛心專研了七年的佛學修習，後來畢業於哲蚌寺的辯經班。邢肅芝最終成為有史以來第一個獲得格西學位的漢人。

邢肅芝花時間學習，並得到欽哲確吉羅卓的灌頂。據稱，他曾學習了一百六十七種灌頂咒，包括他從確吉羅卓那裡學到的最後一課——他稱之為「消失法」。這也許是最神秘、最神奇的修行，我也好想在返回香港大都會之前，學會這門「消失」的隱身功夫。置身宗薩寺，我感覺自己多麼接近那份心靈與存在的狀態。

宗薩寺的利美運動，就像是連接藏傳佛教各個不同教派的超級導體。聽聞霧淞四十年之後，它所釋放的特殊因緣，終於將我牽引至此寺院。唵嘛呢叭咪吽。

Dzongsar Retreat Center / 宗薩寺閉關中心

鮮
為
人
知
的
兩
條
河

TWO LITTLE-KNOWN RIVERS

Feng Huang, Hunan – November 24, 2021

TWO LITTLE-KNOWN RIVERS
Beipanjiang Guizhou to Fenghuang Hunan

Beipanjiang is a tributary of the Pearl River with its geographic source in Qujing County east of Kunming in Yunnan, the furthest point upstream from the mouth of the Pearl River. It changes its name several times as it defines the border between Yunnan with Guizhou, then drops through the famous Huangguoshu Waterfall, then merges with the Hongshui River, which would ultimately become the West River that enters the Pearl River near the Delta in Guangdong.

From Kunming, with a modern highway now in place, it takes only five hours of driving to reach a point where the river cuts through some deep gorges on the border between the two provinces. Guizhou used to be near the bottom of the list of provinces of China in terms of wealth. No more, unless your mindset is stuck in version 1.0, as mine was. During this year, after visiting much of central and coastal China, my mind has been upgraded, like my phone, apps and computer software, now to 5.0.

As if the numerous long tunnels through limestone hills and high bridges over deep valleys along the four-lane highway are not impressive enough, the Yunnan-Guizhou border is now spanned by the highest highway bridge in the world, a record kept from 2018 to this day in the Guinness

World Records. Of the 100 highest bridges in the world, 50 are located in Guizhou with the Beipanjiang Bridge claiming the top spot.

Ma Xuanjun is forty years old, and was recently featured in a report in China's Global Times newspaper. He is Muslim, and the family was originally from Yunnan, but moved to this border village of Du Ge in Guizhou four generations ago due to famine at their former home. The specifications for this high bridge are quite staggering. Ma recites all the figures to us proudly, "The bridge is 1341 meters in length with a span of 720 meters, and a height of 565 meters from the base down to the valley below, equivalent to a 200-storyed building in height…. It cost 770 million RMB, took three years to build and used 25,000 tons of steel, xx number of nails, and yy meters of cable." Ma's exacting figures and dizzying info began to slip in my mind, as well as in my notes.

Ma showed up driving a three-wheel motorcycle truck and stopped by our camper van to chat. He thought we might need to find a place for dinner or to stay for the night, and volunteered his home-stay lodge up the hill across two suspension bridges. At this point, the Nizhu River joins the Beipanjiang at a confluence. During this winter dry season, all the rocks by the river banks are exposed, resembling a gallery of Henry Moore sculptures. In fact, these natural shapes and forms carved by millennia of

Beipanjiang Bridge / 北盤江大橋

river water far surpass anything a human artist could replicate or create. When man meets nature, the latter always has an upper hand.

Earlier, it took us over half an hour to descend from the high bridge to Du Ge Village at the bottom after snaking through a road with many switch-back turns. Then a hazardous side road, very narrow and with acute gradient, took us to a dead end at the confluence of the two rivers. Where we parked our camper for the night is on Guizhou's side, on the east bank of Beipanjiang. A suspension bridge, springing up and down as we walked, took us across the Nizhu River so that we landed on the tip of a piece of land belonging to Yunnan Province, barely large enough to have the two houses built on it, one of which being the restaurant where we had dinner, served with fish caught from below in the Beipanjiang.

Tea break looking over across river / 望河享用茶點

Pipe bridge over Beipanjiang / 水管橋橫跨北盤江

Another suspension bridge, a precarious one that is intended only to support a big waterpipe, swinging side-to-side as we walked, allowed us to cross over gingerly above the Beipanjiang to reach the east bank which again is inside Guizhou. And here is where Ma's home-stay lodge is. However, our brand-new camper van offered superior comfort and we opted not to check in with him.

While the boulders and rocks at the confluence of the two rivers may have battled thousands of years of flood water beating upon it, more recently it has also seen a new type of battle developing some five hundred meters above. As the bridge gained fame as being highest in the world, it started attracting tourists, as well as attention of government officials from both Guizhou and Yunnan. Controversy developed as to the naming rights of the bridge, Beipanjiang or Nizhu, with the former belonging to Guizhou and the latter within Yunnan.

The Yunnan side of the highway was built by Yunnan Province up to the bridge front, whereas Guizhou was in charge of its own side of the highway. But it did not make sense to have each province build half the bridge to connect to each other in the middle, thus the construction fell to Guizhou, with Yunnan covering 52% of the cost and the remaining 48% taken up by Guizhou. This tug of war ended with a draw, as both sides came up with a list of why the bridge should be named one way or another. Finally, after many rounds of negotiations and arbitration, Guizhou won the day and maintained the right to call it Beipanjiang Bridge. After all, it is the source river of the Pearl, ideal for attracting visitors from the prosperous Delta.

Leaving Guizhou, we entered Hunan Province. Near the provincial border is the ancient town of Fenghuang, set in a Miao and Tujia minority nationality region. The pristine and beautiful town was once a poor and remote village by the Tuo Jiang, a river with wooden houses on stilts lining its banks. Due perhaps in part to two of its

Bathing bird & cage / 幫鳥洗澡和洗鳥籠

famous sons, writer Shen Congwen and artist Huang Yongyu, Fenghuang has become a hot spot for tourists today.

Shen's book Bien Cheng (Border Town) is simple and pure, a very earthy love fiction set around Fenghuang in the 1930s, regarding an old man and his granddaughter living along the river. It won major readers' awards and ranked second among the one hundred most popular books of the Twentieth Century in China.

Huang Yongyu, Shen's nephew, is one of China's most renowned contemporary traditional artists. Rising from poverty to become a woodcut artist and later a professor of the famed Beijing Institute of Art, Huang's political persecution during the Cultural Revolution and his eventual reinstatement made him a darling of the modern China art scene. As Shen wrote about his hometown, Huang likewise painted Fenghuang, and maintains a studio home in the town to this day.

The ancient and historic town maintained its old charm mainly because the area, with eighty percent Miao nationality and the remaining being Tujia, was too poor to embrace the economic changes that hit China over the last four decades. So, more by chance than by design, the remains of the town's architectural past suddenly shot up to become one of the most popular *tourist destinations over the last ten to twenty years.*

However, on both banks of the Tuo Jiang, old stilt houses have given way to newer three to four storied wooden buildings, over 95 percent of which are boutique hotels, hostels and home-stay outfits. On the street sides are all tourist shops, restaurants and eateries. We came during the lowest of the low season, and a nice suite cost only 140 RMB, or less than US$ 20.

Arch bridge across Tuo Jiang / 拱橋橫跨沱江

Liu Zheng, the owner of the lodge where we stay, has retired after three years with the PLA. His ten-room outfit is nicely designed and quite posh; most rooms have a balcony looking out onto the fully-lit river bank across the Tuo Jiang at night. "It turns out that we were lucky being poor and without the money to rebuild our houses. Now, these houses turned out to be an asset, as they attract tourists," said Liu with his two year old son on his lap. Liu, who is of Miao ethnicity, continued, "but on popular long weekends and during summer vacation, the prices shoot up five to eight times. Even at that price, rooms are all fully booked in advance."

Today, there is a tiny stretch of the river bank that still has an ensemble of old stilt houses, nonetheless turned into commercial use. I woke up early enough to see the fog and mist before the first sunlight hit the water, arch bridges and houses. Through that small window of a winter morning, I managed to get a glimpse of what Fenghuang must have been like in the good old days, when Shen and Huang grew up in this far-off and little-known town.

For Du Ge and Fenghuang, as with many of the old cities, towns and villages of China, the remnants of the past can only be recorded in books and pictures. And so it is also with rivers like the Beipanjiang and Tuo Jiang. It may be the only means to provide us with a mental picture of that beautiful and pristine space in time, untouched by our modern world.

Stilts supporting houses / 吊腳樓房
Arch bridge / 拱橋

鮮為人知的兩條河

從貴州的北盤江到湖南的鳳凰古城

北盤江是珠江支流，源自雲南昆明以東的曲靖縣，位於珠江上游最遠的地方。北盤江因位居雲南與貴州的邊界，身負「劃定界線」重任，而屢次被更名。這條江河也穿越著名的黃果樹瀑布，與紅河匯合，最終流入西江，再輾轉匯聚成廣東三角洲附近的珠江。

從昆明出發，現在有了現代化的高速公路，方便許多，只要五個小時車程，便可抵達雲南與貴州之交界，北盤江的潺潺河水，流經此地的幾個峽谷深處，準確地劃開兩省邊境。貴州曾在中國財富排行榜上倒數一二，經常是墊底的貧窮省份。但今非昔比，貴州早已大翻身，除非你和我一樣，還停留在落後的 1.0 版的認知中。這一年，陸續走訪中國中部和沿海大部分區域後，我的思想認知已經大躍進和更新一番，一如我的手機、應用程式與電腦軟體，現在都升級到 5.0 版。

四車道的高速公路，爬深走高，不僅穿越石灰岩山丘的長長隧道，還跨過深谷上的高高橋樑，這些工程已足以令人嘖嘖稱奇了，但雲南與貴州似乎還覺不夠，於是在雲貴邊界蓋了座全世界最高的公路大橋——北盤江大橋；從二〇一八年至今，這座橋樑一直保有吉尼斯世界紀錄中的最高橋樑。全球最高的一百座橋樑中，其中五十座都位於

Bridge to Yunnan over Nizhu / 渡尼珠河的橋到雲南　　Bridge to Guizhou and Ma's home / 到貴州和馬選軍家的橋

貴州，而北盤江大橋的高度，位居全球榜首。

馬選軍今年四十歲，穆斯林，原籍雲南，四代前因老家鬧饑荒而舉家遷至貴州都格，一個邊陲小村落，定居下來。馬選軍對當地狀況，瞭若指掌，還曾因此而在不久前被《中國環球時報》報導過。北盤江大橋的規模宏大，氣勢驚人。馬選軍自信滿滿地把這座高橋的「數據規格」，在我們面前如數家珍般，倒背如流：「這座橋全長一千三百四十一公尺，跨度是七百二十公尺，從大橋底座到下方山谷的高度，是五百六十五公尺，相當於一座兩百層樓高的建築……。這座大橋耗資七點七億人民幣，歷時三年完工，總計使用二點五萬噸鋼材、xx 根釘子，yy 公尺長的電纜……。」馬先生的精確數字，和令人眼花繚亂的資訊，開始滑落出我的思緒，也迷失在我的筆記裡……。

馬選軍開一台三輪摩托車，停在我們的露營車旁聊天。他覺得我們或許需要找個地方解決晚餐，或過夜，於是，他毛遂自薦自己的民宿小屋，位於兩座吊橋上的山丘裡。尼珠河就在這裡匯入北盤江。當時正值冬天的旱季，河岸兩旁的岩石，赤裸裸地暴露河床上，巨石與河床，仿若亨利. 摩爾 (Henry Moore) 的雕塑畫廊，把公共藝術與大自然融合為一。事實上，這些由數千年河水涓滴穿石，以大自

然的力量鬼斧神工而成的形狀與姿勢，遠超乎人類藝術家所能復製或創作。當人類遇上大自然，人類永遠只能俯首稱臣。

早些時候，從高橋一路下山到山底的都格鎮龍井村，我們花了超過半小時，兜兜轉轉；山路蜿蜒曲折，途中還必須繞過不少崎嶇的轉折處。接著，我們經過一條險象環生的小路，路面窄且坡度很大，走到底，竟是兩條河流交匯處的死胡同，幾乎行到山窮水盡了。雲貴兩地邊界，其實，近在咫尺，只是必須橫跨吊橋。我們先把過夜的露營車，停靠貴州這一邊，北盤江的東岸。然後，一行人小心翼翼地過橋前進，步行時的顫動，人與橋都晃蕩，上下起伏，我們只能扶著吊橋，搖搖晃晃越過尼珠河，抵達隸屬雲南省的一塊土地上，這地方很小，大概勉強僅容搭建兩座房子，而其中一間，就是我們享用晚餐的餐廳；說起晚餐，當晚主食正是從北盤江捕獲的鮮魚。

還有另一座吊橋等著我們，結構看來也不太牢靠，因為它原來只為了支撐一根大水管，沒打算承載太多人；走在橋上時，左右晃動，我們只能步步為營地越過北盤江上方，抵達東岸，這一回我們又越過了邊界，重返貴州境內，來到馬選軍的民宿旅舍。但相較之下，我們那嶄新的露營車實在比民宿還要舒適太多了，我們最終選擇不和他一起入住民宿。

兩條河匯合處的巨石和岩石，或許已經與滔天巨浪來回衝擊與纏鬥數千年，但近期，則有另一波全新的衝擊，在海拔五百公尺高處，風起雲湧。這一切，從一座被譽為世界第一高橋的聲望開始。想要一睹大高橋的旅人如織，熙熙攘攘，自然也引起邊界兩省，貴州和雲南政府官員的高度關注。於是，攸關大橋的命名直接影響兩地歸屬——

Nature carved sculpture / 大自然刻的雕塑品

北盤江或尼珠河，開始爭議不斷——前者屬於貴州，後者屬於雲南。

在雲南那一側的高速公路，由雲南省修建至大橋前，而貴州則負責自己那一邊的高速公路。只是，一省建設一半橋樑，一直到中間段落再連接起來，似乎太兒戲又不合理，「此路不通」以後，兩省只好協調，由貴州承攬建設工程，雲南承擔百分之五十二的成本，而貴州則負擔剩餘的百分之四十八。接下來，則是命名大事了。兩省各自表態，洋洋灑灑條列大小理由，說明為何這座橋該如此這番命名，兩邊據理力爭。最終，歷經幾輪談判與裁決，貴州勝出，雙方達成共識，保留北盤江大橋之名。畢竟，它是珠江的源頭，有利於吸引來自繁華三角洲的遊客。

我們離開貴州，進入湖南省。靠近省界的，是鳳凰古城，位於苗族和土家族少數民族地區。這座原始而美麗的古城，曾經是沱江邊一個貧窮的偏遠村莊，緊鄰沱江岸邊，櫛比鱗次的吊腳木樓屋。古城小鎮之所以遠近馳名而成今日的旅遊大熱點，某部分或許得歸功於出生此地的兩位著名人士——作家沈從文和藝術家黃永玉。

沈從文的代表作《邊城》，敘述一段以一九三〇年代的鳳凰古城為背景的愛情敘事，內文樸實清新，講述一位住在河邊的老人和孫女的故事，美麗動人。這本膾炙人口的小說，深獲好評，入選中國二十世紀最受歡迎的一百本書中，排名第二。

巧的是，沈從文的侄子黃永玉，是中國其中一位最著名的當代傳統藝術家。黃永玉出身貧困家庭，先成為木刻藝術家，爾後成為頗負盛名的北京藝術學院教授；他在文革期間遭受政治迫害，最終獲得平反複職，這樣的人生際遇，使他成了現代中國藝術界

的寵兒。沈從文書寫故鄉，黃永玉描繪鳳凰，這位才華橫溢的藝術家，至今還在古城上留有一間畫室。

這座歷史悠久的小鎮至今仍能保有古城風情與質樸魅力，主要是因為該地區擁有百分之八十的苗族，與其餘的土家族；因為太窮困，當地的苗族與土家族根本趕不上過去這四十年來衝擊中國的經濟躍進與變革。由此看來，古城之所以古意盎然，主因是機遇，而非刻意，無意間留下的建築設計和遺風遺跡，無心插柳，竟身價上漲，成為這十至二十年間最受歡迎的旅遊景點之一。

然而，沱江兩岸陳舊的吊腳樓房，已讓位給較新的三四層樓高的木頭建築，其中百分之九十五以上是精品飯店、旅館與民宿。街道兩旁盡是為遊客量身訂製的紀念品商店、餐館和小餐廳。我們抵達當地時，是淡季中的淡季，一間舒適整潔的套房，只需一百四十人民幣，折合起來還不到二十美元，價廉物美。

我們下榻的旅館主人劉政，苗族人，在解放軍服役三年後退休。他的十房旅館，裝潢氣派，設計精緻；大部分房間都有個陽台，夜晚時分，可以俯瞰燈火通明的沱江河岸。「事實真的出乎預料之外，

Flimsy bridge Yunnan to Guizhou /
連結雲南和貴州脆弱的橋

Highest bridge in world / 世界上最高的橋

River gorge of Nizhu / 尼珠河河谷

我們算很幸運吧！因為貧窮，沒有錢重建房屋，結果這些老房子居然一轉身成了價值連城的資產，吸引很多遊客來。」主人劉先生的兩歲兒子就坐在他大腿上，他繼續說道：「一到長週末和暑假期間，這裡的房價會翻漲五到八倍。即使價格高昂，還是一房難求，很多旅館房間都被預訂、客滿。」

時至今日，仍可見一小片河岸保有一組舊式高蹺樓房，錯落有致，但已變身成商業用途。冬日清晨，我早早起床，在清晨第一道陽光尚未映照水面、拱橋和房屋之前，先看到薄霧氤氳的小鎮風貌。透過室內那扇小窗，我彷彿窺見了鳳凰古城的昔日好時光，那個孕育沈從文和黃永玉成長的偏遠故鄉，一個曾經寂寂無聞的城鎮。

對都格與鳳凰古城來說，一如中國境內許多老城鎮、老市區與老村莊，只能以書本與圖片，留下往日遺跡的記錄。北盤江、沱江等河流，亦復如是。或許，這些紀錄只能成為我們當下的時空與剎那間，存留心靈深處的圖貌與樣式，完全自外於現代世界，清淨而純然。

Hotels across from hotel / 從飯店望對岸一排飯店

老傳說與新故事

OLD TALE AND NEW STORY

Honghu, Hubei – November 27, 2021

OLD TALE AND NEW STORY

I am now 72. When I was half my age, at 36 in 1985, I led a major expedition for the National Geographic to study the entire length of the Yangtze. This led to discovering a new source for the mighty river, but along the way, I made many other discoveries as well. Not far below the Three Gorges and above the city of Wuhan, I stopped at Honghu of the lower Yangtze in Hubei Province.

Honghu was made famous by the revolutionary stage opera "Red Brigade of Honghu" of the late 1950s. Later the opera was made into a film, first released in 1961. I have a small booklet from those days which uses drawings to depict the story, made to popularize it among children. It tells of a guerilla outfit, led by Han, a woman head cadre, who together with her comrades safeguarded the budding peasant uprising and early Communist movements in the area during the 1930s.

In the spring of 1985 at Honghu, we launched our Zodiac inflatable boat with a twenty-five horse power outboard motor. I had originally ordered a gray boat to keep a low profile. But instead, they sent me a bright red one! The commotion we raised as we arrived at the lakefront of Honghu was phenomenal. Crowds gathered in awe as we inflated the pile of rubber into a 12-foot boat within 30 minutes and sped away.

During migration seasons, there are tens of thousands of birds and waterfowl in and around Honghu. Of wild ducks alone, it has been recorded there were 18 different species. In 1985, we went around the lake to look at both birdlife and duck hunters at work. There had never been any motorized boat cruising this sizable yet shallow lake, with an area of 430 square kilometers. Within minutes, we tore up and damaged seven sets of net laid below by the fisherman.

After compensating the villagers, a guide came onboard to guide us around the labyrinth of invisible net inside the lake. It took us two hours with a guide to find several groups of duck hunters conducting communal hunting at the far end of the lake. Each group was composed of some twenty wooden boats scattered around with two or more people on board each one. Three of these boats were lined up abreast and connected to each other by two long poles. On top of these poles were laid forty-some matchlock cannons, in this case 43, each weighing upward of 50 kilos and measuring three meters long. After camouflaging these guns with weeds and straw,

Little booklet cover / 小紅書封面
Booklet inside page / 小紅書內頁
Setting net in lake / 往湖裡撒網

the boats had been pulled to an open area on the lake with two men hiding on board. They would stay put there for the next few hours.

The remaining boats were then dispatched in all directions to round up the ducks. Over the next few hours, ducks and other waterfowl of all description were slowly driven in the direction of the camouflaged boats until they all settled along in front of the cannons. With a huge series of bangs, the guns were fired off simultaneously and white smoke shot to the sky. Momentarily the sky was filled with fowl taking flight. Boats rowed with double oars darting toward the center of the burst. We moved our Zodiac closer to observe the unfolding melee.

At this time, we saw hundreds of birds floating on the lake as we neared the camouflaged boats. Some birds were still hopelessly trying to take flight. Men with long spears chased these lame ducks without mercy and in no time, front decks were covered with piles of birds. We paddled to the lead boat where a man tallied deliveries with an abacus. The initial count totaled 153 birds, mainly mud hens. At that time of year, most ducks had already migrated out. More birds came in gradually. Mr Xing, leader of this group, assured me that during the height of the season, they could kill a couple thousand ducks with just one blast, surely an economically sound, but ecologically devastating, maneuver.

While I was still recovering from the aftershock of this blast, the rest of the hunters were already busy at work retrieving the lost cannons at the bottom of the lake. Every single gun would fall to the bottom, shallow and visible from our boat. Drying and resetting the system would take half a *day, thus the firing can only happen once each day before they reset hoping for another round of fruitful harvest, or wholesale slaughter as some may call it. The following day, I saw plenty of ducks and mud hens hung up for sale at the local market.*

Later I found out the locals called this type of duck hunting "Pai Cong;" "Pai" meaning lining up, "Cong" referring to the cannons. So, Pai Cong is a line-up of cannons or guns, fanning outward on three boats tied adjacent to each other. This term, however, disappeared before the internet and Wikipedia came on the scene, and is thus known only to people of the past generations.

From jet black hair, to silver gray, to mostly white haired, I finally return to Honghu for a revisit, after thirty-six years. I even brought along segments of the film I took back then in 1985, hoping to share it with the locals. But everywhere I go, people simply shake their heads and say, "No more".

Duck in market / 市場上的鴨子 Duck feather fan factory / 鴨羽毛扇工廠

Spearing fowls / 刺禽鳥
Fowls harvest / 禽鳥豐收

Old empty trimaran & signage /
三體並排的舊空船和標示
Little Grebe in lake / 湖裡小鸊鷉

"No more; it has been at least two decades since such a practice was made illegal and banned," said Shi, the chef in the kitchen where we were having lunch. His restaurant is well hidden in a back street under a bridge spanning a canal. It is the only restaurant within a vicinity of perhaps ten kilometers square, a rarity in China today where any lake that is pristine and beautiful would have been turned into a tourist site long ago.

"No one dares catch or sell wild fish from the lake now, let alone the Jiang Ji wild fowl," Shi added, referring to the mud hens. On the wall of his restaurant is a government printed regulations with about ten items put in place regarding the restrictions on selling wild game meat, with Shi's signature and his mobile phone number at the bottom, stating that he would be held accountable to abide by such rulings.

Signboards, posters and stickers are all over the place, be it in public or private premises. In the room where we dine, they are on the wall, as well as stuck to the lazy Susan we are using. Obviously, the matter is being taken very seriously, as everywhere we go, locals echo the same restrictions. China's government is now taking nature conservation as a state-wide priority.

Honghu itself was first established as a protected wetland of the region in

1996, and was elevated to Hubei provincial protected status in 2000. In 2008, it joined the list of Important International Wetlands, and by 2014 became a national nature reserve.

We parked our camper van at the pinnacle head of a village by the lake front where I can appreciate both sunrise and sunset over the lake. While I saw no ducks or mud hens around the lake, there were quite a few Little Grebes diving in and out of the water, catching small fish as prey. Nearby, I saw one last remaining Pai Cong trimaran-type boat, of course without the guns, sitting by the bank. It looked like it had been abandoned there for ages. The submersible fishing nets we once tore up are no longer to be seen. The government restricted setting fishing nets inside the lake two years ago, and this ban is supposed to last ten years in order for the fish stock to return to health.

In fact, recently there are calls and early steps to retrieve even man-made fish and shrimp cultivation ponds in order to restore the environmental condition to that of decades ago. Those who would cooperate with the government's call would not only be compensated for their ponds at an amount of 7000 RMB per mu (each mu is 0.165 acre), but would also be given a new house as incentive. On average, each family would have 40-60 mu, with some reaching even over 80. This program was started

Sunset by lake / 日落湖畔

Qujiawan old town / 瞿家灣
Ducks on sale / 販售鴨子

on October 1, 2018. Future plan is to maintain the recovered wetland ecosystem habitat as a reserve, and ultimately develop nature tourism around the lake.

In the past, Honghu was known as Small Lobster City, and its cultivated ponds totaled 570,000 mu. Annual yield of these small lobsters could reach over 15,000 tons and they were marketed throughout the country, especially after China developed a mature network of internet purchase platforms. The usual season for these small lobsters is March through October, so I came too late to enjoy them.

Han whom we interviewed has twenty mu of pond and can derive a profit of over 300,000 RMB annually, with around one-third contributed from crab sales. From September onward, crab season will last until November. Crab production would also reach over 15,000 tons, second only to crab yield of Jiangsu Province within the entire country. What fascinated me most is that the crab farmers of nearby Qujiawan would package their crab and label them as being from Yangcheng Lake before selling to some middleman, who would in turn send them all over the country labelled with the famous lake near Suzhou as origin.

Today, each family is allowed only one tiny boat for transport, though these *are no longer row boats, but comes with a diesel tractor engine. Where there are regulations, there are always those who break them. As night fell and we finished our own cooked dinner and were washing our dishes outside our camper with dim lights, we heard nearby boat engines revving up, one after another. In total darkness, several boats were heading out onto the lake. A few villagers are going to set up their nets or retrieve hidden ones.*

Earlier in the day as I strolled the village, I saw nets and shrimp traps drying in some backyards. We also saw fish being dried outside some homes on large woven pans. I thought these must be from the family's own ponds, but certainly not so I now realize. Nonetheless, this is a far cry from thirty-some years ago when loads of wild game birds and fish were being hauled in day after day, year after year, until the capacity of the lake to recover was exhausted.

We took time to drive to the nearby town of Qujiawan. Outside the village are shops with rows of ducks slit up for drying. These, however, are farmed ducks, not wild game like before. This somewhat ancient village is preserved as an education base illustrating the early days of the Communists in China. Many houses now are used to display their former functions and celebrate the who's who of who worked or stayed there during those formative years of guerilla warfare, which are the background to that early revolutionary film from 1961.

While such political education is prevalent throughout China these days, I hope through recounting my earlier years of exploration, some small lessons can also be shared with our future generations. It is important to realize that our cultural and natural heritage are not just given and cannot be taken for granted, but require respect and care. While some of our past can be restored like in the case of Honghu, others may eclipse and never be recovered again. Hopefully, recording the past will also teach us a lesson for the future.

老傳說與新故事

我今年七十二歲。還記得一九八五那年，我只有現在的一半歲數，也就是三十六歲時，我率領《國家地理雜誌》的考察隊伍，探索長江全長。我們最終發現了這條大河流的新源頭，在這過程中，我還另外尋獲許多新發現。我在三峽下方不遠處的武漢市之上，湖北省長江下游的洪湖，稍作停留。

因為一九五〇年代末期一齣革命舞台劇《洪湖赤衛隊》，而讓洪湖一舉成名。後來，這部舞台劇被拍成電影，一九六一年首次上映。我還保留了當年火紅一時的小冊子，內容以圖畫來描繪故事情節，孩子們愛不釋手，簡直是老少咸宜。故事內容講述一名姓韓的女領導，揮軍率領游擊隊，保衛家國，維護一九三〇年代初期的在地農民，農民興起，風起雲湧，也促使早期的共產主義運動。

一九八五年春，我們在洪湖駛用了一艘二十五馬力舷外引擎的 *Zodiac* 充氣船。為免太張揚，我維持一貫的低調作風，定購了一艘灰色的充氣船，萬萬沒想到，他們給我送來一艘鮮紅色的船！人和船一起抵達洪湖湖畔時，頓時引起一陣騷動。我們快手快腳，將眼前一堆橡膠器材與設備，半小時內打氣充飽成一艘十二英尺長的船隻，還加油疾速駛離岸邊，圍觀群眾看得瞠目結舌。

Our Red Brigade Zodiac / 我們的赤衛船 　　　　　　Kids living on boats / 住在船上的小孩

候鳥遷徙時節，數以萬計的鳥類和水禽在洪湖附近展翅穿梭。據記載，光是野鴨就有十八種。
一九八五年，我們繞湖而行，一邊觀賞鳥，一邊留意獵鴨人的工作。洪湖的面積有四百三十平方公
里，湖泊大而淺，過去從未有任何馬達或引擎船隻在湖泊上游駛過，結果，我們的充氣大船才下水
不到幾分鐘，一不小心便把漁夫鋪設水裡的七片大漁網撞毀，損壞殆盡。

補償了村民損失後，一位嚮導員上船，帶我們繞過湖內無形的漁網，避開水內迷宮。嚮導帶著我們，
花了兩個小時，才在湖泊遠方，找到幾組正在集體狩獵的獵鴨人，和他們的幾組船隻。每一組由
二十多艘散置的木船所組成，每艘船上有兩個或兩個以上人員。其中三艘船由兩根長桿相互連接，
並排緊靠。桿子上放置了四十多支火繩槍，當地人稱之為「排銃」，當下有四十三支，每一支重達
五十公斤，長度是三公尺。這些非槍非炮「銃」枝以雜草和稻禾掩飾，安置於一艘「掩護船」上，
船被拖到湖上一片空曠區，再安排兩個人躲藏在內。接下來的幾個小時內，這兩人會一直待在船上
的隱密處。

其他船隻則被派往四面八方去圍捕鴨子。緊接的數小時內，湖上的鴨子和其他水禽被慢慢驅趕到
「掩護船」那一頭，把這群水上生物都聚集到隱身的大砲前。獵物到齊，瞄準目標後，一聲巨響，

43-guns Pai Cong set up / 架設 43 發排衝
Boats gathering / 船隻集結

四十多槍砲齊發，水上煙硝瀰漫，群鳥亂飛，霎時間，家禽慌張逃離。所有小船划著雙槳小船，奔向湖泊中心的「事故」現場。我們把 Zodiac 號再移近一些，希望能近距離觀察正開展的一場殊死混戰。

當我們的船隻趨近那艘發動攻勢的「掩護船」時，我們看到數百隻飛禽浮在湖面上，奄奄一息，也有幾隻正試圖拍翅起飛，垂死的掙扎。手執長矛的船上男子，毫不留情地緊追傷重腿瘸的鴨子，不一會兒，船上的甲板，鳥屍成堆。我們划到領頭的船邊，只見一名男子手拿算盤，手指飛快撥弄算珠，精打細算，準備現場交貨。初步計數，總共捕獲一百五十三隻禽鳥，主要是屬秧雞科的江雞。每年大約這時候，大多數鴨子已遷離。但有越來越多的飛鳥會陸續遷來當地。圍捕小組的負責人邢先生向我保證，旺季時節，他們只需發動一次攻勢，即可獵殺數千隻鴨子，聽來是一場符合經濟效益的生意，但無疑也是破壞生態的策略。

我餘悸猶存，似乎還沒從剛剛的「猛烈砲火」中回過神來，但其餘的獵鴨人早已忙著從湖底中尋回丟失的槍砲彈。每一支槍炮都掉到湖底了，我們從船上俯望湖水，其實淺顯可見。把這些槍砲彈藥等捕獵工具全數晾乾，需要至少半天時間，因此，重新佈局，再戰一回，是一件勞師動眾的獵捕，所以，一天只能進行一次獵擊。若想再來一輪大豐收（也許有人會稱之為大規模屠宰），得

再等一天了。隔日，我在當地市場瞥見許多待售的鴨子和江雞，高掛於攤位上。

當地人把這種獵鴨方式稱為「排衝」；「排」有排隊之意，而「衝」則意味著衝炮。所以，「排衝」指的是一排大砲或槍枝，在相鄰並排的三艘船上，瞄準目標，對外射擊。只是，這特殊詞彙，比互聯網和維基百科還要歷史悠久，在網路辭典出現前，所謂「排衝」，早已消聲匿跡，大概只有老一輩的人知道。

我從青絲烏黑，等到滿頭銀灰，再到蒼顏白髮，終於，足足等了三十六年以後，我終於再度重遊洪湖。我甚至開心得把一九八五年拍攝的電影片段都一起帶來，希望有機會與當地人分享。可惜的是，無論我走到哪裡，人們一聽，皆搖頭回答：「沒了沒了」。

「沒了沒了，這種獵鴨方式已經被禁了至少二十年啦。」我們享用午餐時，餐廳主廚施先生對我們說。他的餐廳位於橫跨運河的橋下後街，地點隱密。那是方圓十平方公里範圍內唯一的一家餐廳，這在今天的中國是極少見的情境，因為大部分樸質原始而美麗的湖泊，不稍多久便名氣大增，搖身一變成為旅遊景點。

「現在沒有人敢從湖里捕撈或出售野魚，更不用說姜雞野禽了，」施主廚補充解釋，就是江雞。在他餐廳的牆上，貼了張政府印製的宣導單，內容嚴禁銷售野味野肉的十大規範，下方還有餐館負責人施先生的簽名和手機號碼，明白表示主人已知悉同意，遵守到底。

類似明文嚴禁的指示牌、海報和貼紙，無論公共場所或私人領域，隨處可見。在我們用餐的包廂裡，這些禁令傳單掛在牆上，甚至連餐桌轉盤上也不放過，唯恐你錯過。顯然，這件事已被認真對待，

因為無論我們走到哪個地方，一旦聊起這話題，當地人的回應一致，禁令不能違。可見中國政府現在已將自然保育議題視為國家級的優先事項來處理。

一九九六年，洪湖首次被確立為該區域的保護濕地，二〇〇〇年時，洪湖正式被提升為湖北省的保護地。直到二〇〇八年，洪湖被列入國際重要濕地清單內，並於二〇一四年成為國家級的自然保護區。

我們將露營車停靠湖邊村莊的制高點上，藉此絕佳位置，好好欣賞湖上的日出燦亮，與夕陽西下的日落風情。雖然我在湖邊不見一隻鴨子或江雞，不過，倒是看到不少小鸊鷉，這群水鳥探頭入水，又潛出湖面，捕捉小魚當獵物。我也在湖泊附近看到最後一艘「排衝」，那是三體並排的船型，船上當然不具任何「武裝配備」，寂寂無聞地，靠岸停放；從外型看來，似乎已被棄置很久。我們曾經撞毀的潛水漁網，也早已不復存在。政府當局在兩年前便已禁止漁網設置湖內，這項禁令必須持續實施至少十年，才能使魚群狀況復原。

其實，近日傳來不少「回收人造魚蝦養殖塘」的呼籲，希望藉此修復破壞，還原幾十年前的環境狀況。願意響應與配合政府號召的農漁戶，除了每畝（一畝約 0.165 英畝）可獲七千人民幣的池塘補償金之外，還祭出「送新房」的獎勵活動。平均而言，每個家庭都擁有四十至六十畝池塘，有些甚至達八十畝之多。這項回收計劃從二〇一八年十月一日開始實施。未來的計劃與目標，希望可以把濕地的生態系統與野生動物棲息地都完整收回，將濕地設為保育地，最後，再把周圍區域發展成觀光湖泊。

洪湖過去素有「中國小龍蝦之鄉」的美譽，養殖池塘總計有五十七萬畝。這些小龍蝦的年產量可達一點五萬噸以上，尤其在中國建立了完善的互聯網採購平台後，漁業產品的銷路更暢通，直接銷往全國各地。小龍蝦一般盛產季是三至十月，所以，我來得不是時候，剛好錯過大啖美食的季節。

我們採訪的韓先生，自家有二十畝池塘，養殖池塘每年讓主人賺取超過三十萬人民幣的利潤，其中，螃蟹就貢獻總銷售額的三分之一。從九月開始的螃蟹季節，將持續到十一月。這一區的螃蟹產量，一般預計可達一萬五千噸以上，僅次於國內整個江蘇省的螃蟹收穫率。令人好奇的是，我發現附近瞿家灣的蟹農會把他們的螃蟹包裝好之後，竟打上「陽澄湖」的大閘蟹標籤，轉賣給中盤商——以蘇州附近著名的陽澄湖為原產地——轉手賣到全國各地。

今天，洪湖一帶的家庭，每戶人家只能允許擁有一艘小船，作為出入運輸之用；這些小船早已不是傳統的手划船，而是以柴油發動的機動船。夜幕低垂，我們自己煮晚餐，吃飽喝足後，在露營車外藉助昏暗燈光，清洗鍋碗瓢盆。我們無意間聽到附近有船馬達聲動靜，一個接一個啟動引擎。看來，上有政策則下有對策。放眼望去，一片漆黑，幾艘船正駛向湖面。一些村民「暗地」裡放網設網，

Sizable pond fish / 大尾池塘魚　　　　　Wooden boat & dried fish / 木板船和魚干

Honghu circa 1985 / 洪湖於 1985 年

其他的則正收回隱藏的漁網。

我忽然記起當天早些時候，當我在村子裡散步時，看到村民在後院裡鋪曬漁網和捕蝦器。另外也看到一些家庭在屋外的大型編織平底筒箕上曬魚。我原以為，這些漁網應該是在自家池塘才會派上用場的器具，至於漁獲，理當也來自自家養殖池塘；但這下，我赫然明白，一切了然於胸，顯然我猜錯了。雖然如此，如此小規模的捕撈，和過去三十年前相比，差得多了。想當初的集體出擊，是如何肆無忌憚地大量獵捕野生鳥禽和魚類，而且是日復一日、年復一年地進行，直到湖泊資源耗盡，無力復原。

我們花了些時間開車到附近的瞿家灣鎮。村外是商店，店裡一排排的鴨子，都被開膛剖肚，掛起晾曬。仔細看這些鴨子，都是養殖鴨，不像以前那些獵捕的野味。這個看來有些古意的舊式村莊，是被保存下來的教育基地，以此闡明中國共產黨人的早期的革命生活。而今，許多老房子都被當成樣品屋，以展示各方功能，其中包括組成游擊戰的那些年，還有自一九六一年間那些革命電影裡出現的背景……。這裡也曾是某某人的某某人或各家名人顯要曾經生活過、工作過，登高一呼過的地方。

雖然，這樣的政治教育至今在中國仍是普遍現象，但我希望藉由重述我早年的遊歷與探索，可以與我們新一代的後生，分享一些心得與體會。我們的文化與自然遺產，不只是給予和成全，也不能理所當然地被予取予求；它們需要被賦予高度尊重與關切，這是無比重要的認知。儘管我們某部分的過去，或許可以像洪湖般，慢慢收復失地、重新復原，但有些地方或許已元氣大傷，甚至恢復無望了。但願我對過去的點滴記錄，能幫助我們對未來有所警惕，恪守教訓。

漂泊大運河──往返於鎮江與蘇州 - 1

GRAND CANAL ODYSSEY

Suzhou, Jiangsu – December 2, 2021

GRAND CANAL ODYSSEY
(Zhenjiang to Suzhou and back) Part 1

"My grandfather worked on a boat on the Grand Canal," said Lu- who is now 56 years old. "I was born, raised and grew up on a boat; likewise my husband," she added. Indeed, Captain Hu who is two years older than his wife and piloting our tug was also brought up on a boat, and is another third-generation boat operator, be it a tug or a barge that is towed behind. Together, they operate LuJiNing 2123, a tug boat we have chartered to study the Grand Canal for a week; "Lu" meaning the province of Shandong, "Ji Ning" for the town by Wei Shan Hu that the couple came from.

Many boats on the Grand Canal today carry the same prefix, LuJiNing, on their registration name as they originate from this village on the lakefront of Hui Hu (Hu meaning lake) where many families became boat operators. Hui Hu was made famous by the revolutionary film "Railroad Guerilla" which depicts the time of the Sino-Japanese War when a locally formed brigade pirated sections of a train with a cargo of winter coats and thus was able to clothe the Red Army for winter battles.

"In our days, it wasn't easy to find a matching mate, so my parents arranged for our two families to become closer relatives," Hu said with an air of hesitancy, implying that their marriage was

arranged. Both families, like those of so many tug boat owners along the Grand Canal at Zhenjiang, were from Shandong. Being from similar backgrounds and the same hometown got them together. In fact, most tug boats and barges are operated by a husband and wife team, yet with a family of three, as many boats come with a pet dog. Ours is called "WanWan", meaning Fortune Aplenty.

"But there are hardly any fourth generation coming into this trade anymore." Hu spoke with a bit of remorse. "My son has no interest at all, and I am afraid this will be the last generation of our family to operate a tug boat, as soon as I retire." His usually stuttering and halting voice suddenly became even more broken.

With a better education, few of those born within the last twenty or thirty years are willing to take up such work and hardship. After all, there are better paying and more attractive jobs being offered in the big cities. Why stay on an ancient and straight waterway with neither excitement nor bright future in sight?

Hu Zaohe's personal story may be a fair case study representing most other boatmen. After all, though he is the oldest among his siblings, two sisters and three brothers, with the exception of his second sister, everyone is

Tug 2123 at mooring /
拖船 2123 號於停泊點
Home meal at tug / 拖船上的家常菜

engaged in working on a boat in Zhenjiang, Yangzhou or along the Yangtze. They only get to meet up for weddings or funerals that bring everyone home. Hu's mother is now 79 and living at home in Shandong.

Hu started learning to live and work on his family's fishing boat at the age of six. His schooling was broken up into many intermittent segments and he did not graduate from elementary school until he was 18. It was during the time around 1972 when all local fishing boats were turned into transport vessels. So, upon graduation, Hu moved on to work on one such communal transport boat, eating what was then called "Big Wok" meals, and being allocated work points according to the old commune system.

In 1986, the communal owned boat system was dismantled and most operators took the opportunity to purchase their own boats. Hu's first boat was only sixty tons and made of cement. He used it as a tug to pull small barges through the canal. Two years later, he upgraded to an 80-ton cement boat. By 1998, after two children were born, the couple moved to Zhenjiang as their new home and bought a 19-meter 135 horsepower tug boat. It was given a lucky number of 100 upon registration. Those early years also saw the couple take time to work on other's boats occasionally, but the pay was meager, barely 1200 RMB per month for the two of them together.

In 2004, four friends together formed a partnership and bought two tug boats; Dantu 007 and Dantu 008. One person would go after the business, the other three would rotate and operate the two boats, and profits were shared among four. They stayed happily together for ten years before parting. During this time, each partner's share reached RMB100,000 per year, a lucrative sum at the time. In 2014, Hu took over Dantu 007 and started looking for business himself, with his income reaching 150,000 to 200,000 yearly.

Three years ago in 2018, Hu and his wife bought a 15-year-old tug boat and fully renovated it. That is the boat we now charter with an almost brand new paint job. His wife cares for it meticulously, swabbing it several times a day. Twenty-six meters in length with a 350 hp engine, it is the current standard of most modern tug boats. While they paid 260,000 Yuan for it, renovation cost them an additional 80,000. Last year, however, he maintained a stable income of close to 200,000.

It was an unusual year as everywhere there was flooding and along the Yangtze the water ran much higher and lasted much longer than in regular years. Many of the "Dragon" barges, with long strings of many boats, could not pass through except with the help of tugs. Thus, those with tug boats benefited, from May to September. Hu's business came mainly from introduction by friends, relatives, or returning customers.

The Grand Canal may indeed be grand, but only in the eyes of historians and those who see it at one of the busy junctions or crossroads in the quaint cities south of the Yangtze, like Wuxi and Suzhou. Beyond these special places, few people bother to make a stop to understand it, except through books and museum exhibits. Of course, poems from the earlier dynasties may add romance and nostalgia, especially through stories like the entourage of Emperor Qianlong's six trips south of the Yangtze travelling via the Grand Canal. But in contemporary times, such images hardly match reality.

We have come to Zhenjiang on the south bank of the Yangtze, and Yangzhou across the river to the north, exactly to have a better look at the Grand Canal. Our first foray to try chartering a boat through a contact in Yangzhou was not successful. An owner with an old beat-up boat, filthy and messy, asked for RMB 2000 per day, and was reluctant to cross the Yangtze into the southern reaches of the canal. Through Ms. Qian, a professor friend who has conducted research on the Zhenjiang section of the Grand Canal, we identified a mooring point of many tug boats sitting idle waiting for work.

We picked the best looking tug, LuJiNing 2123, and ended up with Captain Hu and his wife Lu. Negotiating a price for charter was a tug, of war, as Hu had to factor the distance and days needed to estimate his running costs, mainly from fuel cost per hour, hoping that each day we would run for less than four hours, at most five. That would take us from Zhenjiang to Suzhou in a matter of three days or more, a meager 150 kilometers and a bit over two hours if done by car.

I exercised my long-polished skills in negotiation, suggesting it was not a one-off deal, that we would soon return with loads of students requiring many trips and many tugs, with him serving as middleman so that he may earn more, both money and goodwill. As negotiation got underway, other tug boat owners started strolling by, lending some long ears, and not a few quiet offers. But my eyes were fixated on the cleanest and best-looking tug.

Once a deal was made, we loaded the boat the evening before departure, bringing on board all our accessories, snacks, our own F&B supplies, sleeping bags and mats as Spartan to minimal

Morning brush on next boat / 隔壁船早上刷牙

accommodation, a folding electric bike, and even a folding seat to put over a squat toilet. The following morning, we arrived again at the bank of the Yangtze at 9am. It was then upon settling in that Captain Hu told us that going through the single river lock from the Yangtze into the Grand Canal at Zhenjiang can take anything from a day to two of waiting in line!

But we always have a remedy prepared. Tsomo, my Research Assistant, simply had to call up our contact, Mr. Zhang Kunlun, who is in charge of the river lock entering from the Yangtze into the Grand Canal. Though he was ill in hospital, word soon came through the boat radio that 2123 could skip the line to get inside the lock. I reiterated to Tsomo, our Tibetan staff with a fine degree from Dartmouth College, smallest among the Ivy League schools, "it is not what you know that counts, it is who you know." Better yet, think "Who knew you!", not necessarily "You know him."
`

I always take every opportunity to share my philosophy and thoughts with younger colleagues. Though they may be more computer and internet savvy than me, I boast of longer experience and more past failures, and of course also a few notable successes. With the Grand Canal, I repeated to Tsomo, "so you have seen all these places, have any of these places seen you?" Reminding her that we are here to observe, learn, and digest, hoping someday to leave an impact on this historical water transport artery. However small that impact, perhaps it can take a new angle of interpretation and approach that is unique to CERS.

We soon entered the lock as the last boat squeezed between much larger barges, scratching both the side of the lock and our boat next in line. The huge gate closed behind us and the watermark started dropping as we gradually lowered to the water level of the Grand Canal. As the gate in front opened, we followed other boats and finally entered the canal south of the Yangtze. This would be the only lock for the entire southern channel of the Grand Canal, from Zhenjiang all the way to Hangzhou. To the north, just part way to Anhui would have eleven locks, usually taking upward of two to three weeks in order to line up and pass through all the locks.

As we sailed away from the lock, I was on the bridge sitting next to Captain Hu. Suddenly I saw a slightly faster, motorized barge overtaking us, cutting across our bow as it went pass. At once, I recalled an old story about water ghosts that I recorded while sailing upriver on the Yangtze in 1985. As a rule, ghosts and demons were thought to string themselves along behind a boat and transfer on board when the time was ripe to perform their little evils. It was generally believed that by steering one's boat so as to cut its stern directly in front of the bow of another boat, the string of ghosts would be cut off and end up on the boat behind. In the past, it was a game, which often left the trailing boat's owner jumping, cursing and shooting off firecrackers to pacify his increased string of ghosts.

This practice of using firecrackers is no longer allowed on a boat, yet I still relayed my old story to Hu. "Such ghost stories were prevalent before liberation and when we were little, but today no more," answered Hu. Little did he know that the ghosts in the water may be cut off forever, but now here on board is another ghost, camouflaged in the form of the spirit of an explorer.

漂泊大運河—往返於鎮江與蘇州 -1

「我的祖父在大運河的一艘船上工作，」現年五十六歲的盧女士說。「我在船上出生，在船上被帶大，也在船上長大成人；我丈夫也和我一樣。」她補充說明。比盧女士大兩歲的丈夫，正是駕駛我們拖輪的胡船長，他確實也在船上長大；胡船長同時也是其他船舶的第三代操作員，無論是拖船或被拖在後面的駁船，都歸他一手操縱。這對「船生船長」的夫妻，一起經營「魯濟寧 2123 號」拖輪船，我們租用這艘拖船，為期一週，以此作為我們研究大運河的運輸工具；「魯」是山東省的簡稱，而「濟寧」則是這對夫妻的原鄉，一個位於微山湖畔的城鎮。

今天，大運河上的許多船東，都出於同樣緣由，不約而同為船取名「魯濟寧」，以此為註冊之「姓氏」，昭告船隻背後的經營家族，大多來自微山湖畔的同一個城鎮。微山湖因一部革命電影《鐵道游擊隊》而聞名，影片內容敘述抗日戰爭時期，一個由當地人編制的軍隊，侵佔了一部分火車車廂，車廂裡裝滿的冬衣，正好在寒冷天候下派上用場，為紅軍隊員備齊了過冬的保暖衣物，可以繼續戰鬥。

「在我們那個年代，要找個合適的成親對象，很不容易；所以，我父母就安排我們倆相親，讓兩個家庭成為親家。」胡船長語帶保留，表情有些遲疑不定，似乎暗示他們

My spot at stern / 我在船尾的座位　　Alter with ancestor tablet in cabin / 船倉內神壇上的祖先牌位

的婚姻是早已安排好的。鎮江上的大運河一帶，許多船主大多和胡船長一家的背景相似，祖籍山東。親不親，故鄉人，同鄉情誼使他們更容易凝聚連結。事實上，大多數拖船和駁船都以夫妻檔的團隊經營為主，當然偶有三口之家——很多船都帶著一隻寵物狗隨同。我們船上也有一隻，叫「萬萬」，取個「千萬財源滾滾來」的好名字。

「不過，現在幾乎看不見第四代的年輕人投入這行了。」胡船長的言談之間，難掩遺憾與慨嘆。「我兒子對這行沒有任何興趣，我如果退休，恐怕這就是我們家經營拖船的最後一代了。」平時說起話來結結巴巴的船長，說到感慨處，語言愈發破碎，而悵然若失。

對於近二十、三十年出生的年輕一輩，他們受過優良的完整教育，幾乎沒什麼人願意繼承家族事業，接下艱辛的水運工作。畢竟，大城市為他們提供更多高薪又動人的工作；為何要守住一條平靜無波、日暮途窮、古老又筆直的航道？

胡船長的個人故事，可被視為大多數當地船夫的典範案例，代表性十足。他是家中手足之間的老大，三個弟弟與兩個妹妹。除了小妹以外，其他弟妹都在鎮江、揚州、長江等沿岸水域的船上工作。因

為工作繁忙，兄妹之間聚少離多，難得回家見面時，大多是家中有喜事或辦喪事的時候。胡船長的母親今年七十九歲，仍住在山東老家。

胡船長六歲時，開始踏上家族經營的漁船，從此在船上學習生活與工作。水上與陸地的距離，使他的學校教育斷斷續續，一直到十八歲才小學畢業。大約一九七二年左右，當地所有漁船都轉型成運輸船。於是，小學畢業後，胡船長繼續待在一艘公社運輸船上工作，吃著當時統稱的「大鍋」飯菜，按照舊式的公社制度，分配任務。

一九八六年，公社船務系統解散了，大多數經營者藉此機會，購買自己的船隻，走上了個體戶的經營模式。胡船長的第一艘船，只有六十噸重，材質是類似白堊質的水泥。他用這艘船當成拖船，將小型接駁船拉過運河。兩年後，他購入一艘八十噸的水泥船，事業風生水起。一九九八年，兩個孩子相繼出生後，夫妻倆搬到鎮江，新家也成為工作基地，他們買進一艘十九米長、一百三十五馬力的拖船。更令夫妻津津樂道的是，他們為船隻登記註冊時竟抽到幸運數字 100。早些時候，我們也曾見過這對夫妻偶爾也會到別人家船上打工，但打工的收入微薄，兩人加起來一個月才一千兩百人民幣。

二〇〇四年，水上人家的四個朋友，合資買了兩艘拖船，「丹徒 007」與「丹徒 008」，由一人經營找生意，另外三人則輪流操作執行兩艘船的運作，利潤所得，四人均分。如此經營模式讓他們「過著幸福快樂的生活」十年之久。分道揚鑣後，每個合夥人的份額已達每年十萬元營收，在當時而言，那是一筆為數可觀的收入。二〇一四年，胡船長接手「丹徒 007」，開始創業，當時他的年收入已達十五萬至二十萬人民幣。

大約三年前的二〇一八年，胡船長夫妻買了一艘船齡十五年的拖船，將老船全面翻新整修，我們現在租用的，正是這艘船，船身煥然一新，看來幾乎全新。船長妻子細心保養顧惜這艘生財工具，每天總要擦拭好幾回。這艘船有二十六米長，配備三百五十馬力的引擎發動機，是目前大多數現代拖船的標準。為了這艘船，夫妻倆支付了二十六萬人民幣，裝修又額外讓他們多花了八萬元。但一切已回本，光是去年，他們已開始維持近二十萬的穩定收入。

其實，今年是極不尋常的一年，到處都是洪水泛濫，長江沿岸的水位也比往年高出許多，高水位的持續時間延長許久，令人憂心。不少稱為一條「龍」駁船或大型平底船，得靠其他拖船的繩索，借力使力地拖拉，才能勉強通過運河。因此，從五月到九月，那些擁有拖船的人受益最多。胡船長的生意主要靠朋友、親戚或回頭客的介紹推薦，口耳相傳。

大運河確實山河壯麗，它的氣勢與美，或許只有歷史學家會讚嘆，也或許只在江南古城（如無錫與蘇州）的繁忙街角或十字路口前凝視大河的旅人會激賞；或許再加上書籍與博物館的展示與說明，此外，其實，很少有人會特別費心為運河而駐足停留，好好認識它、了解它。當然，歷史中的前朝皇室確實也曾為此江河吟詩作賦，增添幾許懷舊的浪漫情懷，尤其像滿清的乾隆皇帝曾六次沿大運河南下江南等故事，也耳熟能詳。但與當代對照，這樣的影象與現實之間，相去甚遠，落差極大。

我們來到長江南岸的鎮江，向北隔著江河抵達揚州，千方百計，只為一睹大運河。我們初次嘗試通過揚州的聯繫人租船，但無功而返。後來，一位船主開來一艘破舊的船，看起來髒亂不堪，竟開口要價每日租金兩千人民幣，且還不願跨越長江進入運河南端。所幸稍後我們透過一位對大運河鎮江段深入研究過的教授朋友——錢女士的協助，我們才釐清到底哪一種船才符合我們的行程目的，於是，便找到一個岸邊停泊點，開始觀察許多閒置一旁、等待載客的拖船。

我們挑了最好看的一艘拖輪，「魯濟寧 2123」號，最終才發現，我們上的船隻，就是胡船長和他妻子盧女士的船。我們針對包船價格，一來一往地討價還價，展開一場價格拉鋸戰。我明白胡船長必須考量距離與天數，小心估算運行成本，其中主要關鍵是每小時的燃料成本，他希望我們每天運行四個小時就好，頂多不超過五小時。從鎮江到蘇州，全長一百五十公里，需要三天或甚至更久的時間；但若開車的話，只需兩個多小時。

我在協商過程中，發揮了長期磨練的談判技巧，暗示船主要看長遠的互惠互利，因為未來還有後續交易，我們很快就會帶領大批學生回來，需要多次旅行探索與租借拖船，身為居間協調的中間人，他應當可以贏得更多收入與好名聲。談判如火如荼地進行，其他拖船船東聞聲而來，開始人船簇擁，一邊豎起耳朵聽……報價殺價，熱鬧非凡。不過，談歸談，其實我的眼睛一直緊盯著那艘最乾淨、最好看的拖船。

終於達成協議與共識。出發前一晚，我們帶齊東西先裝船，其中包括所有配件、零食、餐飲用品、睡袋和墊子，維持最低限度的「斯巴達」式極簡克難住宿，也把折疊電動自行車與折疊座椅，包括一個蹲式馬桶。隔天上午九點，我們再次抵達長江岸邊。安頓一切後，胡船長告訴我們，光是從長江穿越河閘，進入鎮江大運河，就可能需要耗上一兩天的排隊久候！

沒關係，我們有備而來，早有對應的補救措施。我那位藏族研究助理措姆 (Tsomo) 只需打一通電話給我們的聯絡人章昆侖先生，章先生正是操作長江進入大運河的船閘負責人。雖然他病倒住院，但不稍多久，船上的無線電裡傳來通關好消息——2123 號船免

排長隊，可直接進入船閘。我的助理措姆，畢業於達特茅斯學院——一所常春藤盟校中規模最小的學校——我藉機提醒她：「重點不是妳認識了些什麼，而是妳認識了誰。」當然更理想的狀況並非「妳認識他」而已，而是想想「有誰認識妳！」

我喜歡把握時機和年輕同事分享我的信念和想法。或許他們比我更精通電腦和網路世界，但我比他們更身經百戰，多了些經驗，也累積不少失敗，當然也不乏一些亮眼成就。面對眼前的大運河，我對措姆反覆叮嚀：「妳現在已經看到所有這些地方了，這些地方有沒有看到妳？」我提醒她，我們來這裡是為了觀察、學習和吸收，期待有朝一日，能對這條歷史悠久的水運大河，留下一份影響。無論影響與衝擊多麼微不足道，至少對「中國探險學會」而言，那會是個獨特的新視角與研究進路。

眼看最後一艘船擠在更大的駁船之間，我們隨即進入船閘，不僅刮到了船閘兩側，也與旁邊一艘船身擦撞了一下。身後大門倏地關上，我們逐漸降低到大運河的水位，水印也開始下降。隨著前面的大門打開，我們跟著其他船隻，終於順利進入江南運河。這將是整個大運河南航道，從鎮江到杭州的唯一關閘。如果往北前行至安徽途中，則有十一個閘門，一般需要兩三個星期的排隊久候，才能一一通關。

當我們駛離船閘時，我和胡船長並肩坐在橋上。一抬頭，忽見一台飆速的馬達接駁船，疾駛橫穿我們的船頭，超越我們，揚長而去。我頓時聯想起一九八五年那時，我在長江上游記錄了一則關於水鬼的老故事。照理來說，一般人以為鬼魂與惡魔會綁成一條線，緊跟船身後，隨時一躍而上，直等時機成熟，便潛入其中，在船上做些小奸小惡的壞勾當。人們普遍認為，如果你能自己掌舵，開著自己的船，直接用船尾超越另一艘船的船頭，就會將鬼魂惡魔的繩串都切斷撇清了，但這下，後面那艘船則倒大霉了，一切鬼怪將跌落至後方那艘船上。過去，這只是個船家們的水上遊戲，後面拖

船船主此時興起便會跳上跳下，一邊詛咒一邊燃放鞭炮，以安撫他船身後不斷增加的連環鬼怪。

其實，在船上放鞭炮，早已屬於被嚴禁的活動，但我還是把我聽來的舊事奇聞，都說給了胡船長聽。「過去解放前，這樣的鬼故事和我們小時候聽的，都是大家耳熟能詳的傳聞，廣泛流行；但今天已經沒什麼人在說了。」胡船長回答。或許水中鬼魂已被永遠切斷，但他不知道的是，船上現在還有另一隻鬼魂出沒，它偽裝成探險家的精靈，伺機而動。

Every morning on Grand Canal / 大運河的每個早晨

漂泊大運河—往返於鎮江與蘇州 -2

Grand Canal ODYSSEY

Shanghai - December 15, 2021

Grand Canal ODYSSEY
(From Zhenjiang to Suzhou and back) Part 2

Lin Yongliang and wife Jin Houyong are both 56 years of age. They came from Hui Hu, a lakefront village in Shandong's Hui Shan County. Lin got on his first boat in his early teens and has stayed on, working on a tug boat along the Grand Canal ever since. Now it has been almost half a century.

We met when we moored our boat next to his tug for the night. Our boat owner captain and wife came from the same village, thus knew Lin and Jin for a long time. Lin seemed curious that someone would charter an entire tug just to have a look at the canal, as it had never been heard of before. The only boats on the Grand Canal are tug boats, and motorized or dead barges, and occasionally a government boat on patrol. There are no smaller tenders, ferry boats, or any pleasure boats. They are simply not allowed to obstruct this important transportation channel. In fact, no boats are allowed to go slower than four kilometers per hour. Upper limits seem irrelevant, as all tugs and barges move slowly, even at full speed.

On his current outing, started on November 13, he has been on the river for three weeks since leaving his home in JiNing Shandong. Behind his tug are nine fully loaded barges, each with a thousand tons of charcoal, making this a delivery of close to 10,000 tons of cargo. That is the

Lin Yonging interviewed by Tsomo / 卓姆訪問林永良

Cargo barge next to cement barge /
貨運駁船隔壁是水泥駁船

maximum load and maximum number of barges allowed on each haul. Any more barges in this train, called a "One-line Dragon", would be too long to enter the river lock between the Yangtze and the canal.

Arriving at the Zhongtian Steel Factory was not really the finish line for Lin and his entourage though it may have been the end of their river road. Lin arrived at the unloading pier on November 26, two weeks after leaving home. In between, they waited at and went through eleven river locks, not including the one at Yangzhou to enter the Yangtze from the northern canal, and then one more to enter the southern canal from the Yangtze to head southward through Zhenjiang, for a total of thirteen locks.

The section north of the Yangtze is just short of 500 kilometers of river distance, and that to the south is only about 100 kilometers. But at Changzhou where the factory is, it would take at least a week to line up to unload his charge, often much longer. Lin would consider himself lucky if he can finish his job by the end of December. It is not unusual to line up and wait two weeks to a full month just to unload one of these "dragons." That is quite unimaginable in today's logistically efficient world where cargo can cross continents in a matter of a day.

With those kinds of delays in off-loading their barges, Lin and his wife would consider it lucky if they can make five or six runs within one year. Alternatively, if they were to rent their tug out for someone else to operate, they might only receive an average of 10,000 RMB for each run. Lin has one of the larger and longer tug boats at 45 meters, each time hauling a load of 1,100 tons, be it charcoal or sand and stones for construction. The boat cost him 800,000 RMB to build and should last for fifteen to twenty years. It was constructed at their hometown of Hui Shan where there are many shipbuilders.

According to Lin, almost one hundred percent of the families of Hui Shan are engaged in operating tug and tow boats, operating as husband and wife teams. Usually both would have the captain license, and when one needs to rest, the other would take over the wheel at the bridge. Every family seems to have their own boat, or multiple boats. Between 2017 and 2018, when the situation was great for business, some families would receive half a million or more in income. Some of the larger boats can take up to 2000 tons of goods, and if luck provided two-way cargo, the profits would be even higher. Coal, charcoal, food and grain, and metal head south to the Yangtze, then sand and stone for construction travel back north to Shandong. Round trip with load would save a lot on fuel cost as compared with a one-way haul, returning with an empty load.

For this trip, Lin handles nine barges with eleven operators on board. Usually, they are also couples between the ages of 50 to 60. Occasionally you find a younger person between 30 to 40 operating one boat alone. Fully loaded, the boat only goes at a speed of four to five kilometers an hour, covering 40 to 50 kilometers per day. Empty boats may travel at 7.5 km per hour. Some boats would run day and night, and could cover a hundred kilometers within 24 hours when there are no locks to cross. Usually north of the Yangtze, there would be one lock every thirty or so kilometers, with each crossing charging 2000 to 3000 RMB. At times, a penalty can be levied reaching 3000 to 5000. A full stretch run can cost between 20,000 to 40,000 RMB for crossing locks alone.

It has been fifty years since coal and charcoal started being shipped over the Grand Canal. More steel factories were built after China unlocked its old communal system. By 2000, there were large fleets of such cargo boats, reaching 4,000 to 5,000 in number. Despite consolidation in more recent years, there are still at least one to two thousand boats around. Though Zhongtian is a medium sized steel factory, boats serving this one factory totaled close to two thousand. Lin felt that, as long as there are steel factories, they won't need to worry about business drying up.

While our conversation with Lin may serve as a case study of shipping and transport on the Grand Canal, I have observed and asked other questions while traveling on the waterway for eight days. Overall, everyone said boating is now more crowded than in the past. In most section, the Grand Canal is like a water highway with four lanes, allowing faster boats to pass slower ones in each direction even at the same time. There are a few narrower passages where, if there is a "dragon" towing nine barges in the way, only one passing lane is available. We got into traffic jams at a few places when passing and had to wait for clearing of the opposite lane. Sometimes, it can be backed up for ten to twenty boats in a snail-paced moving line.

Trash collecting boat / 收垃圾的船
Canal thick traffic near Suzhou /
靠近蘇州運河上船隻頻繁

Over all eight days along the canal, we were only allowed to stay with the main Grand Canal channel, as moving through the side locks would require not only time in lining up, but a special permit to enter each side canals. Likewise, boats from side canals are not allowed into this main water artery of transportation. Not only that, mooring is tightly controlled. It is not unusual that a boat cannot find parking over a great distance of the canal, even between a ten or twenty kilometer stretch. For example, we sailed across the entire city of Suzhou for over two hours and could not find any legal mooring until we were beyond the southern edge of the city.

Speaking of government control, the water of the Grand Canal has greatly improved over the last five years according to everyone we spoke to on our journey, let alone from our own observations. In over a week, we did not see any trash on the river; even a floating plastic bag. On two occasions, we ran into special boats with lever arms extending in front to collect any objects from the canal.

"Every boat on the Grand Canal has had to modify their flush toilet, keeping waste onboard for disposal at designated spots along the banks," Lin said. "The previous practice of dumping into the water is no longer allowed and comes with stiff penalty if caught," he added. To change the toilet to an internal system cost RMB12,000 per unit, with an additional 2,000 for installation. However, once it is completed, the boat owner can receive full reimbursement from the government by producing his receipts and records when re-registering his yearly license.

Fishing along the entire Grand Canal is basically prohibited though I caught glimpses of a few weekend fishermen at more remote and hidden locations. Where factories are not in sight, rolls of willows and other trees line both sides of the bank. Many of these areas have become great refuges for birds. With winter setting in and leaves falling, the taller bare trees show many nests of the Magpies; some are busily consolidating their homes for the arrival of new chicks in the spring. The most abundant waterfowl being the Black-crowned Night Herons, it is not unusual to see half a dozen of these great fishing birds perching on one singular tree, watching carefully over the canal water for any prey. White Egrets are also a fairly frequent sight.

While environmental policy is becoming more strict, including a ban on air horns in order not to disturb residents along the canal banks, some other form of regulation has become more relaxed. For example, over ten years ago, all boats were required to buy various types of insurance. That created opportunities for extortion and rent seeking by government officials to harass boat operators whenever their papers were outdated or expired. Today, no insurance on boats is needed, though I found it strange how they settle disputes in case of accidents.

Unless with first-hand experience, few outsiders realize that China's national priorities are changing fast based on a new level of awareness and with the economy reaching a relatively high stage. Most still assess China based on old images from the past, most of which are not only outdated, but stained with certain biases and often defined by some shaded memories. I include myself in this group, having focused for decades on western China,

As China is marching along to new heights, our impression of China should likewise be revised, rather than being kept behind by some odd political past or self-serving agenda to justify our ingrained prejudice. Spending over a week on the Grand Canal made me realize what mainstream China is about, rather than being carried away by the rhetoric of the media, be it those of China or those from the West. Being a critic or political commentator is easy. To be a constructive engineer or scientist is much harder. Any country should have fewer of the former, and more of the latter.

"When President Xi Jinping visited the Grand Canal, some officials were lobbying to do away with our One-line Dragon barges, saying it was too primitive and slow in a time of supply-chain efficiency," Captain Hu recounted to me as we were about to leave his boat after a week. "Fortunately, one cadre explained to him that, as slow as this mode of water transport is, tug boats are extremely energy-efficient, each towing behind nine barges and leaving little environmental footprint," Hu added with a sigh of relief.

Indeed, if the same 1,000 tons of load on a barge were to be transferred to a 25-ton truck, it would require one truck 40 round trips to haul the same amount of coal from Shandong to Changzhou, in a matter of eighty days of eight-hours driving each day. The fuel and carbon emissions would be far more costly, to both the industry and the world at large. Then imagine, it only requires one tug boat to tow up to nine barges, certainly an equitable and cost effective proposition.

Xi is noted for his love of nature, and implementation of his green China agenda. Without Xi giving his approval, perhaps I too would not be able to see how a centuries-old water channel continues to *provide both a livelihood and life on this largest and longest of man-made waterways, linking China's northern capital of Beijing to another historic city and one-time capital - Hangzhou to the south.*

The Grand Canal in Chinese is called "Da Yun He", meaning Grand Transport River. Today, it is obviously still living up to that name.

Single motorized barge / 馬達動力駁船

漂泊大運河—往返於鎮江與蘇州 -2

林永良和妻子金厚榮，今年都五十六歲，來自山東微山縣湖濱村的微山湖。林在他十幾歲少年時，便已搭上人生中第一艘船，從此便待在拖船上，展開他在大運河中的「航河人生」，推算至今，他已在船上渡過將近半世紀的風霜歲月。

有一晚，我們的船停靠在他的拖船旁過夜，那是我第一次見到他。我們租借的船主夫婦和林永良是同鄉老友，彼此認識多年，交情匪淺。林永良對我們這群人的動機深感好奇，有人租下一整艘拖船卻只為了「看看大運河」？這大概是他前所未聞的事。大運河上的船隻種類不多，只有拖船、機動船與平底的駁船，偶爾會見政府公船在水域上巡邏。除此以外，大運河上不見其他小船、渡船或任何遊艇。這些「非工具型」的休閒船，嚴禁在此出現，不可在這條重要的運輸通道上阻礙大船「辦正事」。事實上，在大運河上的船隻，都要維持一定的前進速度，一般不得低於每小時四公里。至於開多快，似乎無上限，因為所有拖船和駁船即使卯足全力、加速前進，也仍快不了多少。

林永良從十一月十三日開始到大運河上出差工作，屈指一算，他這一次離開山東濟寧外出至今，已在河上待了三個星期。他的拖船拖著九艘載滿貨的駁船，每一艘駁船都載有一千噸木炭，這整批貨的總重量幾近萬噸。這重量是每一次運輸時的最大負載和

最多駁船的數量，依照規定，不得超過此限。拖船拉駁船，駁船載重貨，如此浩浩蕩蕩的「一列船」，被稱為「一條龍」，如果駁船再多，恐怕就進不了長江和運河之間的河閘了。

抵達中天鋼鐵廠時，看起來似乎已是河道的盡頭，但對林永良與他隨行的工作人員來說，還不算是真正的終點站。離家兩週後，林永良終於在十一月二十六日抵達卸貨碼頭。其間，他們已等待並通過十一個河閘，這還不包括從北運河進入長江那段在揚州的河道，然後，又得從長江進入南運河，通過鎮江向南等，總計十三個船閘，一個個關卡，有待慢慢過。

長江以北的河域長度，僅五百公里，以南則只有一百公里左右。但目的地的工廠所在地常州，若要排隊一一卸貨，需要至少一週時間才能完成，有時甚至超過一週。因此，前後數一數，如果能在十二月底前完成所有工作，對船東林永良而言，那可太幸運了。很多時候，排隊久候兩週，或甚至長達整整一個月，最終卻只卸下這些長「龍」中的其中一條。如此天長地久的漫漫守候，已司空見慣。在當今一切標榜高效能的物流世界中，一天內讓貨物跨越全球各大洲已非什麼難事，對比下，大運河中這般「緩慢耗時」的運載，實在令人難以置信。

考量駁船卸貨的這些延誤，林永良和妻子如果能在一年內完成五

Dragon tug with nine barges /
一條龍拖船和九艘駁船
Graffeti under bridge / 橋下塗鴉

至六次的航運作業與目標，那已算是卓然有成的業績。另一個選項是，他們可以考慮把自己的拖船出租，由他人操作，那他們平均每一次出租可以收入一萬元人民幣。林永良有一艘更長的大型拖船，長四十五公尺，每一次可拖運達一千一百噸的重物，品項不拘，無論是用於建築的沙石或電站和鋼鐵廠的煤炭都有。這艘船造價八十萬人民幣，一般可使用十五至二十年。老家故鄉的山東微山縣有許多造船廠，林永良的這艘大船，就是在那裡打造的。

據林永良說，微山縣幾乎百分之一百的家庭都在經營拖船與駁船事業，大多以夫妻檔為經營團隊。一般而言，夫妻倆人都有船長執照，當其中一人需要休息時，配偶便可在橋上換人掌舵，「無縫接軌」。幾乎每戶人家都有自己的船，有的甚至擁有好幾艘船。二〇一七至二〇一八年期間，大環境對企業有利，人人把握商機，有些家庭光是這段期間就賺得盆滿缽滿，有的多達五十萬人民幣或甚至更多。一些較大的船，可以裝載兩千噸貨物，最理想的狀況當然是去程回程都有貨可載，與回程空載的單程運輸相比，雙向載貨不僅節省大量燃料成本，利潤當然更高。一般來說，南運長江下游的是煤炭、木炭、糧食與金屬，而北上山東的貨則以建築用沙石為主。

以這一次的載貨行程為例，林永良要處理共計九艘駁船的業務，船上有十一名操作員。這些操作員通常也是年齡介於五十到六十歲之間的夫妻檔。不過，偶爾也會瞥見一名三十至四十歲左右的年輕人，獨自駕駛一艘船。大船滿載時，船隻能以每小時四到五公里的速度行駛，每天可行駛四十至五十公里；而當空船行進時，一般則以每小時七點五公里的速度行駛。也有一些船，不分晝夜地來回穿梭，在沒有船閘情況下，二十四小時內可行駛一百公里，萬頃波濤，川流不息。通常，在長江以北，每三十公

里左右便設了個船閘，就像繳交過路費，一閘收費兩千至三千人民幣。如果違規的話，可能還會被處以三千到五千人民幣罰款。這麼算來，光是過船閘，全程就要花費至少兩萬至四萬人民幣之間。

大河運輸煤炭和木炭，由來已久，至今已有五十年歷史。中國解除舊的公社制度後，鋼鐵廠林立。隨著需求增多，至二○○○年時，運載重物的貨船隊伍與規模，也「水漲船多」而日益龐大，高峰期可達四千至五千艘。雖然近年來船隻已進行多番整合，但大河水域仍有至少一、兩千艘各類拖駁船，在此穿遊不絕。中天雖是一家中型鋼鐵廠，但光是為這家工廠服務的船隻，將近兩千艘，可見「船忙」之盛況。林永良覺得，只要鋼鐵廠在，就不怕沒生意可做。

我們與林永良的對話，幾乎可作為大運河航運和運輸的案例研究；我另外也在八天的水路探索遊歷中，累積了一些觀察，並提出其他問題。整體而言，幾乎人人都認同，現在運河上的船務來往，比

Factory along canal / 運河沿岸的工廠

Bridges spanning canal at Suzhou /
蘇州橫跨運河的橋

過去更繁忙。大運河的大部分水路，就像一條四線車道的水上公路，速度快的船隻可以同時從四面八方超越慢船。有一些較狹窄的通道，如果看見一條巨「龍」拖著九艘駁船在水路上「拖行」，那麼，當下只有一條通道可行。我們在好幾處水道中親身體驗類似狀況的交通堵塞，擠得水洩不通，不得不等待對向水道疏通後，才能恢復行進。嚴重時，可以同時有十至二十艘船以蝸牛慢爬的龜速，緩緩移動。

這趟為期八天的水路沿線行旅，我們別無選擇，只能留在大運河的主要通道上——因為通過支流船閘不僅耗時排隊，還得有特別許可證才能進入每條運河支流。同理，來自運河支流的船隻，也不允許進入這條主要水道上往返運輸。不僅如此，就連繫船停泊，也備受嚴格管控。在這裡，一艘船在運河上找不到「停車位」而必須停泊遠方，已屬常態狀況，有時候甚至得停靠遠若十至二十公里之遙，也不足為奇。以我們的經驗為例，我們就曾因為苦尋不著停靠點，而繞了整個蘇州市，耗費兩個多小時，直到繞出了城市南邊外圍，才好不容易找到合法的船隻停泊處。

說到政府管控，根據我們在旅途中採訪多人的結果得知，這五年來，大運河的水域比過去改善很多，我們的現場觀察也與這些論點不謀而合。一個多星期的水上生活，我們發現河上不見任何垃圾，連個漂浮塑膠袋或廢棄物都沒有。我們還曾兩度偶遇特殊船隻，船前竟可伸出槓桿臂，類似清除功能，收拾滯留運河上的東西。

「大運河上的每艘船，都必須修改抽水馬桶，將穢物留船上，等到船靠沿岸的指定地點時，才可以清運處理，」林永良繼續補充說明：「以前那種傾倒汙水廢料的做法，現在已經被禁止了，如果違規被抓到的話，懲處會很嚴厲。」將馬桶改成內部裝置系

統，每台成本要價一萬兩千人民幣，還得額外支付兩千人民幣的安裝費。雖然所費不貲，但船主可以在重新註冊其年度許可牌照時，出示這些改裝的收據與記錄，便可獲政府的全額補助。

大運河規矩多，包括沿岸一帶嚴禁釣魚。雖然我曾在偏僻隱蔽處瞥見一些「週末漁民」，但也僅止於此。沒有工廠的地方，沿岸綠樹成蔭，垂柳依依；其中不少地方已成鳥類的絕佳藏身處。秋去冬來，樹葉凋零，喜鵲在挺拔高樹上築巢搭窩；忙著強化家園，準備迎接春天時來報喜的雛鳥。這水域中最常見的水禽是黑冠夜鷺，有時甚至可見六隻大夜鷺齊齊棲息一棵樹上，蓄勢待發，留意觀察運河水域是否有獵物可取。此外，白鷺也是運河區的常客。

雖然環境政策越來越嚴格，包括禁鳴喇叭，以免打擾運河沿岸居民生活；但其他一些形式上的監管，反倒愈加寬鬆。舉例來說，十幾年前，所有船隻都必須購買各種保險；這政策為貪官開了方便門，他們利用船東證件逾期為由，進行敲詐或廉價租借等各種騷擾與威脅行徑。今天，船隻已不需購買保險，雖然如此，我仍倍感不解與好奇，不曉得他們如何解決事故或糾紛。

除非你具備第一手經驗，否則，很少有人意識到，中國因教育及意識層級與經濟力的提升，國家重點與政策正發生急速變化。大多數人仍以過去的舊形象來評價中國，其中大部分觀點不僅過時，而且充滿蔑視與偏見，任由僵化和模糊的記憶所定義；其中包括我自己在內。近幾十年來，我只把探索目標聚焦於中國西部忽視了華中及沿海的改變。

面對不斷邁向新高度的中國，我們對它的印像也理當修正，而不是被一些過往的政治事件或自我設定的議程所牽制，藉此合理化我們根深柢固的偏見。在大運河上待了一個多星期，讓我意識到中國的主流價值為何，免受各方媒體言論所困惑——無論是中國或西方的媒體。成為批判專家或政治評

論員很容易；成為一名建設性的工程師或科學家則要難得多。我以為，任何國家都該少一些評論家，多一些工程與科學人員。

「當習近平主席訪問大運河時，有些官員趁機遊說，想撤銷我們的一條龍拖駁船，他們批評這種駁船托運太舊太慢，不符供應鏈的高效率時代，」胡船長告訴我。再一週後，我們即將下船道別。「還好當時一位幹部對習主席解釋說，這種水路運輸方式雖然慢，但拖船非常節能，一艘拖九艘，對生態與環境的危害很小，」船長補充說明，鬆了口氣。

確實。如果將同等重量的一千噸貨物從駁船上轉移到二十五噸的卡車上，一輛卡車需要四十次往返，才能將等量的煤炭從山東運到常州，以每天開車八小時計算，前後大約需要八十天才能完成任務。由此而產生的燃料和碳排放，對整體工業和世界而言，成本更高、影響更大。然後，轉換畫面，想像一下，現在它只需要一艘拖船，便可拖曳多達九艘駁船，這無疑是一條公平又符合成本效益的解決之道。

習近平對大自然的熱愛，與實踐綠色中國的決心，眾所週知。如果沒有習近平的批准，或許我也無法看到一條擁有數百年歷史的水道，如何在這條最大、最長的人造運河上提供生計、建設生活，將中國北方之新首都北京，與中國南方的舊首都——杭州老城，連接起來。

中文裡所謂「大運河」，顧名思義，意為運輸大河。看來，這大河至今仍不辜負它的名字。

Power plant by canal / 運河旁的發電廠

依
揚
想
亮 出版書目

國家圖書館出版品預行編目 (CIP) 資料

齊物逍遙 . 2022 = Enlightened sojourn/ 黃效文著 . -- 初版 .
-- 新北市 : 依揚想亮人文事業有限公司 , 2022.12
面 ; 公分
中英對照
ISBN 978-626-96174-2-5(平裝)
1.CST: 遊記 2.CST: 中國
690   111020333

齊
物
逍
遙 2022

作者・黃效文｜攝影・黃效文｜發行人・劉鋆｜美術編輯・Rene｜責任編輯・王思晴｜翻譯・童貴珊｜
法律顧問・達文西個資暨高科技法律事務所｜出版社・依揚想亮人文事業有限公司｜經銷商・聯合發行
股份有限公司｜地址・新北市新店區寶橋路 235 巷 6 弄 6 號 2 樓｜電話・02 2917 8022｜印刷・禹利電
子分色有限公司｜初版一刷・2022 年 12 月（平裝）｜定價 1300 元｜ISBN・978-626-96174-2-5｜版權所
有 翻印必究｜Print in Taiwan